Rebooting Capitalism

Rebooting Capitalism

How We Can Forge a Society That Works for Everyone

Anthony Biglan

VALUES TO ACTION

Published in the United States of America
by Values to Action

REBOOTING CAPITALISM/ANTHONY BIGLAN
www.tonybiglan.com

Cover art by David Gee
Interior design by Nita Ybarra
Book production by Judy Hicks

Values to Action
Eugene, OR
www.valuestoaction.com

To Georgia. My partner in life these past fifty years.
I am thankful for her patience and support and her
ability to restrain my worst instincts.
She nurtures every person, pet,
and plant around her and we are all better for it.

Contents

Foreword

I F YOU DIDN'T think the world economy was broken before, then perhaps the coronavirus pandemic has convinced you. Somehow, all of the preexisting problems—the havoc created by global warming, the hollowing out of the middle class, homelessness and mass incarceration, health problems that are perversely more prevalent in rich nations than poor—become more urgent when they might result in us and our loved ones contracting a fatal disease.

Experts of all stripes are rushing to interpret the root of the problem and offer their solutions. The first thing you should know about *Rebooting Capitalism* is that its analysis lies totally outside the economics profession. Instead, it is based on the latest advances in evolutionary science and a tradition of pragmatic problem solving that stretches back to figures such as B.F. Skinner, John Dewey, and William James.

The author of *Rebooting Capitalism*, Anthony Biglan, is well qualified to step into the limelight during this pivotal period in world history. He is trained in the aforementioned pragmatic tradition and has a lifetime of experience making life better in real-world settings such as families, schools, and neighborhoods. He also played a significant role in the battle against the tobacco industry, which continues to be responsible for almost a half million deaths every year worldwide. His last book, *The Nurture Effect*, identifies nurturance as a master variable. Having it results in multiple assets. Not having it results in multiple deficits. If there could be a single policy prescription, it would be to increase nurturance in all its forms.

In *Rebooting Capitalism,* Biglan tackles the large-scale cultural forces that so often manifest as problems at smaller scales. Capitalism in its current form is a big part of the problem because it strongly reinforces practices that benefit some members of society but not society as a whole. The problem with capitalism in its current form is *systemic*. It's not a matter of greedy individuals exploiting the system. Nearly anyone placed within the current system will end up behaving in ways that subvert, rather than promote, the common good.

Systemic problems require systemic solutions. The next thing you should know about *Rebooting Capitalism* is that it *affirms* capitalism in a more enlightened form and also the basic values of democratic governance. This is especially important at a time when more-autocratic forms of governance are being touted as the only way of adapting to collective problems such as a global pandemic.

This is where modern evolutionary science becomes important as an analytic framework. Any process that combines the ingredients of variation, selection, and replication counts as an evolutionary process, regardless of whether it is genetic, cultural, or personal. And evolution doesn't make everything nice. It frequently results in outcomes that benefit me but not you, us but not them, or short-term gains but not the long view. Evolution will take place whether we want it to or not. Unless we learn how to wisely manage evolutionary processes, they will become the problem rather than the solution.

The first step toward managing an evolutionary process requires *establishing the target of selection*. The pandemic and problems that preceded it establish that the target of selection must be *systemic* and *global*. We must select our practices with the global good in mind. There is no invisible hand that converts lower-level interest into the higher-level common good.

The second step is to *orient variation around the target of selection*. It is here that the vibrancy of capitalism makes an essential contribution—but only if markets are constructed to produce the right outcomes. Otherwise, capitalism becomes part of the problem.

The third step is the *identification and replication of best practices*. This requires the rigorous gathering and sharing of information associated with scientific inquiry. Also, *replication must be sensitive to context*. What works here will often require adjustments to work there. It is necessary to experiment, experiment, experiment at all scales—and experimentation is nothing other than a highly managed form of cultural evolution.

Rebooting capitalism will be a daunting challenge, but the first step is *to have a clear sense of what to do*. That is what Biglan conveys in this book, drawing upon a wealth of experience and a theoretical foundation that is far more authoritative than mainstream economics. Reading it is your own next step toward becoming part of the solution.

—David Sloan Wilson, president, Evolution Institute

Introduction

AMERICA IS IN trouble. In the White House, we have a man who almost certainly will go down in history as our worst president. He has appointed many incompetent people, most of whom are working to make matters worse for the majority of Americans and ultimately for the entire planet.

But the Trump presidency is not an aberration, wholly unrelated to what came before. For nearly fifty years, our country has been going downhill. We are the most economically unequal of the developed countries, and the disparity in wealth and income continues to grow. The wealthiest have gained a stranglehold on policy making and economic gains. Millions of people have fallen out of the middle class. Drug overdoses, the tragic endpoint of hopelessness and desperation, have killed more Americans than died in all the years of the Vietnam War.[1]

We are doing a terrible job of ensuring that the next generation of Americans thrives. About 20 percent of our children are growing up poor,[2] and most of them will live their lives in poverty if we continue to do nothing about it. Prevention research has given us the tools to head off problems among children and teens,[3] but effective family and school interventions are reaching only a tiny proportion of the young people who would benefit. As a result, we continue to have far higher levels of crime, delinquency, substance abuse, depression, and academic failure than we otherwise would likely have.

And we are fighting with each other. We argue about politics, climate change, inequality, and health care. Racists are so emboldened that they say things publicly that would have been unthinkable, or at least said only in private, ten years ago—and they encounter approval rather than reproach. Certainly, gains have been made for the rights of women, LGBTQ people, and members of ethnic minority groups in recent decades. Yet even these gains now appear to be in jeopardy. We seem helpless to resolve any of our major conflicts. We talk mostly to those who agree with us, and we attack, criticize, and vilify those who don't think as we do.

The catastrophe of climate change is well upon us. The increasing intensity of hurricanes and the frequency of wildfires have convinced most Americans that climate change is real, menacing, and proceeding faster than experts earlier predicted.[4] Nevertheless, the current administration is working hard to dismantle the few effective policies that the Obama administration was able to enact.

Meanwhile, major corporations continue to harm people. The tobacco industry markets cigarettes that are killing about 480,000 people a year.[5] More than 33,000 people die each year from firearms in the United States.[6] Major segments of the food industry are marketing unhealthful food that is contributing to record levels of childhood obesity and, for the first time, to adult-onset diabetes among children. The pharmaceutical industry is making a major contribution to drug overdoses, thanks to its marketing of opioids.[7] The financial industry continues to make huge profits while evading the kind of regulation that would prevent the industry from gouging millions of consumers and causing another killer recession. Social media companies refuse to take responsibility for misinformation and hatred spread by their users. And the fossil fuel industry continues to expand its production and marketing of fuels, which once seemed a boon to humanity but now threaten to bring a cataclysmic end to the well-being of the planet.

Many people blame our capitalist system for our sorry state, and rightly so. Yet capitalism doesn't have to be destructive. Just like all systems composed of living things, capitalism evolves in response to its surrounding conditions. In the case of capitalism, the conditions are the regulations that tell corporations what they can and cannot do, the values of the people who invent and enforce those regulations, and the values of consumers.

People created these conditions, and people can change them. America's current fascination with wealth and self-aggrandizement was not the core value at this nation's founding. Our more perfect union will be one in which we agree that all of us deserve the basic conditions needed to thrive. We can build a society that ensures the well-being of all its members, eliminates poverty, reduces economic inequality, restrains harmful corporate practices, and slows global warming. We can evolve a society marked by caring and compassion, one that makes the well-being of every person—including those still to come—its foundational value. All we have to do is decide that these are the things that matter to us, and then act accordingly.

The Conservative Ascendancy

We didn't reach our present situation inexplicably. The deterioration of American society is the direct result of a stealthy and very successful advocacy for free market views by what might be called the "conservative billionaire coalition" (though most of them weren't billionaires at the outset).

The late 1960s and early 1970s were not a good time for capitalism in the United States. A guerilla war against capitalism was underway. In 1972, more than nineteen hundred domestic bombings occurred in the United States.[8] Business leaders had good reason to fear for the future of business.

Lewis Powell was one of those leaders. A prominent lawyer who would soon become an appointee to the Supreme Court, he sat on the board of directors of a number of major corporations. His neighbor Eugene Sydnor chaired the Education Committee of the U.S. Chamber of Commerce. Their discussions about the threat to business led Powell to write a memo for the Chamber about what they could do about the problem.

Powell's memo is widely credited with influencing the development of a large, sophisticated, and very successful advocacy movement on behalf of American business.[9] In a dispassionate and well-reasoned analysis, Powell argued that the danger to business came not so much from radical revolutionaries, who remained few in number, as from more mainstream voices:

> The most disquieting voices joining the chorus of criticism come from
> perfectly respectable elements of society: from the college campus, the
> pulpit, the media, the intellectual and literary journals, the arts and
> sciences, and from politicians. In most of these groups the movement
> against the system is participated in only by minorities. Yet, these often
> are the most articulate, the most vocal, the most prolific in their writing
> and speaking.[10]

Powell criticized business leaders for their apathy and inaction in the face of this onslaught: "The painfully sad truth is that business, including the boards of directors and the top executives of corporations great and small and business organizations at all levels, often have responded—if at all—by appeasement, ineptitude and ignoring the problem."

To Powell, the issue was whether the existing business system would endure: "The overriding first need is for businessmen to recognize that the ultimate issue may be survival—survival of what we call the free enterprise system, and all that this means for the strength and prosperity of America and the freedom of our people."

Powell then outlined the steps that business leaders needed to take. He called on all major corporations to assign someone to advocate for business interests. Most importantly for our understanding of what we can do to evolve a more nurturing form of capitalism, Powell called for a *coalition* of all business interests:

> But independent and uncoordinated activity by individual corporations,
> as important as this is, will not be sufficient. Strength lies in organization,
> in careful long-range planning and implementation, in consistency
> of action over an indefinite period of years, in the scale of financing
> available only through joint effort, and in the political power available
> only through united action and national organizations.[11]

Powell detailed what was needed to influence the major sectors of society. In higher education, he called for systematic efforts to build advocacy for business on college campuses by cultivating conservative social science faculty and scholarships to support the development of a cadre of spokespeople for the free enterprise system.

He also advocated for the creation of "staffs of eminent scholars, writers and speakers, who will do the thinking, the analysis, the writing and the speaking," who could increase advocacy for business on television and radio, in scholarly journals, and through books, pamphlets, and paid advertising. Finally, he focused on the political arena, calling for a much more assertive role by business:

> Business must learn the lesson, long ago learned by labor and other
> self-interest groups. This is the lesson that political power is necessary;
> that such power must be assiduously [*sic*] activated; and that when

necessary, it must be used aggressively and with determination—without embarrassment and without the reluctance which has been so characteristic of American business.[12]

Business leaders took Powell's advice. Among the changes their advocacy has wrought are abandonment of laws and regulations that restrain harmful business practices, the steady decline of the middle class, and historic levels of division among us. American culture has shifted from values that emphasize the well-being of our communities to an ethos of wealth accumulation above all other values.

The Invisible Hand

Dominating narratives guide our thinking about most things, including our views of what is possible or impossible, desirable or undesirable. We see our world through the lens of the stories we hear (and tell) about what is important. We can be blind to the things our stories never mention.

The conservatives understood this. As William Simon, one of the architects of the conservative ascendency, argued, "Ideas are weapons—indeed the only weapon with which other ideas can be fought."[13]

The conservative movement found the narrative it needed in the writings of a Scottish philosopher, Adam Smith. In 1776, he published a book titled *An Inquiry into the Nature and Causes of the Wealth of Nations.* Here is his famous statement about the owner of an industry:

> *By directing that industry in such a manner as its produce may be of the greatest value, he intends only his own gain, and he is in this, as in many other cases, led by an invisible hand to promote an end which was no part of his intention. Nor is it always the worse for the society that it was no part of it. By pursuing his own interest, he frequently promotes that of the society more effectually than when he really intends to promote it.*[14]

Many economists have taken Smith's concept as the essential organizing principle for understanding our economic and political system. This concept was central to Milton and Rose Friedman's seminal book, *Free to Choose.*[15] They argued that virtually every aspect of society would benefit from trusting that, as people pursue their own gains in a market, their actions not only deliver goods and services but also enhance everyone's well-being.

Smith's analysis offers an important insight. In a competitive market-place, people will be motivated to make a better or cheaper product because of the financial rewards for doing so. However, in the hands of advocates for free market ideology, Smith's metaphor morphed into a philosophy that makes the achievement of wealth the paramount value in society. Free market economists, acting as allies of wealthy business-people, have taken Smith's insight to extremes, and they have been very effective in taking control of the dominant narrative.

Powell was right that to influence the evolution of society, you need to communicate compelling ideas widely and effectively. However, he was wrong about what ideas would guide society in the best way. He and the free market advocates who followed him promoted a set of beliefs and values that seemed plausible at the time but have proven unable to advance the prosperity, health, social unity, and freedom they promised for the nation. Among the core principles of free market ideology are the following:

- People are rational self-maximizers; when they are free to choose their own actions, unfettered by government, their choices will produce the most good for them and for the society as a whole. In essence, greed is good.

- The worth of a person can be measured by how much he or she earns: some people command huge salaries because they contribute more to the economy, while others are paid very little because their worth to society is measured by what they can command in the marketplace.

- People are poor because of their failure to take initiative.

These principles led to increased selfishness, materialism, poverty, inequality, division, and poor health. In this book, I propose an alternative set of principles that gives a more accurate account of how our economy and political system work. It can guide us to improve the well-being of most Americans.

A Failed Experiment

Over the past half-century, we have conducted a natural experiment. Free market advocates such as Milton Friedman argued that free market capitalism is the only system that can provide both "widely shared prosperity and human freedom."[16] It has not done this. Unfettered capitalism has been a total and complete disaster. The belief in free market ideology has allowed whole industries to engage in practices that harm millions of Americans. At the same time, we have allowed the government to enact policies that have increased poverty and economic inequality, decimated the middle class, fostered an atmosphere of conflict and racism like nothing we have seen in the past seventy years, and ended the feeble attempts that were underway to halt climate change. Since the fall of communism, we have been led to believe that capitalism as it has been practiced in the second half of the twentieth century is simply a given; no other system could be better. Yet, in truth, capitalism in the second half of the twentieth century was on a long slide into selfishness and squalor.

The details of our American malaise have been well documented in recent years.[17] Progressive political leaders have articulated numerous policies that would contribute to the solutions for our problems.[18] Yet many Americans don't see the value of these policies, and even when majorities of voters support them, they are not enacted. Why not?

As I have documented in recent essays, free market ideology has corrupted every aspect of American life.[19] Our business sector's dominant belief is that the return to shareholders is the sole criterion for assessing a corporation's success. Our health-care system focuses on providing expensive and profitable treatments for diseases we could prevent if we invested more of our health-care dollars in prevention. Our universities have joined the culture of material aggrandizement. As their endowments and presidential salaries have escalated, their athletic departments have become a major industry, their tuitions have increased, and student debts have mounted. Meanwhile, their contribution to a solution for the problems the nation now faces remains limited.

Our criminal justice system has set international records for the incarceration of its citizens, while the free market mantra of privatization has created a prison-industrial complex whose profits depend on our failure to prevent crime and recidivism. Religions, which have traditionally been the foundation for communitarian values, have too frequently embraced beliefs and values that harm people. Our media are dominated by monopolies whose platforms encourage messaging that fosters anger, ignorance, and division. Our efforts to combat climate change are undermined by a well-funded network of fossil fuel companies and their lobbyists, who have thus far succeeded in preventing any curtailment of their business. Across the board, regulation is anathema.

Free market thinking is like an invasive weed. It is now so deeply rooted in every sector of society that it chokes out efforts to make our system more nurturing.

We must reform every sector of society. However, the solution is not a complete abandonment of capitalism. Another thing we learned from the twentieth century is that complete state control of the economy is a disaster. Instead, we need to evolve a new form of capitalism, one that makes the well-being of every person its foundational value. This variant of capitalism will engage the full participation of everyone in ensuring that government is moving the nation in the direction of less poverty, inequality, conflict, and illness, and more innovation, compassion, public service, and humility. This version of capitalism is sometimes referred to as *democratic socialism*. In this book, I'll continue to use the term capitalism because I want to emphasize the ways in which corporations could, under the influence of different values, be part of the solution.

Building a Movement

The success of the conservative ascendancy shows that intentional and well-organized efforts to bring about change in American society can succeed. And it gives us a roadmap for how we can evolve a far more nurturing society. With a sort of reverse engineering, we can use some of the same methods to promote prosocial values and the practices that accompany them. However, we cannot expect to create the society we aspire to simply by winning the next few elections. Millions of Americans and thousands of organizations must commit to working for their values through, as Powell put it, "consistency of action over an indefinite period of years."

We are venturing into new territory, but not without a map. Unlike in times past, we have effective tools that can guide us. Thanks to advances in the human sciences, we understand the forces that influence the evolution of our economic and political systems. Corporate capitalism as it exists today evolved because it brought significant material benefits. Corporate practices evolved because, on average, they brought benefits to investors and consumers. We can use that same understanding of how societies and economies evolve to create a system that is far more nurturing of everyone's well-being. We know how to regulate corporate practices. We know what people need to thrive, and we know how to create the environments that nurture well-being.[2]

Fundamental to the problems we face is the fact that free market ideology has undermined our traditional communitarian values. We need to replace free market ideology and its inherent materialism with prosocial, communitarian values—that is, to call on everyone to come together around the goal of ensuring that everyone is safe, respected, and nurtured by those around them. We know this can be done because we've done it before. As Barack Obama pointed out in *The Audacity of Hope*,[20] America has never been the "perfect union" the preamble to our Constitution envisioned. But the idea that we could improve our society is a vision that has inspired Americans to end slavery, extend the full rights of citizenship to women, LGBTQ Americans, and people of color, and end poverty for millions of elderly Americans.

In this book, I will show you how we can use the principles of evolutionary science to evolve a far more nurturing economic and political system. I first explain how evolutionary theory provides the basis for intentionally evolving capitalism—and society as a whole—in a better direction.

Then there is the problem of overcoming doubts about our ability to make a difference. Like many Americans, you may have turned away from politics because you do not trust politicians, feel helpless to make a difference, or find the news of the day too distressing. In chapter 2, I offer some tools to help you get psychologically ready to take action. I show how you can cope with your distress about the state of the nation by getting clear about your values, accepting, rather than avoiding, your distress, and taking action to advance your values. I also offer some tips for overcoming prejudice and persuading others.

We will not evolve the society we want unless we learn to take the kind of collective action that conservatives used to take over our government. So, in chapter 3, I present a framework for making our society more nurturing.

In chapter 4, I describe how we can build a coalition as large and effective as that of the conservative billionaire coalition. Then, in the rest of the book, I present a guide to the reforms needed in all the major sectors of society: business, public health, higher education, public education, criminal justice, religion, and media. For each, I show

how we can examine how well that sector is contributing to—or under-mining—the well-being of people, and I describe the specific steps we can take to shape the behavior of corporations, individuals, and government agencies to enhance well-being and minimize harm.

I also address climate change. The situation is far worse than most people realize. But the reforms we must make in the sectors of society mentioned above are fundamental for achieving the reductions in greenhouse gas emission we so badly need. And the good news is that the society we need to evolve to save the planet will be marked by greater levels of caring, compassion, and well-being than have been seen in human history.

Regulating harmful corporate practices and implementing prosocial policies depends on efficient and effective legislation, so in the final chapter, I address the American political system. Our current levels of corruption and divisiveness are among the consequences of the coordinated effort to promote free market economics. As we make progress in reforming every sector of society so its practices are selected on the basis of their contribution to everyone's well-being, political support for prosocial policies will grow.

Change will be both a top-down and a bottom-up process. At the individual level, it will require each of us to become better at noticing the needs of the people around us, extending empathy and kindness toward them, and joining with others to bring about the changes that are needed. We will promote this by cultivating the skills and values of cooperation and mutual support among parents, teachers, neighbors, coworkers, and children. These skills benefit not only others but the very people who embrace them.

At the same time, change will involve adopting laws and regulations at the local, state, and federal levels that restrain the worst excesses of corporations; reduce poverty, economic inequality, and discrimination; make our families, schools, and workplaces more nurturing; replace incarceration with rehabilitation; end the drug epidemic; and end emission of greenhouse gases.

You may well be skeptical that we can succeed. You have reason to be. We face a gargantuan task. However, the human sciences have made enormous progress over the past fifty years. Through this quiet revolution, we are translating our knowledge into widespread improvements in well-being. We now have knowledge about human behavior and the evolution of societies that will enable us to solve the major problems of society that have vexed us for so many years.

Join me on this journey.

CHAPTER 1:

Selection by Consequences

───────

*There is no question in my mind that [the evolutionary
view of life] is the wave of the future. The main question is how
soon it will arrive and whether it will be in time to avert the
potential disasters that confront us.*

— David Sloan Wilson

EVOLUTIONARY ANALYSIS PROVIDES us with a new way of thinking about how all the features of our society change over time. Yes, American society evolved to be more selfish and harmful to millions of people because it benefited a small group of Americans. But once we understand how systems evolve, we can use that knowledge to guide the further evolution of society toward a new form of capitalism—one that makes the well-being of every person its foundational value.

Variation and Selection

The basic principles of evolution are quite simple. The variation among living things has consequences that select which variations will continue to exist.[1] Here's an example. If you have ever taken antibiotics, you know that you were instructed to take the entire course, even if your symptoms disappeared before you finished them. This is important because the germs the antibiotics are designed to kill vary in how readily they are killed by the antibiotics. In the first few days of your taking the antibiotics, the bacteria that are less resistant are done in. But if you then stop taking the antibiotics, you have selected the more-resistant strains, which may multiply and subsequently prove very difficult to kill.

Any process that has variation and a mechanism that selects a subset of variants is an evolutionary process. Think not only of variation in genes but in the behavior of organisms and in the practices of groups and corporations.

Consider the reinforcing consequences that shape and maintain human behavior. Many people have the impression that reinforcing consequences only involve material things, such as food or stickers. In fact, the most important consequences are the reactions of those around us. An infant learns to look at his mother and smile because of the smiles, cuddling, and cooing that are likely to result. A toddler learns to call the kitty Charlie when her parent says, "That's right, 'Charlie'!" Legislators vote for bills that are favorable to those who give them campaign contributions.[2]

Although a vast literature focuses on the impact of consequences on human behavior, far less empirical research has been conducted on the way business practices are selected by their success in the marketplace. Yet, in a market system, the very survival of business organizations is a matter of whether they can generate profits. Businesses expand or contract on this basis. These are the contingencies we must understand and control if we are going to minimize harmful business practices and maximize beneficial ones.

Multilevel Selection

Until recently, the notion that evolution only involved the selection of genes dominated the thinking of biologists. However, the extraordinary level of cooperation among humans cries out for an explanation. We are the only vertebrate species that has evolved the cooperative groups that led to our taking over the world (for better or worse). So how did humans evolve such cooperative capacities? To answer that, we need to take a deeper dive into evolutionary theory—specifically, multilevel selection.

Evolutionary biologist David Sloan Wilson explains how evolution can occur at different levels, ranging from individual cells to the cooperation of nations. Here is how he puts it in an essay in *This View of Life:*[3]

> *Life consists of units within units. In the biological world, we have genes, individuals, groups, species, and ecosystems—all nested within the biosphere. In the human world, we have genes, individuals, families,*

villages and cities, provinces, and nations—all nested within the global village. In both worlds, a problem lurks at every rung of the ladder: a potential conflict between the interests of the lower-level units and the welfare of the higher-level units. What's good for me can be bad for my family. What's good for my family can be bad for my village. All the way up to what's good for my nation can be bad for the global village.[4]

Wilson encourages us to think about how individual units, such as cells or whole organisms, can function together so that their coordinated action makes the group more successful than any individual could be. The higher-level, multi-individual group process is selected if it achieves sustaining outcomes. If the group process does not work—for example, because individual units do not work toward the success of the group—the group fails, and the coordinated action is not selected. This analysis is relevant to every level of human organization, from sports teams to work groups within organizations to organizations as a whole to industries and business as a whole. It is relevant to local, state, provincial, and national governments, and to the governance of the whole world.

In order to succeed, human groups need to suppress the selfish actions of individuals that may undermine the success of the group. Groups do this by establishing values, beliefs, norms, and goals. Through gossip and group disapproval of the selfish actor, they enforce norms that suppress selfish behavior. Groups can also do this by praising and otherwise rewarding members for behaving in accordance with group norms. Wilson points out, however, that the practices for managing small-group cooperation are more highly evolved than those for governing or regulating larger units, such as corporations and governments.

Wilson's point about the conflict between the well-being of the lower unit and the well-being of the higher unit is critical for our analysis. A wide variety of industries have evolved harmful practices because they were profitable. The critical question we must repeatedly ask is whether the practices of individual companies, whole industries, and the business community as a whole benefit the larger society or do harm to it. This is also the question we must ask about the contribution of any organization to our communities, states, nation, and the whole world. Indeed, in the context of the threat of global warming, Wilson suggests that we need to think in terms of how all the companies and nations of the world contribute to climate change, because the success of corporations and nations in garnering wealth may ultimately harm the planet.[5]

When the answer is that the practices of a given unit (e.g., a corporation or industry) is causing harm, we must arrange consequences that make it no longer profitable for the harmful practices to continue. Yes, I realize this is a tall order, but I think I can convince you that we have the tools to make it happen.

Evolutionary Mismatches

An evolutionary mismatch is a situation in which we have evolved a trait that served us well in the past but causes us trouble in the present environment. Our modern world is loaded with mismatches.

Consider the obesity epidemic. Stephan Guyenet, a neurobiologist, has studied records of the production of sugar in the United States since 1822. His data show that our consumption of sugar climbed steadily from 6.3 pounds per person in 1822 to 107.7 pounds in 1999.[6] Think about this from an evolutionary perspective. I am pretty sure the level of sugar consumption in 1822 was already way above the level humans consumed for the previous ten thousand years, during which many of our genes were selected.

This is an example of an evolutionary mismatch. We evolved to find sugar reinforcing, undoubtedly because the humans who originally found it reinforcing got good at finding and eating foods high in calories, and thus they were more likely to survive. However, few places in nature had large amounts of the stuff. That changed when we learned how to massively increase the production of sugar. Our current obesity epidemic is the result of the fact that we simply weren't built to consume that much sugar.

Our modern world is so vastly different from the one in which we evolved that mismatches are all around us. Throughout this book, I present examples of how corporations and other organizations have evolved practices that benefit those actors but harm others. Virtually every sector of society has mismatches between the power and influence that advocate for free market ideology and the systems we have for ensuring that corporations function to benefit everyone.

We have evolved massive corporations because they greatly expanded our ability to have things that are highly reinforcing but did not exist in prior years. In response to harmful corporate actions, many nations have evolved public policies designed to reign in harmful practices. However, corporations have evolved well beyond the borders of individual nations, and international law has not kept up with this expansion. This, too, is an evolutionary mismatch.

Perhaps the newest and most threatening mismatch is the evolution of social media on the Internet. Two billion people are now on Facebook, and a huge network of antisocial actors is being richly rewarded by promoting misinformation, racial animus, and violence.[7] Yet governments are barely aware of these developments, and we have not evolved effective ways of addressing the harm this network is doing. I discuss the challenge this poses to evolving nurturing societies and what we can do about it in chapter 9.

Once you start seeing how frequently the accelerating evolution of technology and industry has caused mismatches, you can see that we need to evolve strategies to ensure that harmful results of new technologies and industries are identified and policies are put in place to prevent their harm. For example, even though we have no idea where developing artificial intelligence practices may take us, the expansion of these techniques is far outstripping our analysis of the threats they may pose and our development of methods for preventing harm.

The Evolution of Corporations

Capitalism hasn't always involved corporations. But over the past two hundred years, corporations have become the dominant feature of our economy. No effort to make capitalism more nurturing will succeed unless we understand how corporations evolved and how we can influence their evolution in a direction that enhances everyone's well-being.

The incorporation of business enterprises is a practice that arose through variation and selection. It is an example of selection at a higher level of organization. As with other instances in which cooperation benefited the larger group, corporations survived and expanded because they enabled outcomes that were harder to achieve by individuals or groups that lacked the size, structure, and legal protections that corporations slowly obtained.

Corporations have three defining features that contributed to their selection. First, they can issue shares so many people can contribute capital to an enterprise. This enables the accumulation of larger amounts of capital than traditional businesses could typically accumulate.

Second, investors in corporations have limited liability. This means they are not responsible for liabilities of the company beyond the money they put in. For example, if you buy shares of Tesla Corporation and the corporation loses a huge lawsuit due to some proven negligence, the most you can lose is the amount of money you invested. Limited liability facilitates raising capital. However, given the current values context in the United States and many other countries, limited liability is also a contingency that favors investors not caring whether the companies they invest in harm other people.

Third, and most controversial, the law considers corporations to have personhood. That means the law treats a corporation as an artificial person. In some aspects of corporate activity, this is essential. How can a corporation write a contract if it does not have the same rights and responsibilities as an individual citizen? It wouldn't work for you to sign a contract with an individual member of the corporation; that person might leave the company. The corporation, not any one member of it, promises to provide a product or service. If the corporation violates the terms of the contract, you want the courts to hold the corporation responsible. I address the more controversial applications of corporate personhood below.

Corporations are a relatively new development. In 1800, the United States had 335 corporations, most of which were chartered for a fixed period to engage in a narrowly defined set of activities, such as building a canal. However, businesses and states increasingly found that corporations facilitated profitability and economic development, and they selected this variant because of its economic benefits. As of 2001, 1.6 million corporations were operating in the United States.[8]

Originally, states granted charters to corporations for a fixed period of time and a specific purpose, such as the building of a canal. However, over the course of the nineteenth century, some states loosened their control over corporations because they believed they were losing business to other states. Despite this trend, in 1903, nearly half the states were still limiting corporate duration to between twenty and fifty years.[9]

To summarize, what evolved over the past two hundred years was the modern corporation, with its three cardinal features: (1) the ability to issue shares, (2) investors' limited liability, and (3) being an artificial person. By issuing shares, corporations enabled more people to participate in an enterprise and enabled the corporation to amass more capital.

Free Speech of Corporations or Legalization of Corruption?

The notion that a corporation is an artificial person has troubled many people ever since the Supreme Court ruled that this means corporations have free speech rights and can spend money to get candidates they support elected. As I noted, for some purposes, treating a corporation as a person is essential. However, the extension of this concept to the notion that corporationshave the same free speech rights as humans is an idea that could only have evolved in the context of relentless free market advocacy.

A series of Supreme Court decisions whittled down the concept of corruption to quid pro quo corruption. *Quid pro quo* means a person giving money to a candidate or officeholder gives it with the express understanding that the politician will take a specific action in exchange for the money. For example, "I will give you $1,000 for your campaign if you agree to vote for Senate Bill 554." If I create a political action committee (PAC) and spend millions of dollars supporting your election, we are supposed to believe that will in no way influence you to vote for my interests.

The most recent decision undermining limits on corruption came in *McCutcheon v. Federal Elections Commission*. The issue in this case was whether it was unconstitutional to put limits on how many candidates a person can give money to. The plaintiff, Shaun McCutcheon, an Alabama businessman, sued to overturn this limit. The limit under existing law was $117,000 in a period of two years. McCutcheon's lawyers argued that such restrictions limited McCutcheon's right to free speech. The district court ruled against McCutcheon, arguing that the limits were justified by the need to limit corruption or the appearance of corruption. However, in a five-to-four decision, the Supreme Court agreed with McCutcheon that the law was unconstitutional. In writing for the majority, Chief Justice Roberts wrote:

In assessing the First Amendment interests at stake, the proper focus is on an individual's right to engage in political speech, not a collective conception of the public good. The whole point of the First Amendment is to protect individual speech that the majority might prefer to restrict, or that legislators or judges might not view as useful to the democratic process.[10]

But why is the proper focus the First Amendment? Undoubtedly, free speech is fundamental to our democracy. As a lifelong member of the American Civil Liberties Union and the former president of the Oregon affiliate, I believe protecting the right of people to advocate for their beliefs and interests is essential to our freedom.

However, a collective conception of the public good is also a founding principle of our democracy. The Declaration of Independence asserts that we have "certain unalienable Rights" and that "among these are Life, Liberty and the pursuit of Happiness." The preamble of our Constitution states that among the purposes of our Constitution are establishing justice, ensuring domestic tranquility, promoting the general welfare, and securing the blessings of liberty. Surely, we can measure the value of ensuring free speech in terms of its contribution to these outcomes, rather than placing it above them.

By placing free speech above the value of the common good, Roberts tipped the scale of our social values in favor of the wealthy. To do so, he had to defy a mountain of empirical evidence that shows that human behavior is influenced by its consequences. Despite empirical evidence to the contrary, he asked us to believe that a politician who receives thousands of dollars in campaign contributions from the Koch Brothers does not realize they oppose laws that would reduce fossil fuel use, and they expect him (or her) to vote accordingly. Are we to believe these contingencies do not influence this politician's votes?

By restricting the idea of corruption to quid pro quo corruption, Roberts blithely ignores the fact that campaign contributions influence politicians. Roberts chose to ignore it, not so much by claiming that consequences do not affect behavior as by arguing that concerns about free speech override concerns about "a collective conception of the public good."

Extending the rights of free speech to corporations—entities that hardly existed when our country declared independence and the forefathers wrote our Constitution—was certainly not in the minds of our founders. Thus, the decision is contrary to principles that many conservative justices endorse, which is that we should interpret the Constitution in terms of the original meaning given to its words.

To sum up the situation, there are now no limits on what wealthy people and corporations can spend to get politicians to adopt their preferred policies or to eliminate laws and regulations they don't like. Until recently, the wealthy and corporations have been able to do this covertly, thanks to the lack of laws requiring disclosure of their funding. Specifically, so-called super PACs can spend unlimited amounts of money supporting candidates as long as they don't coordinate with the candidates' campaigns. Furthermore, although super PACs must disclose their donors, they have been able to accept money from "dark organizations," which are not required to disclose their donors.[11] At this writing, a case before an appellate court would require disclosure of donors who are giving to these dark organizations. But, given the takeover of the Supreme Court by Federalist Society jurists, we should not be surprised if the Supreme Court reinstates the dark money allowance when the case reaches it.

Have these developments increased the influence of wealthy individuals and corporations? Of course! Consider the gap between what polls show Americans want and our current public policy.

- **Taxing corporations and the wealthy.** According to a 2017 Pew Research Center poll, 52 percent of Americans favor raising corporate taxes, while only 24 percent think they should be lower. Forty-three percent say we should raise taxes on families making $250,000 or more, while 24 percent say we should lower them.[12] Despite what the public wants, however, the Republicans passed a tax bill that gives 62 percent of its benefits to the wealthiest 1 percent.[13]

- **Minimum wage.** According to *HuffPost*, 53 percent of those polled support raising the minimum wage, while only one-third oppose it.[14] Yet the federal minimum wage is only $7.50 an hour. If the minimum wage had simply kept up with inflation since 1968, it would be $11.64.[15] Its value has steadily eroded over the period in which conservative business interests took over policy making.

- **Citizens United.** In *Citizens United v. the Federal Elections Commission*, the court ruled that corporations have the same free speech rights as individual humans. That decision demonstrated the power of the conservative billionaire coalition. It handed over control of political influence to corporations, despite the fact that 78 percent of Americans say they do not like the decision.[16]

- **The Paris Climate Agreement.** The Trump administration's withdrawal from the Paris climate accord is supported by only 29 percent of Americans, with 46 percent opposing it.[17] Ultimately, this action will harm millions, indeed billions, of people. But it does not hurt the fossil fuel industry, which has played such a big role in creating the political system we have today.

Also consider the success of the financial lobby in preventing many of the regulations Congress was going to develop under the Dodd-Frank law. The purpose of this law was to implement regulations that would prevent another financial meltdown like the one in 2008. However, the law left to government regulatory agencies the task of writing 398 rules that would be the heart of the act. According to *The Nation,* the top five consumer protection organizations had twenty lobbyists advocating for regulations that would protect consumers under Dodd-Frank, while the banks had 406.[18] Commercial banks spent $18.6 million to defeat Dodd-Frank. Since its passage, they have spent $50.7 million to ensure that its regulations would not harm the industry. The result has been that, three years after enactment of the law, the agencies had written only 148 of the 398 regulations.

The Evolution of Harmful Corporate Practices

The practices of corporations are selected by their consequences, and in the past fifty years, the primary selecting consequence has been profits. Indeed, the Business Roundtable, a bastion of Fortune 500 companies, explicitly embraced conservative economist Milton Friedman's dictum that corporations should make the maximization of profits their sole purpose.

This singular focus has resulted in the creation and marketing of harmful products and services. When concerns about those harms arose, the quest for profits selected public relations, lobbying, and political activities that protected companies from being held liable for their actions or from losing the opportunity to profit from harmful practices.

The most egregious example of the evolution of harmful corporate practices is the tobacco industry's development of cigarettes at the turn of the twentieth century. (See https://evolution-institute.org/how-cigarette-marketing-killed-20-million-people/ for details.[19]) Cigarettes proved to be a profitable product because they delivered nicotine to the brain more rapidly than did pipes and cigars, which made it more likely a smoker would become addicted. As an economist at Philip Morris put it: "Today's teenager is tomorrow's potential regular customer, and the overwhelming majority of smokers first begin to smoke while still in their teens."[20] Over the course of the twentieth century, the tobacco industry evolved increasingly sophisticated marketing practices, to the extent that, by the middle of the twentieth century, about half of men and a third of women were addicted to cigarettes. Since the mid-1950s, when the carcinogenic effects of smoking were proven, more than 20 million Americans have died of smoking-related illness. The industry was able to maintain its business despite the carnage because it evolved effective public relations to prevent the public from understanding the harm of smoking, as well as a lobbying and political program to prevent government from curtailing its lucrative business.

There are many other examples of corporations evolving harmful products and practices. The food industry has evolved increasingly irresistible foods. Food scientists have discovered how to put just the right amount of sugar, salt, and fat into foods to get children to demand them. And they are marketing these foods very effectively. A report from the Rudd Center for Food Policy and Obesity reported that the industry spends $1.8 billion a year marketing to children and adolescents.[21] Most of this is spent marketing food products that are high in fat, sugar, and salt and have little nutritional value: fast foods, high-sugar cereals, sugar-sweetened beverages, candy, snacks, and deserts. Only four-tenths of 1 percent of the companies' marketing is spent advertising fruits and vegetables. In addition to ads, product placement in movies and TV shows is quite common. One study found that a total of 1,180 brands appeared in the most popular movies between 1996 and 2005.[22] The result is that America has a historic level of childhood obesity. About one in five children is obese.[23] In six states, more than 35 percent of children are obese or overweight. As a result, we have children developing what used to be called "adult onset" diabetes. For the first time in history, children in the current generation are likely to have a lower life expectancy than their parents.[24]

The story is pretty much the same in the pharmaceutical industry, the gun industry, the financial industry, the fossil fuel industry, and, yes, the technology industry.

- Although the pharmaceutical industry has created many highly beneficial drugs, it has increasingly engaged in practices that enrich the companies to the detriment of the health and well-being of the population. Companies have promoted over-use of opioids, anti-depressive medication, antibiotics, and psychostimulants for attention-deficit hyperactivity disorder.[25] Their marketing of opioids alone led to more than 59,000 deaths due to overdose in 2016. That would make it the eighth leading cause of death.[26] They have also lobbied to prevent any regulation of the enormous increases in the price of drugs.[27]

- An average of 35,000 Americans a year were killed by guns between 2012 and 2016; the rate rose from 33,000 in 2012 to 38,000 in 2016.[28] In that same five-year period, an average of two hundred people a day were injured by guns. The economist Ted Miller at Pacific Institute for Research and Evaluation estimated that the cost of gun violence is about $229 billion per year.[29] The gun industry, with the help of the National Rifle Association, has figured out how to expand its market by promoting fear of bodily harm among women and fear that the government will take away people's guns. It has also gotten good at marketing guns to children. Its lobbying resulted in a law that prohibits lawsuits against gun manufacturers for the automatic weapons they sell that are used to commit mass murder.

- No industry has embraced free market ideology more fervently than the financial industry. The result has been that the laws and regulations established during the Great Depression, which prevented serious recessions for sixty years, have been whittled away. We were told that the regulation of banks was unnecessary because, in an unregulated market, everyone would be able and motivated to minimize losses and maximize gains. The result was the Great Recession of 2008, which cost the world economy trillions of dollars, threw millions of Americans into unemployment and homelessness, and contributed to 4,750 suicides[30] and 18,000 cancer deaths.[31]

- In chapter 10, I document how climate change is a bigger threat to the world than scientists predicted even ten years ago. Temperature increases, ice melting, sea-level rise, severity of storms, and species extinction are all exceeding predicted rates. The fossil fuel industry knew humans have caused climate change but worked successfully to keep people from believing it. It used the public relations and political tactics developed by the tobacco industry to prevent any significant effort to reduce the use of greenhouse gas emissions.

- Then there is the tech industry. In chapter 9, I document how your favorite technology monopolies—Facebook, Google, and Amazon— have contributed to the obliteration of our privacy, the evisceration of journalism, the amplification of hate and division, and the election of Donald Trump.

In a series of essays for the Evolution Institute, I document these facts in detail.[32] All these problems are simply the result of the evolution of corporate practices in the context of a society dominated by the belief that the only goal of corporations should be to maximize their profits. The pursuit of those profits has selected products and marketing practices that caused harm, public relations that hid the harm being done, and political tactics that bought off politicians to prevent interference with their business practices. In every case, the industries have gained but society as a whole has lost—as have millions of people.

The Lucrative Benefits for the Conservative Billionaire Coalition

If I am correct that the actions of people and organizations are selected by the consequences of their actions, we should find that the advocacy of the coalition of conservative billionaires reaped many benefits. If not, why would they have continued to pour money into their effort? Figure 1.1 is an illustration of how they benefited from their advocacy over the past forty-five years. It is from an analysis by Emmanuel Saez and Gabriel Zucman, economists who have been studying the ways in which the very wealthy are steadily increasing their share of the earth's riches.[33] The Powell memo was written in 1971, and the first conservative president, Ronald Reagan, was elected in 1980. Notice how the proportion of U.S. household wealth in the hands of the wealthiest one-tenth of 1 percent of the population took off in the 1980s. The efforts of the conservative billionaire coalition have produced very satisfying results—for them.

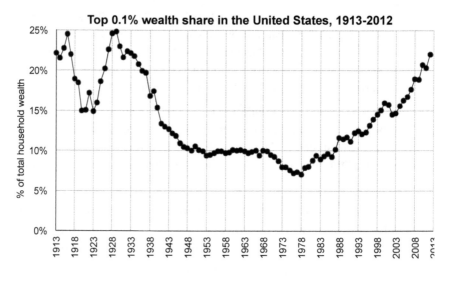

FIGURE 1.1

We also need to consider whether corporations have benefited from the ascendancy of free market thinking. Figure 1.2 was compiled by an organization in Switzerland called Areppim. It shows that corporate profits must been steadily increasing since the 1980s. But even more significant is the increasing gap between those profits and the amount of tax that corporations must pay. During the conservative ascendancy, corporate taxes have steadily declined.

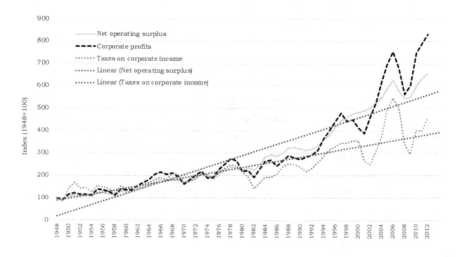

FIGURE 1.2

Evolving a More Nurturing Form of Capitalism

What does an evolutionary analysis have to offer for addressing our problems? Can we use the principles of evolutionary theory to create a society that does a better job of ensuring everyone's well-being? I hope to show you that we can. The key to the change we need can be stated quite simply. We need to change the consequences of people's and organizations' behavior so that they select prosocial outcomes. Of course, actually bringing about change is a bit more complicated. Let's start with a look at changing the practices of corporations.

Changing Consequences for Corporations

At the level of the organization, we have two ways to change consequences that will result in the reduction of harmful practices: (1) make the practice too costly to continue and (2) make alternative beneficial practices more profitable than a competing harmful practice.

The no-profit principle. It is not unusual for governments to fine a company for a harmful practice. Recently, the pharmaceutical industry and the financial industry paid large fines for misbehavior.[34] However, in neither case did the companies that were fined lose money. The fines were just a cost of doing business, and they clearly did not end the harmful behavior. If we want to change the consequences so that a company stops engaging in a harmful practice, we need to ensure that it will lose money on the practice.

Currently, efforts to stop any particular harmful corporate practice are played out in the context of the acceptance of the capitalist system as it evolved in the twentieth century. Although those who oppose practices such as marketing cigarettes or fossil fuels recognize that the underlying reason for continuing harmful practices is the profit gained by those companies, even that awareness seldom reaches the root of the problem. In a sense, the problem is not the practice; the problem is that the practice results in profits, and profits are currently seen as the only relevant outcome.

For example, when the attorneys general of forty-eight states sued the tobacco industry over the deaths of hundreds of thousands of people, the industry and the states attempted to negotiate a settlement. One of the things the attorneys general proposed was that the industry pay a fine for every percentage of the youth population that began smoking.

For example, if Marlboro influenced 3 percent of the under-eighteen population to begin smoking in a particular year, they would pay a fine for each percentage point. The industry strongly resisted this proposal, and the attorneys general abandoned it.

Yet it was the perfect contingency. The agreement that was eventually reached prohibited billboard advertising and the use of cartoon characters, among other things, as ways to reduce youth smoking. However, the problem wasn't those methods of marketing to young people. The problem was that the industry profited from getting youth to smoke. As soon as these marketing methods were cut off, the industry increased its magazine advertising. Subsequent research showed that the industry was still reaching and influencing large numbers of youth. Getting young folks to smoke continued to be vital and lucrative to the industry because the fundamental contingency—the profitability of marketing to youth—remained the same.

Opponents of harmful practices face knee-jerk hostility toward almost any regulation. The public now considers the idea of regulating corporate practices so antithetical to economic well-being that we must go to extraordinary lengths to convince people that a particular practice is detrimental. The default assumption is that most corporate practices are beneficial and most regulation is harmful.

We come to the fundamental contingency to consider in any analysis of corporate harm: the profits of the industry. In every instance of corporate harm, the practices of the corporations have evolved because they were profitable. I am referring not just to the development and marketing of a harmful product but to the lobbying and public relations that prevent our legislators from enacting effective regulations.

Progress in evolving a form of capitalism that minimizes harm and benefits most people will be impossible to achieve if we continue to fight separate battles in each of the industries doing harm. When we see the generic features that select harmful practices, we will be able to move society away from its current default assumption that regulation is bad and toward a framework in which all corporate practices are measured in terms of their harms and benefits, and practices that are proven harmful are no longer profitable.

Thus, I propose a general framework for preventing harmful corporate practices. The standard should be that experts assess a specific practice, such as marketing cigarettes to teenagers, in terms of the harm it does, and if the evidence clearly shows harm, as it did in that case, the practice faces regulation. In every case, it would be possible to assess the costs to society of that harm, and to ensure that the company would have to pay more to engage in the practice than it could earn in profit by continuing the practice. With that contingency in place, it simply wouldn't make financial sense for a corporation to do something that hurts people.

Positive consequences for useful corporate behavior. In a variety of instances, it may also help to ensure positive consequences for certain prosocial corporate practices. In particular, providing tax incentives for a company to systematically assess and report on its impact on the community could lay the groundwork for that company increasing practices that benefit the community. Another example would be to provide tax incentives for food companies to market fruits and vegetables. That, combined with taxation on unhealthful food, could significantly improve children's nutrition. Unfortunately, in the current political environment, corporate lobbying mostly determines the tax incentives corporations obtain; the public benefit or harm resulting from these incentives is not considered.

Here, too, we need to get many more people to see that beneficial and harmful practices are selected by their consequences. Promoting positive consequences for beneficial practices will increase such practices—whether this involves an ongoing assessment of the well-being of employees, customers, suppliers, and the community; increases in worker participation in corporate governance; or corporate contributions to community development.

These principles are also relevant to other types of organizations. In the case of nonprofits, the relevant change will not be a matter of affecting profits, yet the practices of these organizations are nevertheless shaped by financial consequences. Indeed, we need to create contingencies that increase support for the efforts of nonprofits to advance well-being. For example, we could create a special class of nonprofits that are contributing measurable benefit to disadvantaged populations. A greater tax deduction could be given for contributions to these entities.[35]

Nurturing Individuals' Prosocial Values and Behavior

Obviously, we are going to have a tough time changing the consequences for corporate actions if most people continue to believe that material self-aggrandizement is good for society and caring for others is unnecessary. It is essential to evolve a society in which most people are working to enhance the well-being of their group. At every level of society—from the family to nations to the entire world—we need people and organizations that are prosocial. We need them to work for the well-being of others and to ensure that any group or organization they are a member of contributes to the well-being of the larger society. However, prosocial people don't just naturally appear. They need to live in environments that nurture prosociality.

What do I mean by nurturing environments? I've written a whole book on the subject.[36] Here is the short version. First, people need to live in family, school, work, and community environments that minimize toxic social and biological conditions. Toxic social conditions involve conflict with others, which promotes antisocial behavior.[37] They also involve social isolation and loneliness, which contribute to premature death among the elderly. Toxic biological conditions include air pollution, consumption of unhealthful foods and, increasingly, the consequences of climate change.

Second, people need lots of positive reinforcement for prosocial behavior. I am not talking about candy or stickers; I mean warmth, caring, kindness, approval, listening, hugging, respect, and recognition—all vital ingredients to keep people persevering, innovating, caring for others, and learning. We thrive on reinforcement.

Third, we need to limit influences and opportunities that encourage problem behavior. Influences include the marketing of cigarettes, alcohol, unhealthy food, and guns. Opportunities for problem behavior include children being home after school with only their peers and no adult supervision.

Fourth, we need environments that cultivate psychological flexibility. This involves an orientation toward life that focuses on living our most important values, and, in light of what is working, persisting in or changing what we do to live those values. It also involves being willing to have unpleasant thoughts and feelings in the process of doing difficult things that are consistent with our values. In the next chapter, I show you how psychological flexibility can help you cope with the current state of the world while contributing to the evolution of the kind of society you want.

In sum, we need to nurture the well-being of those around us. We need to see, recognize, celebrate, and promote acts of kindness, caring, cooperation, patience, forgiveness, forbearance, and love, as well as contributions to others' well-being. We need to do this in families, schools, neighborhoods, work organizations, casual encounters in the public square, and public discussions—whether online, in mass media, or in encounters in our day-to-day lives.

In doing this, we can have a virtuous cycle in which the cultivation of nurturing increases people's prosociality, and as more people embrace prosocial values and behaviors, more and more environments become nurturing.

The Values of Billionaires

One group of individuals is particularly important for determining the further evolution of our economic and political system: billionaires. Becoming a billionaire is not a reinforcer in the way that food and water are: humans don't need to be billionaires to survive. What can a mortal billionaire do with a billion dollars? Mark Zuckerberg, the founder of Facebook, was estimated to be worth $60.4 billion as of February 2019, at age thirty-four.[38] If he lives to be ninety (on average, wealthier people live longer), he will have to spend more than $1.32 billion a year to use all his money in his lifetime. Do you believe he would be less happy if he had only $50 million a year to spend?

In fact, research has been done on whether money can buy happiness. It turns out that the added pleasure or happiness money produces drops off rather dramatically when you get beyond the basics. Two winners of the Nobel Prize in economics, Daniel Kahneman and Angus Deaton, used data from 450,000 people who took part in a survey that the Gallup Organization conducted regarding income and two aspects of well-being. The first aspect, emotional well-being, involved the daily frequency and intensity of emotions such as joy, sadness, anger, and affection. They found that people with higher incomes reported more emotional well-being, but only to a point. Having an income above $75,000 a year did not lead to more happiness, less sadness, or not feeling stressed.[39] The other aspect of well-being involved how satisfied people are with their lives. Kahneman and Deaton found that people with higher incomes reported higher levels of satisfaction with their lives.

No billionaires participated in this study. But on the life satisfaction measure, even the highest earners ($160,000) were at only about 7.5 on a 10-point scale. So being a billionaire may make you more satisfied with your life, but it apparently won't reduce your stress or sadness or make you any happier than a person who earns $75,000 a year. Perhaps we can have high levels of well-being in terms of happiness, caring relationships, low levels of depression, and so on, with only modest levels of economic well-being. But in our current society, many people at the low end of the income continuum would benefit from increased income.

In any case, becoming a billionaire is a socially and verbally constructed reinforcer. Its value to those pursuing billionaire status is not in the material goods they can buy but in how they relate wealth to other things, such as being famous, being influential, being less likely to have harmful things happen to them, and feeling that people who dislike or doubt them will be proven wrong.

I am not saying that every billionaire seeks money for the reasons I just cited. People may have many noble reasons for behaviors they engage in to fill their bank accounts. If you study the biographies of some very wealthy people, you will find that they made their money in the process of building or pursuing things that interested them. Steve Jobs was one of the richest men ever, but he seemed to care little about material goods. According to Walter Isaacson, Jobs bought a large house but never got around to buying furniture for it. His passion was innovative technologies. His wealth was a byproduct, although he clearly saw it as a measure of his success.[40]

Indeed, for many billionaires, wealth seems more important as a measure of their status and success than for the material goods it can buy. When Ted Turner wrote a check for $100 million to the United Nations, he said his hand was trembling because he knew his ranking on the Forbes Fortune 500 list would drop. Donald Trump said money is "a scorecard that tells me I've won and by how much."[41]

In recent years, the theory that individual pursuit of prosperity would benefit everyone has morphed into a culture that lionizes the accumulation of wealth above all other values. Read some of the tell-all books about Wall Street excess. For example, Turney Duff, author of *The Buy*

Side, describes how hedge fund managers happily engaged in insider trading, taking the most profitable trades for the firm by buying stock in advance of clients making large purchases.[42]

You can read a report from the Institute for Policy Studies that documents the loophole in tax law that allowed the top twenty U.S. banks to pay $2 billion in bonuses to their top executives and deduct it as a business expense.[43] These values have influenced a large network of rich and influential people, along with their highly paid allies. The people in this network share beliefs, norms, and values that promote the accumulation of wealth at a cost to many others. They tell each other that the aggressive pursuit of wealth is good for them and good for everyone else. As a result, even as public awareness of the growing problem of poverty and income inequality reached new levels in 2016, we elected a president who is a virtual caricature of self-aggrandizement.

Free market economic theory, as propounded in the second half of the twentieth century, fostered a view of the accumulation of wealth that encouraged materialistic values and undermined values having to do with the well-being of others. It promoted the socially constructed belief that the best measure of not only our success but our contribution to society is the accumulation of a fortune.

Empirical evidence supports this. Since advocacy for free market economic theory took off, the proportion of Americans who endorse values having to do with amassing wealth has exceeded the proportion who say they value helping others, contributing to their community, and growing as a person.[44] During the same period, an increasing number of high school students said money is important, buying things you don't need is OK, and doing your own thing is a good idea.[45]

Bringing about a change in our political and economic system is not just a matter of changing public policy. Indeed, public policy will change only when we influence many people to think about our economic system differently. As long as the dominant view is that the pursuit of wealth benefits everyone, the well-off are the job creators, wealth is a reflection of personal worth, and allowing some people to become staggeringly rich is good for the country, we will continue to make policies that minimize taxes on the wealthy, reduce regulation of business practices, and enable money to dictate policy making.

In chapter 5, I present examples of the way some corporate leaders' values have changed as a result of counseling they received to help them with anxiety. As people's compassion and self-compassion increased, they adopted more prosocial corporate behavior. One key to such change is increasing the power of social networks that influence corporate leaders. In chapter 5, I describe the conscious capitalism and B Corp movements, which are creating such networks.

Much of what I recommend in this book involves policies that can prevent harmful business practices and increase the economic well-being of poorer people. But we will not persuade anyone to adopt such policies unless we change the beliefs, attitudes, and values of a significant number of influential people. Later in this book, I show how we can do this. But for now, let me simply say that it is ultimately a matter of what we choose to value. We can value a society that allows some people to become fabulously wealthy at the expense of others, or we can embrace the value of ensuring that all people live in conditions in which they can flourish.

Evolutionary Principles Can Guide the Further Evolution of Society

When we get good at seeing how selection by consequences affects people, groups, organizations, and entire nations, we will have the tools to influence the further evolution of society. The key question is whether we will continue to allow profit and wealth maximization to be the selecting consequence above all others or create a system in which the behavior of individuals and practices of organizations are selected in light of their benefit to general well-being. In recent essays, I describe how making wealth maximization the dominant value has selected harmful corporate practices, corrupted much of society, increased our divisions, and utterly failed to deliver on the promises of free market ideology.[46] Later in this book, I discuss how the principle of selection by consequences can help us evolve a far more nurturing society.

CHAPTER 2:

Your Readiness for Advancing a Nurturing Society

We've got to find a way that's more compassionate,
softer, that allows us to move forward towards the kind
of lives that we really want to live.

— Steven Hayes

WHAT DO WE do about the mess we are in? We commit to a long-term, multipronged effort to reform all the major sectors of society. Sound daunting? It is. You have every reason to put this book down and watch TV. However, I don't think you would have gotten this far if you weren't passionate about making the world a better place.

For most of us, our dominant reaction to the current situation is distress, which often leads to either avoiding the whole situation or attacking those we don't agree with. Neither is good for us or helpful in getting to where we want to go. In the past three years, I have talked to hundreds of people who are angry at those who are fomenting hatred and division, frustrated at our apparent inability to influence them, and hopeless about what to do. It is understandable that millions of Americans have effectively turned their backs on political participation.

In this chapter, I want to address your psychological readiness for the long journey that will be needed if we are to take consistent and effective action during, as Lewis Powell put it, "an indefinite period of years." I can show you how to more effectively deal with your distress while simultaneously enriching the meaning in your life and making an important contribution to bringing about the changes in capitalism that are so badly needed. And because we will not change the nation's direction unless we get better at dealing with prejudice and persuading others, I share what we know about reducing prejudice and present a brief primer on the principles of persuasion.

Your Psychological Readiness for Pursuing Your Values

In my experience, at least two things get in the way of our taking effective action to promote the kind of society we want. One is that we find the current situation so distressing that we simply avoid paying attention to what is happening to the nation, our community, or our climate. The other is that we simply don't know what to do. In this section, I give you ways to deal with the distress you feel as you get clear about what you most value and get ready to take effective action. And in the remaining chapters, I cover things you can do to help create a society that does a better job of ensuring everyone's well-being.

What follows, then, is a short course on psychological flexibility as it applies to your values and actions about citizenship, your community, and the environment. I am indebted to Steven Hayes for his new book, *A Liberated Mind*, which informs much of what I write.[1]

Psychological flexibility can be thought of as personal pragmatism. We choose to do what works to live our values, even when our minds tell us we cannot succeed. In other words, we persist or change our behavior not because of what our minds tell us but in light of what seems to be working in living our values.

If you are like me, you often doubt your ability to make a difference in influencing change in society. However, hopelessness and despair don't have to be the enemy of effective action. If you wait until you feel strongly that you can prevail, you may wait a long time. Our thoughts are simply not a good guide to what we can accomplish. Accept your discouraging thoughts; thank your mind for them. Then do what seems likely to make a difference.

Months may go by without our working for things we value. However, our lives are richer and more meaningful when we make the pursuit of our values an everyday occurrence. In essence, I am proposing a pragmatic philosophy that involves acting in the service of our values, not because it is easy or we are sure we are right, but because we choose to make our lives about those values.

Let's start with your thoughts and feelings. Being highly distressed about the state of the nation is understandable. Indeed, your distress speaks to your caring for the nation and the people in it. But how can you best cope with your distress, and, at the same time, work to make a difference?

A first step involves simply noticing your thoughts and feelings related to the problems this book addresses. If you have gotten this far, you probably had quite a number of distressing thoughts and feelings as I described the problems we have. You may have noticed that you tend not to want to have these thoughts and feelings. In the past, as a psychologist, I was oriented toward helping people not have distressing thoughts and feelings. But the research on acceptance and commitment therapy (ACT) changed my thinking, and, indeed, the way I respond to my own thoughts and feelings. It turns out that it's more productive to relate to our distress using the skills involved in psychological flexibility.

The first psychological flexibility skill is *defusion*, a made-up word that means stepping back from your thoughts and feelings rather than being fused with them. For example, if you hear or read about an event in which someone has been ill-treated—a child molested, an immigrant parent separated from her child—see if you can step back from what you are thinking and feeling and just notice it. One way to do this is to say, "I am having the thought that this child has been molested. I am having the feeling of sadness about this poor child."

To practice this skill, you might read some of my essays on the sorry state of American society, looking for examples of problems that distress you.[2] For each one, write down the feeling you have as follows: "I am having the feeling that..." Do this for ten different problems. Try the same thing with troublesome thoughts that come up each day. With daily practice, you can get good at seeing your thoughts and feelings rather than seeing the world through your thoughts and feelings.

We now come to the second skill: experiencing your transcendent self. Notice something about what you've just done. Suppose I read your list and ask you, "Who is having these feelings?" You naturally say, "I am." Notice that the "I" is not any of those feelings. There is a sense in which the "you" who has these experiences and has had many other experiences is different from any of the thoughts and feelings you experience. See if you can notice that this observer self is not something that you can look at in the way you look at your thoughts and feelings. It is the "you" that looks. That observer self never changes. In a sense, it is a safe place from which you can experience all the things that are there to be experienced.

The third skill is acceptance of whatever thoughts and feelings you have, without judgment and without any effort to change, avoid, or get rid of those thoughts and feelings. Here some accepting ways to orient toward stressful thoughts and feelings:

- Hold your experiences the way you hold a delicate flower in your hand.

- Embrace your experiences the way you embrace a crying child.

- Carry your experiences the way you carry a picture in your wallet.

The fourth skill is *mindfulness*. Jon Kabat-Zinn, the developer of *mindfulness*-based stress reduction, defines it as "paying attention in a particular way: on purpose, in the present moment and non-judgmentally."[3] Many people use various forms of meditation to increase their *mindfulness*. However, Hayes points out that any practice that helps you focus on the present moment for the purpose of living your values is a form of mindfulness. For example, simply getting into the habit of paying close attention to what is going on in the present moment can facilitate your acting in ways that are consistent with your values. A mindful approach to living encourages us to pay attention to what our values imply for every facet of our lives. To advance nurturance in our society, how shall we interact with the people we work with or those who wait on us? What will we say or do when we see things that harm children? What do our values imply about how engaged we will be in civic affairs?

I believe these four skills lay the groundwork for you to become better able to deal effectively with the problems we currently have in our communities and society. The fifth psychological flexibility skill is getting clear about your values. As you get better at paying attention to distressing thoughts and feelings, see if the process puts you in better contact with what you really care about. For example, if you hear about another mass shooting, you may notice yourself having thoughts about how we need gun control legislation and feeling angry toward the organizations trying to prevent sensible gun control legislation. What does this say about what you value? Safety for everyone? Concern for children? You can use this new way of having distressing thoughts and feelings to help you get clear about what is really important to you. From this perspective, you have no reason to fight these feelings or avoid them.

Here is an exercise that can help you develop the skills of defusion, transcendence, acceptance, mindfulness, and choosing your values. Each day for the next week, look for things that concern you about the state of the nation, your community, or the environment. Each day, try to find about five things. Make a table like the one below. Make a brief note about the event or news report that concerned you and the thoughts and feelings that came up. Then, in the fourth column, write what your thoughts and feelings tell you about what you value.

Event that concerned me	I had the thought that:	I had a feeling of:	What do my thoughts and feelings tell me about what I value?

Do this activity for a week and see if the impact of your thoughts and feelings changes. I suspect you will find that your ability to pay attention to your thoughts and feelings from the observer perspective strengthens your awareness of what you most value.

Uncomfortable thoughts and feelings are part of a process of moving toward committed action, which is the sixth psychological flexibility skill. Committed action is a matter of engaging in specific behaviors that are consistent with your most deeply held values. The rest of this book is about the actions you can take to contribute to creating the society you want. In each chapter, I describe specific steps you can take to help evolve a society that works for everyone. But before I get into these, here are some considerations about developing effective habits of committed action.

Developing new habits is best done in small steps. Trying to do too much at once is a recipe for failure. Whether you decide to go to the gym for an hour every day or completely change your diet, you put yourself at risk of failing and may end up completely abandoning the effort if you take on too much. If you are not accustomed to doing things to bring about societal change, your best bet may be to spend no more than fifteen minutes a day on whatever you choose to start working on. And even in doing that, go easy on yourself. If you don't do as much as you had planned, you may need to use your defusion and acceptance skills on the thoughts you have about being a failure or the feelings of hopelessness you have about being able to make a difference.

As you read the action implications in each chapter, make a note of the ones you *might* want to adopt. If you have feelings of being overwhelmed, notice them, and also note that the very act of reading this book is an important and challenging step in contributing to the change we need. Then, when you have finished the book, look back over the *possible* actions you listed and pick one or two you feel will best advance your values.

One more thing has come out of the research on psychological flexibility: *compassion.* Psychologist Paul Gilbert defines compassion as "a basic human kindness, accompanied by an awareness of the suffering of oneself and other living beings, coupled with a wish and an effort to relieve it." Recent research shows that when people become more compassionate toward themselves and others, their compassion benefits them and those around them.[4]

It is easy to be compassionate toward those we love. The real change will come when we are compassionate toward those who differ from us and maybe even frighten us. The payoff of compassion can be seen when those who feel like enemies become our friends and allies, or at least stop thinking of us in negative ways.

It is clear that people can learn to become more compassionate toward both themselves and others, including those with whom they disagree. Hooria Jazaieri and nine colleagues at Stanford University published a study in which they tested whether people can learn compassion.[5] They randomized a hundred adults either to a nine-week course in compassion or a control group that took the same training, but only after the first group had taken it. The course included training in meditation about compassion toward others and toward one's self, as well as about receiving compassion from others. The training led people to have significantly greater compassion toward themselves and others and to be more willing to receive compassion.

Similarly, James Yadavaia, Steven Hayes, and Roger Vilardaga tested whether people could become more compassionate toward themselves.[6] Their approach to doing that was based on ACT. They used an exercise to help people see the problem with trying to control one's thoughts. It goes like this:

"Don't think about chocolate cake!"

Try this for a minute. Really. Take a minute to see if you can do it.

Done? If you succeeded, it was probably because you thought about something else. But do you think that will work to suppress self-critical thoughts or thoughts about the state of the nation all day long?

Yadavaia and his colleagues taught people to step back from self-critical thoughts by imagining that the thoughts were written on leaves floating by in a stream. Participants were prompted to notice when they stopped seeing the thoughts on leaves and instead slipped back into believing the thoughts. Their assignment was simply to go back to putting their thoughts on the leaves.

A particularly powerful exercise involved people imagining they were small children again and were asking their parents for what they most needed psychologically. They then imagined being an adult and giving their young self what they needed. Finally, the program focused on self-kindness as a value and prompted participants to make a commitment to be kind to themselves.

The program increased people's self-compassion and reduced their distress and anxiety. It also enabled them to become more psychologically flexible. Indeed, the way that self-compassion helped to reduce distress and anxiety was by increasing psychological flexibility.

To summarize, your assignment for making your way in the world and getting ready to improve your country: (1) get good at noticing your thoughts and feelings, (2) keep noticing how the *you who observes* your thoughts and feelings is a safe place from which to observe everything that happens, (3) practice accepting your thoughts and feelings without judgment, (4) articulate your values, (5) cultivate your ability to act in the present moment in ways that are consistent with your most important values, (6) take action in pursuit of your values, and (7) apply these skills to strengthening your compassion for yourself and others.

I cannot emphasize enough how valuable this approach to living is. These skills have changed my life as well as the lives of my family members, my clients, and hundreds of thousands of people around the world. If you have problems with depression, anxiety, obesity, tobacco, alcohol, or other drug use or any other psychological or behavioral problem, you can find these skills enormously beneficial.

So I urge you to pursue psychological flexibility. You can find many additional exercises for cultivating these skills on the Portland Psych Therapy website. You may also find it useful to identify others who are into this way of being. You can go to the Association for Contextual Behavioral Science website to explore the rich array of resources that are helping millions around the world cultivate this new form of consciousness. Also, I highly recommend three other books: *Get Out of Your Mind and Into Your Life*[7] and *A Liberated Mind*[8] by Steven Hayes, and *The Happiness Trap* by Russ Harris.[9]

In my view, psychological flexibility and compassion not only define the kind of world we need to evolve but also define the way in which we can get to it. If you are already a political activist, you may not feel that you need these skills, but I submit that they are the key to achieving the changes you are working so hard to achieve. I say this not only because it will lower your distress as you work for change, but because this way of living will make you more effective in reaching the millions of people who need to be persuaded that a caring and compassionate society is far more likely to provide them with what they need than the materialistic, competitive, and angry society they currently inhabit.

Ultimately, the development of psychological flexibility is a radical approach because it gets to the root of our American malaise. Our national life has come to be suffused with materialistic and selfish values that erode our interpersonal and community relations. In response, we can seek to make all our relationships more nurturing.

You may not change the course of history, however, you can make your life more meaningful if each day you act to make the world more like what you want it to be. If you are saddened by the hate and ridicule that our current national life seems to be fostering, you can move against it through acts as simple as listening to a stranger you meet and affirming his or her worth. Indeed, affirming a person's values is the first step in persuading them to adopt a new belief.

Why Caring Relationships Are Foundational for the Society We Seek

It might seem that promoting values such as compassion, empathy, kindness, and caring is irrelevant to achieving the many public policies we need, such as a higher minimum wage, stronger government regulations, and a tax system that reduces economic inequality. However, the individual and policy level are intimately related. How likely are Americans to vote to forgo some personal benefit in the interest of ensuring that we have fewer poor people if they feel no empathy toward poor people?

It will be particularly important to encourage these values and actions among the wealthy, since wealthier people are less likely than poorer people to be compassionate. In an article in *Scientific American*, Daisy Grewal summarizes the evidence.[10] Drivers of luxury cars are more likely than drivers of cheaper cars to cut drivers off. When people were asked to compare themselves with either people who were worse off or better off, the ones who compared themselves with those who were worse off were more selfish. Surveys of people about their compassionate feelings showed that less-affluent people reported greater compassion than wealthier people. Wealthier people were also more likely than poorer people to say greed was "justified, beneficial, and morally defensible"— exactly the viewpoint the conservative billionaire coalition has been promoting for forty years. Finally, wealthier people were less good than poorer people at recognizing others' emotions and less likely to pay attention to people they were interacting with. In other words, if you are my servant, you need to be watchful to be sure I am satisfied; I could fire you. I, on the other hand, don't have to worry about how you feel.

The problem, then, is to figure out how we can cultivate these values and the goals and behaviors that go with them in entire populations— including wealthy people who place personal wealth above concerns about disadvantaged people. (And I recognize that some wealthy people already embrace compassionate values.)

Significant progress is underway. Behavioral scientists around the world have developed hundreds of treatment and prevention programs and have shown through thousands of careful experiments that they reduce human conflict and promote nurturing relationships. I reviewed this evidence when working on a recent National Academy of Medicine report.[11] Our reach is well into the millions.

Another reason for optimism about changing values comes from Dennis Tirch, a psychologist at The Center for Compassion Focused Therapy. He has practical experience in helping wealthy people become more compassionate. I asked him to give me his take on the possibility that we might help businesspeople become more compassionate. Here is what he said:

> At our training institute and practice, The Center for Compassion Focused Therapy (CFT) in Midtown East in New York City, we see clients from a wide range of socioeconomic backgrounds, yet many of the people who seek us out are high-net-worth individuals, and people working in advanced executive positions. When I tell my colleagues that training in compassion has been one of the most successful and popular methods we have used in working with hedge fund managers, CEOs, and partners in corporate law firms, they are often surprised. We have found that intelligent, successful people are often inspired by the science that demonstrates the power of compassion in transforming our lives and our minds. We know from years of research that increased compassion for self and others can lead to greater well-being at every level, from our immune system functioning to our ability to overcome our social fears. Within the context of a warm, accepting and supportive psychotherapy or coaching relationship, many of our clients come to understand how living their lives from a place of compassion for self and others can enhance their experience of meaning and purpose in life.

> Compassion training can lead to enhanced performance and greater satisfaction at the level of teams and organizations as well. As the work of Monica Worline and Jane Dutton has demonstrated, cultivating compassion in business organizations enhances their strength and functioning.[12] The Compassionate Mind Foundation in the UK has created an initiative for training compassionate leadership, having its first conference for compassion in business in 2018. Combined with the work of the Center for Compassion and Altruism Research and Education at Stanford University and The Greater Good Science Center in Berkeley, California, this represents a growing momentum towards

training business leaders and organizational cultures in compassion. At the Center for CFT, we are seeing how strongly compassion training can change lives and business performance, up close.

While it might not be obvious at first, compassion isn't about being soft or weak. Compassion is an evolved human motive that represents our sensitivity to the presence of suffering we notice in the world and in ourselves, coupled with a commitment to take action to alleviate that suffering. When our compassionate mind is awakened and takes charge of our thoughts and actions, we are able to respond with greater courage, authority and flexibility. These qualities that are essential to effectively negotiating high- pressure situations, and to living effectively.

For example, I can recall working with a CEO who had begun mindfulness and compassion training to deal with chronic depression and anxiety. After cultivating self-compassion and greater psychological flexibility, much of her presenting problem was successfully addressed. However, she remained in compassion focused coaching to help her resolve some thorny questions about how to deal with restructuring the firm she led. After engaging her compassionate mind, she chose to take steps that would preserve thousands of jobs and ensure the long-term viability of the business rather than strip the company of its assets for short-term profit. While this choice might have seemed less than aggressive in maximizing immediate gains, her decision led to much greater return on investment in the longer term for her shareholders, the preservation of the welfare of thousands of families, greater public goodwill, and a strengthened corporate culture. (Details of this case have been anonymized and changed to protect the identity of those involved.)

Compassion, cooperation, mindfulness, and strongly interconnected human relationships are essential for the functioning of individuals, businesses, and communities. Current trends towards vulture capitalism" and institutionalized selfishness will fail in the long run, and it is the responsibility of psychology to help our governmental and business systems realize how we can get back on the right track.[13]

Caring relations are foundational for evolving a society that works for everyone. By helping people become more compassionate toward themselves as well as others, we can create a society in which an increasing number of people support policies that diminish harmful corporate practices and enhance the well-being of a growing proportion of the population.

A Way Forward

In this troubling time, how can we move forward as a nation to address the erosion of the middle class, the precarious situations of millions of Americans, and the pervasive loss of optimism about the future?

I think we need to address this both as individuals and through organizations. At both levels, we need to get better at reducing prejudice and discrimination and at persuading others to join us in working toward a more nurturing society. If you are with me so far on the psychological orientation we need in order to get this done, let's consider how we can use psychological flexibility to reduce prejudice and how we can become more effective in persuading others.

Addressing the Problem of Prejudice

When I began to work on this section of the chapter, I looked through my files for things I'd written on this topic. I found the following, which I wrote in 2008.

- I don't know how many times I cried the week Barack Obama was elected. I was, of course, not the only one. There was Jessie Jackson, tears running down his cheeks as he stood in Grant Park, listening to our new president.

- The next day, I was walking up the street near the University of Oregon in the pouring rain, huddled under my hood. A young black man was walking toward me, also hunkered down under his hood. Our eyes met, and he gave me the biggest, warmest smile. No hint of suspicion or reserve. We both knew the world had changed. I called Georgia and tried to describe it, but I choked up talking about it.

- All over America, millions of people felt a new sense of pride and wonderment. Around the world, millions of oppressed and demoralized people felt empowered.

It makes me sad to read this now, given the current sorry state of race relations. It turned out that many white people were threatened by having a black man in the White House. Over an eight-year period, undoubtedly aided by the growth of the Internet, the network of prejudiced groups grew. Then, when Trump was elected, they felt increasingly empowered to speak publicly about their prejudices and act on them.

I don't claim that what I have to say here about combatting prejudice will sway those who are entrenched in hate groups. But I think combatting prejudice is vital to bringing the vast majority of people together around values and behaviors of mutual acceptance, respect, and compassion.

My reading of the research leads me to conclude that three principles could help us address the problems of prejudice and discrimination. First, we need to create situations in schools, workplaces, and other settings where people can interact in congenial ways, identify and affirm common values and goals, and work together to achieve those goals. Second, we need to promote psychological flexibility that encourages us to notice and accept that we may have prejudicial thoughts, but that we can act on the basis of our most important values. Third, we need to increase the amount of entertainment, news, and social media that tells stories promoting acceptance of people who are different from us.

Bringing people together around shared values and goals. Elizabeth Paluck and Donald Green reviewed prejudice reduction research and concluded that one of the best strategies for reducing prejudice involves bringing people together to work for a common goal, in such a way that each person contributes to the group's success.[14]

The best evidence for this strategy comes from research in schools. An approach known as *cooperative learning* has consistently been shown to reduce intergroup prejudice. In it, students work together in small groups in situations where each group member has a unique contribution to achieving the group's product. This is called *positive interdependence*, whereby goals are structured such that individuals can attain their goals if (and only if) others in their group also reach their goals. This changes patterns of peer interaction; instead of competing with, ignoring, or harassing one another, peers promote each other's success. Cooperative learning teaches skills and norms for respectful and cooperative interactions in groups.

My colleague Mark Van Ryzin recently did a study in which he helped half of middle schools in a sample implement cooperative learning.[15] His sample of schools was so small (fifteen) that I didn't expect him to find much impact. I was wrong. He found that in the schools that did cooperative learning, students got along better. Victimization of marginalized students was reduced. Non-white students got more academic support from their peers. Stress and emotional problems were reduced, and so was deviant peer group formation.

This strategy has potential for work organizations. Currently, the dominant approach to addressing discrimination in workplaces is diversity training. And although there is evidence that diversity training has benefits,[16] there is still much room for improvement. Unfortunately, many work situations are not structured so that shared goals are articulated and work groups cooperate to achieve them. This is why Paluck and Green call for more research in real-world settings, rather than in university laboratories. If we know that people from different groups are likely to encounter each other in workplaces, and that strategies that encourage people to cooperate in achieving shared goals and values can work, we should be doing numerous experiments in workplaces to test and refine these strategies.

ACT for addressing prejudice. Many people are motivated to not be prejudiced—not because they fear disapproval but because they genuinely desire to have warm relationships with others. Research by David A. Butz and E. Ashby Plant shows that people who personally value positive relations with others expect to have positive interactions and report having interactions that both they and the other person find positive. Even when they feel anxious about the interaction, rather than avoiding the interaction or worrying about acting out of prejudice, they lean into the interaction and seek common ground with the other person.[17]

This research is consistent with what ACT researchers have found. Rather than getting people to not have prejudicial thoughts, they teach them to accept their thoughts as thoughts and get clear about their values. The result is that people are more willing to acknowledge their prejudicial thoughts and more willing to act in caring ways toward people who are different from them.

I think I need to say a little more about what it means to accept a thought. It doesn't mean you believe it. It doesn't mean you should like it. It *does* mean you should notice that a thought is a thought, and not the thing the thought is about. In the midst of being worried and anxious about an unpleasant interaction you had with someone, it may help to notice that your worries are thoughts going through your head, not the actual events that just happened.

In one study, Steven Hayes and his colleagues looked at whether the stigmatizing attitudes that drug abuse counselors may have toward their clients could be dealt with through ACT.[18] Drug abuse counselors work with a tough population. Clients often don't show up for sessions and they frequently don't do what therapists suggest. Relapse is common. As a result, many counselors find themselves irritated with their clients and burned out in their work. Hayes reasoned that people become counselors because they want to help people. When they get angry or irritated with their clients, it is so inconsistent with their image of themselves as a caring person that they try to stifle their feelings. That just makes them feel more frustrated.

The research team randomly assigned counselors to receive either a one-day workshop on ACT or a similar-length workshop using traditional multicultural training that emphasized becoming aware of stigmatizing attitudes and the importance of changing them. A third (control) group got instructions about biological aspects of drug abuse.

The counselors who got ACT were encouraged to notice and accept their negative thoughts and feelings about clients. But in accepting them, they were also helped to see them as thoughts and feelings, not facts. At the same time, they were prompted to reconnect with the values that got them into their work, such as being able to help others.

In comparison with the control group, both the multicultural training and ACT groups had reduced stigmatizing attitudes toward clients immediately after the workshop. However, three months later, while the ACT group continued to experience a decline in these attitudes, the multicultural group had seen an increase in such attitudes and was, by then, no different from the controls. Moreover, at the three-month follow-up, the ACT recipients were significantly less burned out than were those in the multicultural group. Although people in the ACT group continued to have some stigmatizing attitudes, they rated them as less believable than did counselors in the other group. Hayes's analysis of the data indicated that it was the reduction in the believability of their stigmatizing attitudes that led to the reductions in burnout. Apparently, being willing to have stigmatizing attitudes but not believing them, and then re-committing to one's values with respect to helping people, is more effective than struggling to not have such attitudes.

A study by Jason Lillis and Steven Hayes on prejudice among college students provides another example of how this happens.[19] College students who received training in ACT became more accepting of their prejudicial thoughts; however, they came to view them as thoughts, not as reality or the truth. They indicated as many prejudicial thoughts as people who did not get the ACT intervention, but ACT helped them clarify their values about people of other races. The result was that the ACT participants became more willing to spend time with people who were different from themselves and to participate in experiences involving cultural diversity.

Some studies have shown that people who are asked to interact with someone of a different race or ethnic group may be worried that they will appear prejudiced. Plant and her colleagues found that people who were trying to not appear prejudiced, out of fear that others would disapprove, avoided "sensitive" topics. However, their efforts failed; the people they interacted with and unbiased raters of their behavior perceived them as acting prejudiced.[20]

Think about how an ACT perspective could help. It would encourage you to notice prejudicial and worried thoughts about interacting with someone from a different group, but to focus on what your values are. Yes, you may be afraid you will say or do something that makes you look prejudiced, but what do you really want in the interaction? The Lillis and Hayes study showed that when you get clear about your values and don't struggle to not have any given thought, you are more likely to approach such an interaction effectively.

The power of media. Another effective strategy that Paluck and Green identified is entertainment media. Movies, TV, and books that tell stories about stigmatized people can help people experience empathy and compassion for stigmatized people. For example, *To Kill a Mockingbird,* which is widely read in schools, helps young people empathize with the unjust treatment of the accused Tom Robinson, as narrated from the vantage point of an innocent child who has not learned to be prejudiced.

Recent research provides striking support for this thesis. Loris Vazalli and his colleagues in Italy studied the impact of the Harry Potter series on prejudice among young people.[21] They found that high school students who had read the Harry Potter books and seen the movies had significantly more positive attitudes toward gay people than did those who had not been exposed to the Harry Potter series. They also found that an online sample of college students in the United Kingdom who had read the Harry Potter books had more positive attitudes toward refugees than did students who had not. Finally, in an experimental evaluation of the effects of the Harry Potter series, the researchers randomly assigned fifth-grade students to read either portions of Harry Potter books or unrelated material. The children who read the Potter excerpts developed significantly more positive attitudes toward immigrants than did the other group.

Then there is social media. In chapter 9, I describe how the advent of social media has amplified division and hatred at unprecedented levels. We are witnessing a mismatch between the evolution of social media and the cultural practices we have developed thus far to prevent division and hate. I discuss ways we can begin to address this problem.

To summarize, we can do a lot to reduce prejudice and discrimination. As we go forward in trying to make our society more nurturing, we need to help schools, work organizations, neighborhoods, and communities make more and better use of strategies for increasing people's ability to interact compassionately and cooperatively with all kinds of people. We also need to create entertainment media that promote tolerance, compassion, and caring.

Persuading People

The principles of personal pragmatism suggest that if you are seeking to influence people, you should use the most effective strategies—even if those strategies run contrary to your strong inclination to criticize or argue. Matthew Hornsey of Queensland University in Australia has shown that people reject criticism from anyone they do not see as a member of their group.[22] For example, in one study by Hornsey and his colleagues, 188 Australian university students viewed a set of comments from a person who criticized Australians for being "intolerant of immigrants and racist toward indigenous Australians." The researchers told one group of students that the criticism came from an Australian and told another group it was from someone in the United States, Canada, or England. When students believed the critic was a non-Australian, they were significantly more likely to dislike them, think their argument was not constructive, disagree with them, and reject the idea of any need for reform of discrimination. They rejected the outsider's argument even when government statistics and scholarly citations buttressed the criticism.[22] In sum, Hornsey and others found that criticism can actually make members of a criticized group more resistant to criticism.

On the other hand, taking the perspective of people you disagree with does work. It enables you to step back from being entangled in their statements and helps you communicate with them. This is not the same as agreeing with them. It is a matter of searching for common ground.

As a candidate for president, Barack Obama spoke of the racial divide in the United States in a speech that has come to be called "A More Perfect Union." In it, he captured precisely what I mean by taking the other's perspective:

> I believe deeply that we cannot solve the challenges of our time unless we solve them together—unless we perfect our union by understanding that we may have different stories, but we hold common hopes; that we may not look the same and we may not have come from the same place, but we all want to move in the same direction—towards a better future for our children and our grandchildren.[23]

He explained the perspective of both white and black people, without criticizing either group. After describing the injustices that have harmed and impeded black people's progress, he suggested a distinctly pragmatic way of thinking about it:

> Anger is not always productive; indeed, all too often it distracts attention from solving real problems; it keeps us from squarely facing our own complicity in our condition, and prevents the African-American community from forging the alliances it needs to bring about real change. But the anger is real; it is powerful; and to simply wish it away, to condemn it without understanding its roots, only serves to widen the chasm of misunderstanding that exists between the races.

He then took the perspective of many white people:

> Most working- and middle-class white Americans don't feel that they have been particularly privileged by their race. Their experience is the immigrant experience—as far as they're concerned, no one's handed them anything, they've built it from scratch. They've worked hard all

their lives, many times only to see their jobs shipped overseas or their pension dumped after a lifetime of labor. They are anxious about their futures, and feel their dreams slipping away; in an era of stagnant wages and global competition, opportunity comes to be seen as a zero-sum game, in which your dreams come at my expense. So when they are told to bus their children to a school across town; when they hear that an African American is getting an advantage in landing a good job or a spot in a good college because of an injustice that they themselves never committed; when they're told that their fears about crime in urban neighborhoods are somehow prejudiced, resentment builds over time.

Like the anger within the black community, these resentments aren't always expressed in polite company. But they have helped shape the political landscape for at least a generation.

The Hornsey studies show one reason that taking the other's perspective can help.[24] Recall that people reject criticism or disagreement from people they feel are not a member of their group. However, when they feel that someone outside their group is genuinely sympathetic to them and their interests, they soften and are more willing to accept input.

One of the best examples of how this can work comes from research on motivational interviewing. Bill Miller, a psychologist at the University of New Mexico, discovered that people who have a drinking problem can be influenced to reduce their drinking if a therapist or counselor interviews them in a supportive way.[25] The therapist asks sympathetic questions about how the client's life is going and paraphrases what the client says in ways that communicate empathy. The therapist avoids confronting the person. People can be more willing to listen to people who communicate caring for them.

Through judicious reflective listening, the therapist helps the client notice the discrepancy between his or her goals and current behavior. For example, the therapist might explore ways the client's drinking has interfered with his or her relationship with his or her spouse. If the client seems resistant, the therapist accepts that, too, rather than argue.

Peter and Susan Glaser, experts on interpersonal communication and persuasion, published a book called *Be Quiet, Be Heard!*[26] The title captures their strategy in four words. You can be more influential with people if you listen to them with empathy and show them you're paying attention to what they think and feel. If you don't already do this, you might start by listening to children and family members and friends. When you come in contact with people you disagree with, you can practice thoughtful listening and connection and see if you can find common ground around values you share.

Geoffrey Cohen and David Sherman reviewed considerable evidence showing that affirming the values of others makes them more open to what we have to say.[27] For example, in one study, when people who had expressed prejudice toward Arabs were asked a question that enabled them to describe something positive about themselves (e.g., "When were you creative?"), they were more willing to believe an Arab's description of discrimination that he or she had experienced.[28]

I have to confess that I am puzzled by the number of people who voted for Trump and still stand by him. A year into the Trump presidency, I saw a CNN piece on Trump voters in Youngstown, Ohio.[29] Five voters—two of them black—said they were quite satisfied with him. One explanation might be cognitive dissonance: people don't like to be inconsistent, especially if they have taken a public stand. They would rather stick to their position than admit they made a mistake.

And here is another consideration. Youngstown has suffered enormously in the past thirty years. It went from a city full of well-paying manufacturing jobs to one with an unemployment rate of 7.4%.[30] The population was 95,000 in 1990; it was 64,000 in 2018.[31] Try taking their perspective. As I elaborate on in chapter 11, their government—which has been both Republican and Democrat over the years—has failed them. They are understandably angry and disheartened. Along comes Trump, who speaks to their anger. Specifically, he speaks to their anger at the kinds of people who supported the policies that led to the demise of Youngstown—who promised better and gave them worse.

Finally, lest you think it is not really possible to bring people together from across the political and opinion spectrum, you should know about the work of the America in One Room experiment. This project has shown that, through carefully structured discussions in small groups, you can bring together people who have quite diverse opinions on the major issues of the day.[32]

We Can Do This

You can reduce your own distress and make a greater contribution to working our way out of the mess we are in by adopting a mindful, accepting approach to your own thoughts and feelings rather than arguing in your head or with people you disagree with. Instead, get clear on your values and take steps to advance them. That may be a matter of finding organizations you support and putting your energy and resources into their success rather than fighting Trumpians in your head. In your contact with people you disagree with, try reflective listening and see if you can find shared values.

If we are going to repair the nation, we must understand the perspectives of the millions of people who have been harmed in the past forty years and address their concerns. This isn't a matter of getting into arguments with them about how they feel about immigrants or minorities. It is a matter of joining them around policies that will improve their circumstances—policies, by the way, that also will improve the well-being of minority group members and immigrants.

I was born on D-Day, June 6, 1944—the day the Allies invaded Normandy. Stephen Ambrose has written about D-Day.[33] After describing the efforts of Americans across the country to make the weapons to help win the war, he tells what happened when news came that the Allies had landed in France. All over the nation, people stopped what they were doing and waited anxiously for news of whether our forces would succeed. Ambrose takes us to a café in Montana. When news of the landings came over the radio, everyone fell silent. They waited for more bulletins. We were united.

I hope we can channel that same sense of shared care and attention now—this time, to come together around a positive vision of the society we want to build, one that ensures everyone's material and social well-being.

Humans have a strong evolutionary history that makes us prone to work together against a common enemy. But it will not work to have our enemy be our fellow Americans. Attacking each other will simply maintain the atmosphere of divisiveness and model the very behavior we are trying to reduce. So, if it takes enemies to motivate an effective movement, let them be climate change, economic inequality, conflict, and division. Let us fight with empathy and compassion for ourselves and others. For these are the qualities that will bring people together and preserve our sanity as we work toward a more nurturing world. In the end, these are the very qualities we must seek as a nation.

In the remainder of this book, I describe the reforms needed in the key sectors of society. There is no guarantee that we can achieve all the reforms needed, but if we make our lives about the values we have for ourselves and our society, we are not only far more likely to achieve our goals, we are far more likely to experience compassion for ourselves and those around us and to have greater meaning in our lives.

Action Implications

Personal

Start small and build a habit.

What can you do to bring about the changes you desire? Taking civic action is a little like trying to develop any new habit—exercising more, saving more, losing weight. If you have not done much in the way of participating in civic affairs and politics, you may face two obstacles. First, you may feel overwhelmed by all the things that are needed and not know where to start. Second, you may feel hopeless.

Here is where the pragmatic approach to life will come in handy. First, don't struggle with feelings of hopelessness or being overwhelmed. Trying to control them won't work. They are a testimony to your caring about the nation and the depth of trouble we are in. Second, start to develop a habit of spending a little bit of time each day doing something that could help move us forward. Just like trying to exercise more, you don't want to start with three hours in the gym. That will make the new habit feel so aversive that you will soon find a way to wiggle out of it. Instead, devote fifteen minutes a day to doing something for the nation.

In 1974, I began the practice of getting up and writing for fifteen minutes first thing in the morning. It was initially hard to get into the groove of writing, but I eventually got to the point where I could click into whatever I was working on without fussing about whether I needed to read something first or whether what I had to say was worth writing. I have published about 250 papers and several books since then. Start a habit.

In your first fifteen-minute stint, make a list of things you could do. One thing you could do is to find statements on the Internet that promote the kind of world you want and forward them to others on Twitter, Facebook, etc. Another is to identify organizations you think are making a difference. Give money to them. Encourage your friends to do so. Build an online social network of people who are working to address the nation's problems.

Read more about a pragmatic approach to living.

- Chapter 5 of my book *The Nurture Effect*[34]

- Other readable and helpful books on a pragmatic way of living:

    ○ Russ Harris's *Happiness Trap* and *ACT with Love*[35]

    ○ Steven Hayes's *Get Out of Your Mind and Into Your Life* and *A Liberated Mind*.[36] In the latter book, he brings everything he has learned about psychological flexibility together. It is a profound description of a pragmatic way of living that I believe is fundamental to the changes we want to see.

    ○ Dennis Tirch's *The Compassionate-Mind Guide to Overcoming Anxiety*[37]

Stop paying attention to arguments against things you like and attacks on your views.

These kinds of attacks are designed to do two things: (1) get people who might be sympathetic to side with the attackers and (2) get progressives so pissed off that they counterattack in ways that further drive disaffected white people toward Trump. Need proof? Look no further than Thomas Edsall's June 28, 2018, article in *The New York Times,* "Don't Feed the Troll in the Oval Office."[38]

Cultivate your skills in listening to and taking the perspective of others.

A place online that can help you get better at listening is the Living Room Conversation.

If you are a behavioral scientist...

Do research on positive messaging to find the most effective ways to promote prosocial values. Do research in the "real world" on strategies for reducing intergroup conflict and prejudice. The evidence from laboratory studies indicates what will work, but it needs to be translated into practice action on a large scale. The funding, promotion, tenure, and recognition and awards systems in the behavioral sciences need to be restructured so that funds are available to do such studies and the scientists doing them are rewarded.

If you are an educator...

Use cooperative learning strategies and programs such as the PAX Good Behavior Game[39] to promote cooperation and caring in schools.

Policy

Become an advocate for good public policy.

Having led efforts to get people to advocate for political candidates, I know that many articulate people have strong feelings about the direction our politics should go but are quite hesitant to advocate for their political views. I hope the suggestions I give for pursuing sanity in an insane world will help you get more comfortable and effective in persuading others.

One immediate and simple thing you can do is try to shift conversations away from enumerating the many ways in which groups and political leaders are doing things you don't like and toward both the positive values you share with others and the things people and organizations are doing to improve our situation.

Organizations

Join Values to Action (valuestoaction.com).

I created this nonprofit organization to form a network of people who are working to bring about the reforms needed throughout society. By joining, you can participate in building the movement to bring about change. In the remaining chapters of this book, I suggest ways in which the major sectors of society can be reformed. I am assembling networks of people who work together at the local, state, national, and world levels to advance the value of caring for every person. As you read the rest of this book, think about what it would be like to become part of such a movement.

Support groups that are working to reform capitalism. Check out the following websites:

- Conscious Capitalism
- Run for Something
- Democratic Socialists of America
- Indivisible
- Democratic Legislative Campaign Committee
- Democratic Congressional Campaign Committee
- Democratic Senatorial Campaign Committee

CHAPTER 3:

A Framework for Making Our Society More Nurturing

We here highly resolve…that government of the people,
by the people, for the people shall not perish from the earth.

— Abraham Lincoln

L EWIS POWELL UNDERSTOOD that in a free society, if you want to influence how things work, you have to do it with ideas; you have to convince people that what you advocate will work for them. For Powell and his associates, free market theory provided the ideas. In its time, it was a reasonable theory. However, fifty years of behavioral science research have brought us to a point where we know far more about why people do what they do. We also have a deeper understanding of what humans need to thrive and how we can create the conditions that nurture their thriving. And we have decades of experience showing us how free market theory has failed to deliver on its promises.

In this chapter, I introduce an alternative set of ideas about both the society we want and how we can get there. My framework has five components. First, we need to have a clear and compelling vision of the society we want. I propose that we pursue a society in which people and organizations are caring, compassionate, and motivated to help one another. Second, we need to be clear about the conditions that nurture such prosocial behavior. Third, we need a system for gauging how well we are doing in moving toward the society we envision. Fourth, we need to create conditions that select the beneficial actions of corporations and other organizations and minimize the selection of harmful practices. Finally, just as Powell proposed for his business colleagues, we need a strategic plan for influencing every sector of society to move toward an economic and political system that nurtures everyone.

The Society We Want

In recent years, the bulk of public discussion has been about the awful things that are happening. We have a daily diet of news stories and op-ed pieces, each with a different angle on what a wretched president we have and how bad things are getting. However, I am convinced we will not evolve the society we want by complaining about the one we have or attacking the people who disagree with us. We need a positive vision of where we want to go as a nation, a vision that can mobilize people and organizations to take effective action. I envision a society that values everyone's well-being more than it values the accumulation of wealth by a small slice of society.

I have rooted my approach to this positive vision in the enormous knowledge that has accumulated about what human beings need to thrive. It draws strength from my association with a broad and growing coalition of behavioral scientists who are working to translate that knowledge into worldwide benefit.[1] The growing evonomics movement has influenced me greatly.[2] This movement, which I discuss in chapter 7, uses evolutionary theory to understand not only the evolution of capitalism but the evolution of human society in general. It provides an empirically based framework for guiding the further evolution of society toward the nurturing conditions I seek to promote.

The 2009 Institute of Medicine (IOM) report on prevention, which I participated in writing,[3] also inspired my thinking. The IOM report put it this way: "The scientific foundation has been created for the nation to begin to create a society in which young people arrive at adulthood with the skills, interests, assets, and health habits needed to live healthy, happy, and productive lives in caring relationships with others."

Finally, my approach is informed by my contacts with thousands of people I have spoken with since I published *The Nurture Effect*. They have convinced me that a huge, growing, and diverse group of people and organizations around the world understands that we can create much more caring and compassionate societies by using the tools of behavioral science.

In essence, we have a choice. As a nation, we can continue to encourage the pursuit of individual wealth as our paramount value, a pursuit that in fact benefits only a few, or we can choose to build a society that values the well-being of *every* person. The difference between these two visions comes down to what we think matters more: looking out for ourselves or caring for others.

Social psychologist Tim Kasser has led the way in helping us understand these contrasting values. In a recent review of the research,[4] he described the constellation of attitudes, values, and behaviors he labels *materialism*. People with materialistic values desire and seek wealth, possessions, image, and status. They agree with statements such as "I like a lot of luxury in my life," "I'd be happier if I could afford to buy more things," and "The things I own say a lot about how well I'm doing in life."

The alternatives to materialistic values are those I would label as *nurturing;* other reasonable labels are *prosocial* and *communitarian*. These values include (1) having satisfying relationships with family and friends (e.g., "I will have a committed intimate relationship."), (2) concerns about the community ("I will assist people who need it, asking nothing in return."), and (3) personal growth and self-acceptance ("I will have insight into why I do the things I do."). Kasser tells us that all around the world, people who have materialistic values are unlikely to have prosocial values.[5] Materialism versus nurturance seems to be an either/or proposition.

People who endorse materialistic values tend to have a greater number of psychological and behavioral problems than other people.[6] They are more likely to think of themselves in negative terms and less likely to feel calm or happy. They tend to have problems with depression and anxiety, and they rate their physical health and life satisfaction more negatively. They are more likely to engage in compulsive buying and risky health behaviors, such as smoking. They are also more likely to act in self-serving ways, take advantage of others, and care little about others' needs. As citizens, they are less likely to be egalitarian and more likely to hold prejudicial views toward people in other groups and to try to dominate others. Couples who share materialistic values rate their relationships more negatively than other couples.[7]

Given all these negatives, why would people embrace materialistic values? There are at least two reasons. First, because they feel threatened. Kasser has done some clever experiments that show that people are more likely to endorse materialistic values when they are encouraged to think about threatening topics such as dying, having others snub them, or being poor.[8]

Kasser's evidence lines up with an evolutionary analysis. In our evolutionary history, during particularly dangerous periods—for instance, when food was scarce or another group was threatening your group—you might have been more likely to survive if you looked out for number one. This also explains why more-materialistic people embrace values such as fame and popularity. People with friends are better able to survive during threats and shortages. In an inhospitable world, you had better get what you can get when you can get it.

A second reason people embrace materialism is because marketing is telling them that having many possessions will solve their problems. Frequent exposure to advertising and the materialism of others makes people more likely to endorse materialistic values.[9] If you live among people who focus on what they own and their social status, you will be inclined toward those values. Besides, how often do you see an ad for being nurturing?

When I delved into this research, I realized that many of the policies that free market advocates have put in place pay a double dividend. Cutting government spending has not only benefited the wealthy directly by reducing their taxes, it has undermined policies and social programs that can reduce poverty. By doing so, it has increased the threat and stress felt by many people, which tends to drive them toward materialistic values. It makes them more oriented toward being consumers—a twofer from the standpoint of those with products to sell!

Think about what this implies about promoting materialistic values. They do not seem to be good for society. When we encourage people to focus on achieving wealth and acquiring material goods, it does not even benefit them, let alone the people around them.

Many practices of our current capitalist system undermine cooperation and nurturance in families, schools, communities, and our national life. I have in mind the promotion of economic policies that have eroded the economic well-being of millions of Americans, the marketing of guns through appeals to fear, the marketing of harmful drugs, the portrayal of immigrants as criminals and job stealers, and the free market ideology that argues that the selfish pursuit of one's own economic interests will benefit everyone.

All these practices grew to prominence due to their financial benefit to wealthy people and corporations. I don't believe that corporations adopted them *because* of the harm they do. The corporations simply set out to profitably market products and services. Ironically, it is as though an invisible hand is producing harmful byproducts of these corporate practices, without people seeing the relationship between the practices and the harm they cause.

In short, far from contributing to caring, prosocial relationships, free market advocacy has argued strongly against the idea that we should care about each other. In the process, it has undermined policies that would promote nurturing families, schools, and neighborhoods and has weakened Americans' commitment to the well-being of others. The first step for the society we seek is to articulate our vision of a society in which materialism gives way to a focus on nurturing our own and others' well-being.

Lastly, with respect to pursuing our own vision, it is important to remember the strategy that conservatives took in advancing free market principles. As Paul Pierson, a leader of the Olin Foundation, put it, "Perhaps we should think instead about challenging [progressive views] by adding new voices,"[10] rather than directly attacking existing voices. Similarly, we will not advance the values, goals, and practices we desire by attacking the voices for conservatism but by advancing a compelling vision of the society we wish to create.

Nurturing Prosocial Behavior

People and corporations will act in ways that benefit those around them and society as a whole, but only if we create the conditions that select prosocial behavior and actions. In this section, I focus on how we can cultivate individuals' prosocial behavior. I address corporate behavior later in this chapter and throughout the rest of the book.

People Are Quite Prosocial—Given the Right Conditions

Humans are, in fact, prone to being cooperative, compassionate, and caring from the start. Michael Tomasello is one of the leading developmental psychologists in the world. He and his colleagues have studied how even infants will help others and demand fairness. They found that babies who had not yet learned to talk would help an adult who was putting toys away.[11] In a clever experiment, they showed that a baby who watched one puppet help another get a rattle out of a box, while a second puppet slammed the box closed, preferred the helpful puppet.

Similarly, adults will often act for the benefit of others even when it does not maximize their gains. For instance, consider the Ultimatum Bargaining Game.[12] Two people play it. One player allocates a given amount of money between them. The other player then has two choices: accept the first person's decision and take the allocated share or reject the decision, in which case neither person gets any money. It turns out that the most common move of the first player is to propose a fifty-fifty split of the money, a response that does not maximize that player's gain. The helpfulness of babies I just described suggests that this inclination to share is the product of the evolution of altruistic tendencies in humans.

There is one group for whom the general tendency to be cooperative and share is less common: economists! Students of economics who played the Ultimatum Bargaining Game tried to keep more money for themselves.[13] Moreover, professional economists report giving less money to charity than do people in other professions.[14] Apparently, learning that you are inherently self-interested can become a self-fulfilling prophecy.

The idea that people are selfish maximizers is simply inconsistent with what we know about human evolution. Humans evolved for thousands of years in hunter-gatherer groups of fewer than fifty people.[15] The survival of these groups depended on effective cooperation in gathering food and finding and killing game. Groups that weren't as good at cooperating were less likely to survive, compared with more cooperative groups. As a result, evolutionary forces favored group cooperation.[16]

The Evolution of Antisocial Behavior

You may reasonably ask why, if we are such great cooperators, there is so much interpersonal aggression. One reason is that exposure to threat brings out selfish tendencies. Children raised in threatening environments are more likely than children raised in safer environments to develop aggressive traits, associate with deviant peers, and engage in criminal behavior.[17] In short, humans have also evolved the capacity to become more selfish in a dangerous environment; under these circumstances, being aggressive has survival value.

In addition, antisocial behavior is shaped in groups that cooperate to achieve aims that benefit the group at the cost to the larger society. Juvenile crime develops in small groups of deviant peers who bond with each other over their anger at being socially rejected by mainstream peers.[18] The dynamics are the same in terrorism. Disaffected young men bond with each other around an ideology that justifies their hatred of a society that has made them feel rejected; the Internet has amplified this process.

The ascendancy of the coalition of conservative billionaires is another example of these dynamics. A small group of very wealthy people cooperated to take control of public-policy making in ways that benefit them but harm the rest of society.

As this analysis and the current state of selfishness in American society suggest, we cannot simply depend on our evolutionary inheritance to ensure that people will be prosocial. We need to nurture such behavior in families, schools, workplaces, and our public discussion. I describe nurturing environments in chapter 1. These are environments that minimize toxic biological and social conditions, richly reinforce all kinds of prosocial behavior and values, limit opportunities for problem behavior, and promote psychological flexibility.

Values and Goals from an Evolutionary Perspective

If we are going to evolve a more nurturing society, we also need to figure out how to promote the values and goals that would advance this agenda. That requires an understanding of how social groups establish and maintain values. As I indicate in chapter 1, much of what motivates people is verbally and socially constructed. By that, I mean that what we value is the result of what our social community encourages us to value. For example, the student who studies hard to get an A probably lives in an environment in which parents and peers value and approve of good grades.

Similarly, antisocial values and behaviors develop in environments in which peers approve of such behavior. Tom Dishion and his colleagues showed this in a study of pairs of adolescent boys.[19] The youths were asked to discuss topics such as how to solve problems they were having with parents or peers. The boys who laughed at each other's deviant talk were more likely to commit delinquent acts over the next two years than were boys who didn't convey that kind of approval.

In sum, considerable evidence shows that people's value systems arise largely from social relationships that teach them to value some things and not others. Those who believe the pursuit of great wealth will necessarily benefit everyone exist in a social network of other people who believe the same thing. If all your friends and family laugh when you say you want to devote your life to making your community better for other people, but show interest when you talk about making a lot of money, your values and ultimately your behavior will likely be influenced accordingly.

However, as I indicate in chapter 1, you can *choose* to pursue values that are contrary to the values of those around you. One of the things ACT therapists do to encourage people to get in touch with their most deeply held values is ask them to imagine what values they would choose if they found themselves in a world where everyone would continue to approve of them even if they lied, stole, or cheated. People generally realize that they still value prosocial outcomes. They want to help others and be kind, caring, and compassionate. Of course, if you embrace such values, you are likely to want to join others in pursuing those values.

A Public Health Approach to Measuring Our Progress

Why so much attention to public health in a book about economics and capitalism? Because the ultimate benefit of any economic and political system is its benefit to human beings and the ecosystem on which their well-being depends. The public health framework allows us to gauge how well our society is doing in this regard. Our current economic system is not only failing to deliver economic well-being to families; it is undermining our health, our freedom, our social relations, and our unity. Public health provides the tools not just for measuring well-being but for implementing the policies and programs that can steadily contribute to improving well-being. Indeed, economists such as Anne Case and Angus Deaton have increasingly turned to measuring the impact of economic policy on health.[20]

As I finish this book, my wife and I, like many millions around the world, are "sheltering in place." Just about everyone on the planet is getting a lesson in the importance of public health. We are anxiously tracking the number of Covid-19 cases and number of deaths that result. We are fighting this pandemic with the tools that public health experts have evolved beginning in the fourteenth century. But beyond epidemics, public health has become a general framework for thinking about and taking effective action to improve all aspects of human well-being, from wealth and income to depression and cardiovascular disease.

Two core concepts of public health are *incidence* and *prevalence*. Originally, public health professionals were concerned about the incidence and prevalence of infectious diseases. For example, they tracked the incidence, or rate of occurrence of new cases, of the plague or cholera, and the prevalence, or total number of people who had one of these diseases. However, we can assess the well-being of the population much more generally than just by considering disease. We can measure the prevalence of people who are living productive lives and the prevalence of people who are satisfied with their lives. We can track the prevalence of those who are depressed, are lonely, or have left the workforce. And we can assess the prevalence of people who are psychologically flexible, in the sense that they pragmatically pursue their values even when their mind pulls them away from doing so.[21] We can assess the incidence of divorce, of physical and sexual abuse of others, and of conflict in workplaces. If you are interested in any aspect of well-being, chances are that aspect is being measured.

After identifying a disease, public health officials turn to the question of what risk factors contribute to the disease. For example, after lung cancer became common in the twentieth century, public health officials began to measure its incidence and prevalence so they could figure out how to reduce it. When Ernst Wynder showed that cigarette smoking caused lung cancer, officials began to track the prevalence of smoking so they could know if they were reducing smoking.[22] Once it became clear that young people needed to be prevented from taking up smoking, officials began to track the incidence of young people starting to smoke.

In short, every aspect of human well-being is measurable. We can use these measures to gauge how nurturing our society is and whether we are improving well-being or diminishing it.

Over the past fifty years, we have accumulated a wealth of information about the things that affect people's health and well-being. You might be surprised by what we have learned. It turns out that if we are interested in reducing the likelihood of people dying at an early age, we need to be concerned first and foremost about whether they live in nurturing conditions.

PROPORTIONAL CONTRIBUTION TO PREMATURE DEATH

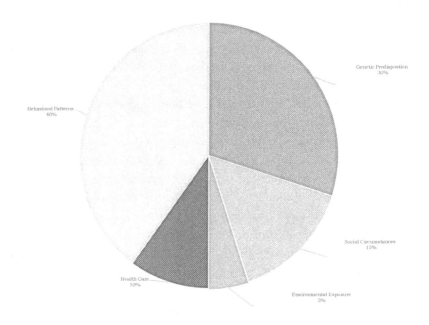

FIGURE 3.1

Figure 3.1 shows causes of premature death.[23] Notice that social circumstances cause 15 percent of premature deaths. These include situations such as poverty, social stress due to conflict with family members, and loneliness—in other words, environments that are not nurturing. Moreover, 40 percent of premature deaths arise due to behavioral patterns, such as smoking, drug abuse, physical inactivity, poor nutrition, antisocial behavior, and depression. Furthermore, these unhealthful behavior patterns are largely the result of social circumstances. In short, if we are interested in having people live longer, we need to improve their social circumstances and prevent all the behavioral problems that contribute to early death.

If we want a society in which most people are thriving, we will want a society that carefully measures all aspects of human well-being—not just physical disease but the social circumstances and behavioral patterns that harm individuals and the people around them. We need a society that nurtures people's prosocial behavior.

Public health efforts have been greatly strengthened by the advent of experimental evaluations, which are helping us to select increasingly powerful ways to help people. The most commonly used experiment is the randomized controlled trial. For example, if we want to know if a family intervention can reduce the aggressive behavior of children, we can identify families who are concerned about their children's aggressive behavior and randomly assign half of them (the experimental group) to get the program, while the other half (the control group) does not get it. If six months later, the children in the families who got the program are less aggressive, we can be reasonably sure that the difference between the groups is due to the program. Why? Because randomly assigning families to the two conditions made it likely that the two groups would have the same level of children's aggressiveness. (In such studies, it is common to treat the families in the control group after comparing the results between the two groups.)

Randomized controlled trials have only been widely used in medicine and behavioral science for the past seventy years. The Cochrane Collaboration, which tracks randomized trials in medicine and behavioral sciences, identified more than 150,000 as of 2004.[24] Thanks to these types of trials, we have increasing confidence that we can develop effective interventions to help families, schools, workplaces, and communities.

The reason I am telling you this is that experimental methods can accelerate the evolution of effective cultural practices. Through experiments, we can steadily improve our ability to deal with problems that involve human behavior. A good example of this is the work of the Arnold Foundation. They believe the government's effectiveness will improve if we evaluate government programs with randomized trials. They find that it is very often possible to evaluate an ongoing program by using a randomized trial.

For example, Jon Baron of the Arnold Foundation described a randomized trial they funded to evaluate Bottom Line,[25] a counseling program to help low-income first-generation students get into college and succeed. They found that the program increased the percentage of students who enrolled in college by 5 percentage points (from 90 percent to 95 percent), increased continuous college enrollment by 10 points (from 71 percent to 81 percent), and increased the percentage of students enrolled in four-year colleges by 14 points (from 63 percent to 77 percent). Those numbers may seem small, but if such support were provided to 100,000 students living in poverty, it would mean that 5,000 more young people would enroll in college, 10,000 more would be continuously enrolled, and 14,000 more would be enrolled in four-year colleges.

Such experimental methods are also essential for getting rid of social programs that don't work. For example, consider the Scared Straight program, which was based on the idea of taking delinquent youth to a prison and having prisoners berate them and warn that they would end up in prison. It was widely promoted for more than twenty years. When it was finally evaluated in experiments, the program was found to actually *increase* juvenile offenses.[26]

Contrast the growing movement to use experiments to incrementally improve the efficacy of government programs with the dogmatic free market theory that government programs are necessarily ineffective and can be replaced with private sector programs. Perhaps privatizing a government function will work, but we should evaluate each case experimentally to find out.

Thus, a public health framework is fundamental to evolving a society that sees to the well-being of every person. By measuring well-being in terms of the incidence and prevalence of psychological, behavioral, and health problems, as well as the environmental conditions, such as poverty and inequality, that affect well-being, we will know whether our communities are getting better or worse. If we do not do this, we will be flying blind.

Influencing Corporate Practices

So far, I have focused on the values and behaviors of individuals and the conditions that select prosociality. However, we can also use evolutionary analysis to understand how to affect the practices of corporations and all other groups and organizations. Indeed, if we want to change the shape of capitalism, this is what we must do.

Capitalism is a set of practices, including beliefs, values, norms, and goals, that justify, guide, and encourage certain practices and vilify, disapprove, and discourage other practices. Capitalism evolved from earlier practices because of the benefits it conferred on individuals and groups that adopted capitalist practices.

In recent essays, I show how corporations have selected harmful practices because of the financial consequences of those practices—they were profitable. To put it simply, changing corporate practices is a matter of changing the consequences of those practices.

When we understand this, we can use the tools we already have to sort out which practices contribute to the general well-being and which undermine it. I have described how the tools of public health can help measure the well-being of Americans. We already measure the number of people who die due to the marketing of cigarettes, guns, unhealthful food, and opioids. We measure the proportions of people living in poverty, lacking health insurance, and facing discrimination. And we are beginning to predict how many human lives (and those in other species) will be lost due to greenhouse gas emissions.

With these tools and our understanding of what influences the selection of corporate practices, we can construct a framework for the regulation of capitalism. First, we can measure the extent to which a particular practice is contributing to ill health or any other aspect of well-being, such as depression, anxiety, or exposure to harassment or discrimination. Second, we can examine the extent to which a harmful corporate practice is profitable to the company, and we can penalize the company to the extent that the practice *causes it to lose money.* Keep in mind that the fines imposed on the pharmaceutical industry for their marketing of opioids were generally far less than their profits; the fines were simply a cost of doing business and did not end the practice.

Greater use could also be made of positive consequences. The purpose of tax incentives is to influence corporate practices. In most cases, lobbyists for corporations engineer the incentives; their purpose is seldom to achieve some public good. We need an organized experimental analysis of the ways in which tax incentives could influence prosocial actions of corporations. For example, a tax incentive could be given to companies that systematically assess whether any of their practices harm significant proportions of the population.

In this new version of capitalism, society will not view regulation as bad or good per se. Instead, groups will propose regulations when the harm of a practice is clearly established, and governments will evaluate the impacts, both good and bad, of a proposed regulation. In the process, the nature of the contingencies we use to influence practices will evolve, with a greater number of effective regulations going into effect based on the contribution of those regulations to the general well-being. This will, of course, require a shift in the prevalence of prosocial, communitarian values.

Moreover, as I indicate in chapter 1, we can also provide incentives to organizations for engaging in beneficial practices, such as the marketing of more healthful foods. In addition, we can create and strengthen social networks that promote prosocial values, goals, and behaviors.

Influencing Every Sector of Society

Of course, the problem is more complicated than simply changing the contingencies for corporations. Consequences affect the very process of regulating corporate practices. Thanks to the lobbying and largesse of wealthy people and organizations, regulatory practices, if they existed at all, were made favorable to corporate interests. But the capture of government by business interests would not have been possible unless leaders of numerous sectors of society had come to believe the flawed thesis of free market capitalism.

Which brings us to the last component of my framework for evolving a more nurturing form of capitalism—and, for that matter, a more nurturing society in general. If we want to reverse the course of recent evolution and bring about a society dedicated to the well-being of every person, the history of the conservative ascendency provides a road map.[27] Like Powell and those he influenced, we can articulate a set of principles about the kind of society we want. And in doing so, we will be on much firmer ground, thanks to the enormous amount of evidence that has accumulated about what people need in order to thrive and how we can create conditions that enable them to do so.

Just as the conservative billionaire coalition influenced every sector of society to embrace free market ideology, we need to influence every sector to embrace the value of ensuring everyone's well-being and to adopt policies and practices that move them toward greater promotion of the common good.

In the remainder of this book, I present a strategic plan for evolving a more nurturing form of capitalism. I write not just to inform you but to invite you to join a movement to create such a society. In the next chapter, I make the case for creating an unprecedented coalition across all sectors of society and all segments of the population because we need a coalition that is bigger and more powerful than the conservative billionaire coalition if we are going to prevail. Then, in chapters 5 through 11, I describe the ways that key sectors of society need to be reformed.

This is not a book to be read and forgotten. What I have tried to do is create the first draft of a how-to manual for an unprecedented movement to reform capitalism so it works for all—including the children still to come. Each of the remaining chapters has specific action implications. But more than that, I invite you to join the Values to Action community, which is working to make these reforms a reality. I think my ideas for this movement are good ones, and with your active involvement, we can take the steps I suggest we need in each sector of society, refine them, test them in actual practice, and evolve increasingly effective strategies. Join this movement. It will enrich your life at the same time that it heals our nation.

Action Implications

Personal

Join Values to Action (valuestoaction.com).

Join us in advancing the reforms needed throughout society. Each of the remaining chapters in this book details the reforms needed in a sector of society and ways we can achieve those reforms.

Each of the following chapters will give you specific things you can do to evolve a more nurturing economic and political system.

Policy

We need policies at the federal and state level that improve our monitoring of well-being.

Ultimately, we should monitor most facets of well-being at the community level—just as we do for economic outcomes. In this way, communities can track progress in improving specific aspects of well-being and continue or change what they are doing in light of observed outcomes. In each of the following chapters, I describe policies that will contribute to the change we need.

Organizational

Identify organizations working to improve any aspect of well-being.

There is a vast array of such organizations, but as I discuss in the next chapter, they are not working together in the way that is needed.

CHAPTER 4:

The Values to Action Coalition: The Foundation for the Change We Seek

---

Strength lies in organization, in careful long-range planning and implementation, in consistency of action over an indefinite period of years, in the scale of financing available only through joint effort, and in the political power available only through united action and national organizations.[8]

— Lewis Powell

LTHOUGH THE ADVOCACY of the conservative billionaire coalition has been beneficial to many wealthy people, it has been disastrous for millions of Americans and people around the world. Even after the coalition increased its share of the wealth from about 7 percent in 1978 to more than 20 percent in 2013,[1] it got a tax bill passed in 2017 that gave 82 percent of benefits to the top 1 percent.[2] Think of it as an organism that has grown increasingly big and powerful and developed an insatiable hunger for more power, not unlike the plant in *Little Shop of Horrors* that takes over the shop and demands "FEED ME!"

What can we do? The massive changes we need to achieve in society require that we build an extraordinary coalition of organizations,[3] bringing them together around a vision of society that has a form of capitalism that works for everyone. All sectors of society must work together to make American society one in which everyone's well-being is given a higher priority than the material aggrandizement of a few. It is exactly this kind of coordination that resulted from the Powell memo.

The foundation for building this new, progressive coalition is a network of behavioral science organizations that have identified the factors that undermine human health and well-being and the programs and policies that can help people thrive.

Modern marketing and advocacy tell us we need a name for the coalition. I am tempted to call it the progressive billionaire coalition. Certainly, a strong case can be made that numerous very wealthy people share our values, and that without their money and influence, we will be hard pressed to succeed. However, a progressive billionaire coalition still implies that it is the very wealthy who should run society. So how about the Values to Action Coalition?

An Evolutionary Take on Why We Need a Coalition

An evolutionary analysis underscores why a coalition of unprecedented size and diversity is needed. Consider the evolution of the conservative billionaire coalition. In the past half century, a number of wealthy people took coordinated action to create a network of foundations, think tanks, advocacy organizations, and media groups to foster support for free market economic theory. Their coordinated action was shaped and maintained by the steady accretion of power and wealth that flowed to them. Each success in preventing a policy they didn't like or getting one they liked implemented reinforced their coordinated efforts at the same time that it gave them even greater leverage in policy making. For example, the Citizens United decision of the Supreme Court gave corporations virtually unlimited power to advocate for their preferred candidates, thus further strengthening their political influence.

The success of the coalition in advancing free market ideology is an example of multilevel selection. Recall that, depending on the consequences, selection can occur at the level of individual units (e.g., cells, people, or groups) or at the level of larger units at a higher level (e.g., a corporation, an industry, or a network of business organizations such the chamber of commerce).

David Sloan Wilson describes the tension between selection at different levels. For example, the behaviors of an individual within a group may be selected by rewards to the individual, such as more food for that person. However, as small human groups evolved, groups that were able to suppress the selfish behavior of individuals so they cooperated for the good of the group were more likely to survive.

Humans' genetically driven cooperative tendencies and the cultural practices of groups (e.g., rewards for cooperation, sanctions for selfish behavior) evolved because of their contribution to survival. Over the centuries, even larger groups, such as corporations, evolved because they conferred benefits that could not be achieved without this higher level of cooperation.

The conservative billionaire coalition has taken this to an even higher level. They discovered that greater wealth could be achieved by forging an unprecedented level of cooperation among wealthy individuals and organizations that is laser focused on policies that are economically beneficial to them. However, their selfish success has not benefited society as a whole. Their selfish actions are not unlike the selfishness that a group member might have exhibited in a prehistoric hunter-gatherer group, which then needed to be suppressed in the interest of that group's survival. If we want the whole of humanity to succeed, we need to get the conservative billionaire coalition to act in the interests of the whole and limit its ability to make policies that benefit it at the expense of the rest of society.

Contrast the conservative billionaire coalition with the much less organized array of advocacy groups, political organizations, billionaires, and foundations working on one or another facet of the changes we need. These groups are working in generally uncoordinated and often competitive ways to address one or another problem. There are groups working to address racial discrimination, climate change, poverty, gender inequality, tobacco use, guns, healthful eating, the availability, quality, and affordability of health care, and so on.

These groups are competing for money and members. Often, they are in conflict with one another, arguing that their cause is more important than other causes. For example, within the Democratic Party, there is a tendency to pit those emphasizing addressing discrimination and the rights of minorities against those emphasizing economic issues. These controversies are encouraged by the news media, which loves a good fight because it attracts an audience and benefits them financially (another example of selection by consequences). But as long as people are encouraged to believe they must choose between these issues, it will be hard to achieve the broad coalition needed to overcome the control of public policy by the conservative billionaire coalition. We need to have all these forces come together in a much more effective fashion than they have thus far.

Contrast the fragmentation and raucous quarreling among progressive groups with the disciplined, coordinated efforts of the conservative coalition. Their focus on policies to increase their wealth has led them to subordinate every other consideration. A president who is a sexual predator and liar? Never mind, we need tax breaks for the wealthy. A senate candidate in Alabama who is revealed to have sexually molested teenage girls? We can't lose that seat in the Senate; we need tax breaks for the wealthy. The loss of health care for millions of Americans? That's OK; we want to cut the tax on wealthier people that Obamacare implemented. In the past fifteen or so years, we have seen the conservative coalition shed virtually every principle other than those that support policies that would increase their wealth.

What would happen if all the people concerned about one or more of the problems we face as a nation formed a coalition around a clear vision of the kind of society we want to build and committed to work *over an indefinite period of time* to build the society we aspire to? We would finally succeed in changing the direction of the nation, our economy, and the well-being of our people, and do it just as effectively as the conservative billionaire coalition did.

Three Reasons a Grand Coalition Is Vital

Why does our success depend on creating such a big coalition? First, the major psychological, behavioral, and health problems we face as a society (e.g., human conflict, crime, academic failure, substance abuse, obesity, cardiovascular disease) are interconnected, but our strategies for dealing with them generally have not been. Second, our strategies for dealing with them ignore fundamental conditions (e.g., poverty, inequality, and discrimination) that make all the problems more likely. Third, the organizations working on these problems are not speaking with one voice about how we can address all of these interconnected problems. Let's take a closer look at each.

Interconnections Among Problems

In 2000–2001, I led an interdisciplinary study of adolescent problem behavior at the Center for Advanced Studies in the Behavioral Sciences at Stanford University. We brought together evidence that had been accumulating for a number of years, which showed that adolescent problems were interrelated.[4] Youth who use substances or fail in school are more likely than other youth to have other problems, such as antisocial behavior and depression. Yet our research and practical action to deal with these problems is quite fragmented, with some research groups and treatment providers focused on depression, while entirely different research groups and treatment providers are focused on other problems, such as drug abuse, teen suicide, and antisocial behavior.

Progress has clearly been made on this issue, especially by prevention researchers who have shown that multiple problems can be prevented by comprehensive programs that address multiple influences on these problems.[5]

However, the fragmentation in our approach to our problems remains, and it extends beyond youth. The major sectors of society that have responsibility for enhancing well-being include education, health care, human services, religion, and criminal justice. The success of each sector is enhanced when the other sectors are effective.

We have evolved research and treatment organizations focused on different facets of well-being, with little attention to or coordination with the efforts of other organizations addressing other problems. Here are some examples:

- **Schools.** A school's success depends on the effectiveness of the other sectors. Schools struggle to effectively teach children who come to school with myriad problems, including exposure to abuse and trauma, untreated depression, substance abuse problems of their parents, and antisocial behavior. Programs to address the problematic behaviors children exhibit in schools have made definite progress. For example, Positive Behavioral Intervention and Support, the Good Behavior Game, and Positive Action have all shown value in reducing problem behavior in schools.[6] However, most of the problems that children bring to school would also benefit from effective family interventions. Yet I can tell you from extensive experience working in schools and family interventions that most schools have virtually no coordination with or assistance from agencies that provide family interventions. Greater coordination is needed.

- **Family interventions and the criminal justice system.** Families are harmed by our current criminal justice system, although research is just beginning to document how children are harmed when incarceration undermines family stability and traumatizes children.[7] Among the outcomes this situation portends is that many children will themselves develop problem behaviors that lead to incarceration. Yet, as far as I can tell, the criminal justice system has paid little attention to the way in which its practices harm families. Greater cooperation between the family service and criminal justice systems would help each system be more successful. Criminal justice should be concerned about making effective family interventions available to high-conflict families, which produce a large proportion of the offenders. For example, Mark Eddy and his colleagues developed an intervention to help people who are incarcerated and have children become more effective parents.[8] Such efforts should be part of every prison system.

- **Health care and prevention.** It has been estimated that 95 percent of health-care dollars are spent on treating disease.[9] Yet a huge proportion of the diseases being treated could have been prevented.[10] Health would be improved and much money would be saved if the health-care system made use of family and school interventions that can prevent problems known to have an impact on physical health: cigarette smoking, excessive alcohol use, antisocial behavior, depression, attention deficit hyperactivity disorder, and child abuse.

- **Drug use disorders and family functioning.** Drug addiction undermines effective parenting. Yet about 80 percent of people who are addicted to drugs are unable to get treatment.[11]

- **Churches.** A church that provides social support and guidance to a child in a poor and struggling family may contribute to that child's overall development and thereby make the schools more likely to succeed. Yet very little coordination occurs between the religious community and the human service sector.

At the local level, judges, school superintendents, public health officials, and religious leaders need to band together to ensure that the community provides material and social support to families and makes sure that evidence-based family, school, and community interventions are reaching those who will benefit from them.

There is solid empirical evidence in support of this view. The Communities That Care Program has shown that when community leaders are helped to understand the major risk and protective factors that contribute to problem development and to implement evidence-based preventive interventions, they can significantly reduce the rates of delinquency and drug abuse.[12]

Think about this also at the state and national levels. At these levels, each sector has people who are trying to make their system more effective by seeking more funding and evaluating and refining their policies and practices. However, to a great extent, these systems are more focused on dealing with problems after they have developed than on preventing problems. And they tend to narrowly focus on the proximal influences on problems, such as family conflict or bullying in schools, and ignore how the larger context affects not only the problems they are chartered to address but all the other problems.

Of course, one of the reasons each of these sectors is less effective than it could be is because each is starved for resources. For example, twenty-nine states provide less funding for education than they did ten years ago.[13]

The various sectors find themselves competing for the limited dollars available to address social problems in a nation that is currently under the mistaken belief that funding of social programs is a waste of money.

In addition, we do not pay people in human services, education, or criminal justice what we should. The average pay for a preschool classroom teacher nationally is $26,420.[14] The median salary for an elementary school teacher nationally is $54,890. The median pay for a behavioral health specialist who might provide services in a health-care or human service setting is $16.17 an hour, which comes to about $32,340 annually.[15] The median annual income for parole officers is $54,228.

Now if your thinking has been influenced by free market ideology, you may be inclined to think these are quite reasonable salaries. That is because we have been repeatedly told that markets provide the best way of determining the value of a job. These jobs pay less than what lawyers (median annual income of $115,820), family physicians (mean annual income of $172,963), CEOs of large corporations (mean annual income of $13.8 million), and hedge fund managers (the top ten on Forbes list averaged $200 million) make because they are inherently less valuable.[16]

That argument obscures two things. First, the jobs in education and human-services-related sectors are largely funded by the government to provide services the society needs. They are not well paid in our current society because a half century of advocacy undermined belief in the efficacy of government. Second, some of the CEOs of our major corporations are not only not benefiting society, they are harming it. For example, Martin J. Barrington, the CEO of Altria, the maker of Marlboro cigarettes, was paid $11,997,585 in 2017.[17] John Pierce, Betsey Gilpin, and Won Choi estimated that the company's advertising between 1988 and 1998 led to 1.2 million young people beginning to smoke Marlboros, which will result in 300,000 deaths.[18]

Moreover, if you have been influenced by the conservative billionaire coalition over the past several decades, you may also think that none of these human service sector systems are very effective and investing in them is a waste of money. I agree that they could be more effective. For example, they could do a better job of measuring their impact and improving their effectiveness over time. And they could make greater use of the prevention and treatment programs and policies that behavioral scientists have come up with in the past forty years.

But where is the money for continuously evaluating the effectiveness of public sector efforts or the money to train people in these interventions? Each sector is fighting a battle for resources, often in competition with the other sectors.

Addressing Root Causes

It is time for the leaders in each of these sectors to come together and advocate not only for the resources needed to improve the success of each sector but for the policies that would reduce poverty and discrimination, which are making these problems more common and more intractable. Most efforts to deal with the problems do not address root causes such as poverty and discrimination. Here are some examples:

- Efforts to reduce incarceration have focused on sentencing reform but done little to prevent crime by reducing poverty or reducing discrimination in arrest, prosecution, and incarceration.

- Efforts to improve education through curricular reform and improvements in social-emotional learning have proven effective.[19]

However, public support for public schools has eroded, and funding for schools has declined.[20]

- Health-care outcomes could be improved if social determinants of health, such as poverty and discrimination, were prevented, yet the health-care system is largely uninvolved in addressing the social determinants of health.[21]

- Progressive political groups are failing to get progressive candidates elected because their forces are concentrated narrowly on winning the next election in places where polling suggests they can prevail. Little effort has been made to organize a broad coalition focused on the fundamental economic policies that have hollowed out the middle class. See chapter 11 for a more extensive critique of Democrats' failure to address the economic problems of the working class.

- Now that an unprecedented epidemic of opioid overdose is well underway, we begin to see the development of an effort to combat drug addiction. Yet this tragedy has been unfolding ever since the pharmaceutical industry promoted overmedication with opioids, and since a huge swath of Americans slipped out of the middle class. A root cause has been overlooked because free market advocacy hollowed out the middle class and gave the pharmaceutical industry much more influence over policy than the public health sector has.

- In addressing the problem of poverty in the state of Washington, the Bill and Melinda Gates Foundation invested more than $1 billion to improve education and reduce homelessness.[22] Their focus is on remediating the impacts of poverty on families' health and children's cognitive development. This is undoubtedly valuable. Evidence indicates that the projects they have funded can reduce intergenerational poverty.[23] However, their approach does not address the public policies that created the levels of poverty found in the state of Washington and in the rest of the nation. (This may be less a problem of myopia about the root causes of poverty and more a problem of opposition to the policies needed to reduce inequality. After all, Bill Gates has given considerable money to conservative Republicans such as Mitch McConnell and Marco Rubio.[24])

All these examples point back to our failure to focus on social and economic well-being. We have been poking our fingers in the dike to combat drunk driving, too much incarceration, poor education, chronic disease, discrimination, and drug addiction, one problem at a time. All the while, we are ignoring the deterioration of the values of cooperation, respect, and support for others' well-being, as well as the deterioration of the basic social and economic conditions that were the bulwark of Americans' well-being.

Speaking with One Voice

We will not change the direction of this country until all sectors of society and all the organizations working on specific problems create a coalition that advocates for values, goals, policies, and programs that can rebuild the middle class and reduce poverty, economic inequality, and discrimination.

Successful coalitions to bring about change in American society are not unprecedented. Doris Kearns Goodwin describes the Progressive Era between 1890 and 1920 that advanced the well-being of millions of Americans through its many reforms.[25] These included:

- Passage of the Sherman Antitrust Act and the Clayton Antitrust Act, which prohibited the creation of monopolies

- The progressive income tax

- Increased protection for union organizing

- Creation of the Federal Reserve and the Federal Trade Commission

- Restrictions on how many hours a child can work

- Establishment of an eight-hour work day for railroad workers

- Creation of the Food and Drug Administration, which, for the first time in U.S. history, began to regulate the food industry in the interests of public safety

Similarly, the civil rights movement brought about a revolution not only in the rights of black people but ultimately in the rights of many other groups.

You might think of our national situation this way. It is as though a tornado has torn through the entire nation and devastated almost every community. It is necessary for us rebuild the nation. And in doing so, we can create the communities of the future.

Go to a community in middle America that has been ravished by a tornado and you will find people working together to repair the damage and rebuild the community. For example, when Greensburg, Kansas, was devastated by a tornado in 2007, the citizens rebuilt the major buildings to the highest standards of sustainability and adopted renewable energy practices.[26] And when Joplin, Missouri, was completely devastated by a tornado in 2011, Greensburg GreenTown, a nonprofit organization that had helped make Greensburg sustainable, helped Joplin take the same course.

In the current era, it is not as much our physical structures as our social relations that have been devastated. But out of this wreckage, we have the opportunity to build a far more compassionate, sustainable, and healthy society.

Coalition Building within Behavioral Science

We behavioral scientists are becoming more assertive about how policy makers should use our knowledge to foster well-being. The National Prevention Science Coalition (NPSC) was created under the leadership of Diana Fishbein to educate policy makers and society about the tremendous potential of well-researched programs and policies. We are working to ensure that policy makers and community members understand that these programs and policies can ensure that most young people arrive at adulthood with the skills and values needed to lead productive and caring lives.

Since NPSC was created, I have been involved in the creation of an even larger coalition. The Coalition of Behavioral Science Organizations currently consists of six organizations: The Association for Behavioral Analysis International, The Association for Contextual Behavioral Science, The Association for Positive Behavior Support, The Evolution Institute, The National Prevention Science Coalition, and The Society for Behavioral Medicine. Our goal is to get increasingly effective at speaking with one voice about what humans need to thrive and the fact that the behavioral sciences are the key to creating the environments that support everyone thriving.

A Coalition on Behalf of Nurturance

As I hope I have convinced you, the conservative billionaire coalition has taken America down the wrong path. We have become a more selfish, divided, and stressful place. Few Americans are satisfied with the state of our society.

However, the very success of the conservative billionaire coalition provides our most important model for how we can reverse the changes that nearly fifty years of advocacy for free market economics have created. Just as their coalition worked to get every sector of society to embrace the belief that the pursuit of individual wealth will necessarily benefit everyone, we need to take control of public discourse by coming together around a vision of the healthy and nurturing society that most people desire and that behavioral science has shown can be achieved.

Our goals need to include reform of each sector of society. We need to bring the values and practices of each more in line with what the majority of Americans want for their communities and nation. We need to promote ethical business practices that make our collective well-being one of the goals of every business. We need to build a health-care system that does a much better job of preventing disease and treating everyone who needs treatment. We need to make higher education, once again, an engine of growth and equality. We need a criminal justice system that focuses on prevention and rehabilitation, not punishment. We need the media to promote prosocial values and public policies. We need to ensure that every sector is doing what it can to reduce greenhouse gas emissions. And finally, we need to reform our political system so it works for all.

In the remainder of this book, I lay out the reforms I believe are needed in each of the most important sectors of society and describe the steps we can take to achieve them.

Action Implications

Personal

Become an advocate.

As you read the rest of this book, look for ways you can promote the reforms you feel are needed in every sector of society.

- Join the Values to Action coalition (valuestoaction.com).
- We are creating a broad network of people who are committed to the reform of every sector of society. The remainder of this book sketches out what is needed in each sector and how we can advance the needed reforms.

- Get good at speaking up.

- I know so many people who care passionately about the issues we are discussing but who hesitate to get involved in organizations working on these issues or to speak up in public discussions. If you are a scientist, you have probably been taught to be cautious about your claims. It is always possible that someone will criticize you for being "WRONG!" This is where the psychological flexibility I talk about in chapter 2 is so important. If your values are to see this nation move in the direction of greater nurturance, speaking up about what we know about human well-being and how to promote it is the single most important thing you can do advance your values. Psychological flexibility is not a matter of being sure that what you are doing will work or that everyone will applaud your efforts. It is a matter of taking actions that are likely to advance your values, even when you feel anxiety or doubt. I say this from the standpoint of fifty years of having plenty of anxiety and doubt in the process of speaking up.

If you are a behavioral scientist...

You can support the growth of the behavioral science coalitions I describe above. The National Prevention Science Coalition is developing policy briefings on how human well-being can be advanced. The success of this effort will depend to a great extent on behavioral scientists communicating the facts to citizens and policy makers at the state and local levels. One of your contributions to this movement for nurturing can be to become a spokesperson influencing the people and organizations you can reach.

Policy

Analyze how the laws regarding nonprofit advocacy impede the advancement of prosocial goals.

I am far from an expert on this, but given that the rights to almost unlimited advocacy have been conferred on corporations, it seems to me that we need a class of nonprofit organizations that can advocate for policies that will benefit everyone. Our reform movement should enlist some good lawyers to work on this problem.

Organizations

Identify organizations you are connected with at the national, state, or local level and link them to the Values to Action coalition.

Find at least one that could be part of a coalition. Identify the role it could play in advancing well-being and advocate for its getting involved.

Create local coalitions across the sectors of society discussed in the remainder of this book.

Increasingly, communities are organizing to improve well-being using a collective impact model, in which all sectors of the community are invited to participate in taking steps to build greater supports for well-being.[27] These efforts are coordinated by a backbone organization that organizes the efforts of each sector. Values to Action can help you do that.

If you are a behavioral scientist...

Become active in the Coalition of Behavioral Science Organizations. We intend to be more assertive about what behavioral science has to offer in creating the kind of society that research shows can improve just about everyone's health and well-being.

CHAPTER 5:

Businesses That Nurture

Just as people cannot live without eating, so a business cannot live without profits. But most people don't live to eat, and neither must businesses live just to make profits.

— John Mackey, founder of Whole Foods

WHEN I HAVE described this book to friends and colleagues, some have reacted quite skeptically to the idea that capitalism could ever be nurturing. After all, the fundamental contingency in a market system is making a profit. And a business can do many things to make a profit, some of which will harm consumers and third parties. Is it possible, then, that we can evolve a society in which businesses are nurturing? I am convinced it is.

As I see it, the criteria we need to judge whether any business is nurturing is whether it benefits the six stakeholders that are affected by it:

1. **Customers.** Do customers benefit from its products or services?

2. **Employees.** Do employees benefit from working for the company?

3. **Investors.** Do investors make a sufficient return on investment? (A word about "sufficient" below.)

4. **Suppliers.** Do suppliers benefit from supplying the business with the parts and services it needs?

5. **Society as a whole.** Do communities, regions, states, the nation, and the world benefit from the activities of the company or does the company cause more harm than good?

6. **Climate.** It has become crystal clear to those of us who are following the evidence on climate change that we now must consider the impact of every business on our climate.

I would argue that we have the tools to measure the impact on each of these groups in terms of harm and benefit. For customers, we can assess whether any are harmed, such as in the cases of smokers, gun owners, those eating unhealthful foods, patients taking prescription medications, people investing in collateralized debt obligations, and those suffering (or who will suffer) from the effects of carbon emissions from burning fossil fuels. We can also assess the benefits to customers.

In every case, we must balance the harms against the benefits. In the case of the tobacco industry, the harm of smoking clearly outweighs any benefit. But for many businesses, the balance is less clear. For example, antidepressant medications appear to have benefit for people who are severely depressed, and so we would not want to prevent their prescription for people with severe depression. However, evidence of the harm caused by less-depressed people becoming addicted to them, as well as the use of behavioral therapy (which has none of the risks of medication) as an effective treatment for depression, suggest the need for regulations to curtail their ready availability for people who are not severely depressed.

We also must deal with the balance of benefits and harms *among* these stakeholders. One could argue, for example, that customers, employees, and investors are currently benefiting from fossil fuel consumption, while society as a whole is being harmed.

I do not claim that my framework of standards for regulating business is complete. It is only a starting point for moving toward reductions in the harms of business and the evolution of more-nurturing businesses. However, the standards I suggest can be used to refine measures of harms and benefits and analyze the balance between the two.

With greater clarity about harms and benefits, we can have the debates that inevitably arise in a democratic society about where we will draw the line—which practices we should deem sufficiently harmful to necessitate regulations to prohibit or curtail them. I submit that this is a far more useful framework than the default and empirically unsupported assumption that unfettered capitalism will always benefit everyone.

In sum, if we choose to make everyone's well-being a foundational goal of our society, we must measure the impacts of all our business activities and regulate businesses in light of accurate measures of both their benefits and their harms.

Nurturing Businesses

In this section, I describe emerging business practices that are organized to achieve not just profits but benefits to all the people affected by the business—investors, customers, suppliers, and citizens in general. The success and spread of these practices are evidence that we can have a business community whose practices are selected by their benefit to all stakeholders.

Nurturing in the Construction Industry

After I published *The Nurture Effect,* I got an email from Dr. John Austin. I had never heard of him, but he is one of the leading figures in using behavioral science to help businesses improve worker safety. After reading my book, he felt that what I was saying about the value of nurturing environments could be relevant to work organizations. I was somewhat surprised he thought that, but was at the same time, excited to explore the possibility. I agreed to participate in a workshop that he and Bob Cummins were doing for construction and manufacturing organizations. Could an industry dominated by men possibly be interested in nurturance?

The workshop was held in Grand Rapids, Michigan, the hometown of Gerald Ford, who succeeded Richard Nixon when Nixon resigned. I had never been to Grand Rapids, but a walk around the town on a sunny day in September and a visit to the Gerald R. Ford Presidential Library and Museum impressed on me that this was traditional "rock-ribbed" Republican country. There was a brand of Republicanism in the Midwest in the middle of the twentieth century that was far more moderate and focused on the well-being of communities than on the amassing of great wealth.

In preparing for the workshop, the three of us concluded that the entry into a conversation about nurturance for this group could be a description of the stressful and coercive family, school, and community environments that lead to so many psychological and health problems. Based on research I had been doing on male adolescent development, I suspected that many men in the construction and manufacturing industries had had difficult childhoods. If so, many would be prone to feeling threatened and quick to react with anger and suspicion to any negative input. A company that took a "command and control" approach to worker safety would likely get a fair amount of resistance and pushback from people with this kind of history.

I was delighted to discover that the participants in the workshop were quite open to this analysis. They were already well into the alternative to command and control—namely, positive reinforcement for behavior that benefits the worker and coworkers rather than punishment for unsafe behavior.

I was particularly impressed to learn about CSM Group of Companies, which manages the construction of hospitals, schools, food and beverage facilities, industrial facilities, and commercial properties in twenty-six states. They had been working with Austin for eight years. Their vice president of Environmental, Health and Safety, Kevin Kirk, described how he got their construction sites to improve their housekeeping. (As I learned, *housekeeping* refers to how materials and equipment at a site are organized to make accidents less likely; the opposite of good housekeeping is to have materials and equipment strewn haphazardly around the site.) Kirk was able to improve housekeeping simply by having each site email a picture of its location each week. He then gave recognition to sites that were in good order. When people realized that this procedure carried no threat, positive reinforcement worked; no punishment was necessary.

They also had been working with Suzann Foerster, an executive coach, for seven years. Foerster brought innovative approaches that included mindfulness, having difficult conversations, and providing performance feedback.

Construction is a dangerous business. According to the U.S. Department of Labor, Bureau of Labor Statistics, in 1980, there were 7.5 deaths per 100,000 full-time equivalent (F.T.E.) employees, with construction ranking as the most dangerous occupation. In 2014, there were 3.3 deaths per 100,000 F.T.E. employees, with construction ranking as the second most dangerous occupation. Katrina Reed of CSM Group told me that 5,147 workers were killed on the job in 2017. On average, that was more than ninety-nine deaths a week, or more than fourteen a day.[1]

CSM Group has much lower injury rates. The standard measure is the total recordable incident rate (TRIR), which reflects the percentage of employees who experience an injury in a year. In the construction industry, the TRIR is currently 3.2 incidents per hundred workers. The rate for CSM Group is 0.0 per hundred workers, and the rate for companies that work with them on construction they manage is 1.14.

As I delved into how CSM Group works, I realized that nurturance in this company goes far beyond simply keeping workers from being injured. For example, in an essay he wrote to employees of his company, Steve East, the chairman of the board of CSM, said he wanted to promote emotional safety, such that people feel safe saying what's on their minds, have a sense of trust, know it's OK to fail, and know they won't be judged. He argued that emotional safety "will foster a vibrant, innovative, and collaborative environment. It will change the game."

Indeed, East told me they had recently updated their strategic plan to include only one strategy. He called it the "nurture approach":

Engage, nurture, and empower people who are gritty and care to:

- Be innovative

- Be inclusive

- Be exemplary

- Be one

East argued that the company's most valuable asset is the people who work there. He gave me numerous examples that supported his claim. I'll quote them directly:

- No tolerance of bullying, as demonstrated by separating from [firing] employees who engage in threats of any kind. Unfortunately, this [bullying] is a common practice in construction and manufacturing alike.

- A culture that values and invests heavily in education and learning. If an employee wants to take a course or go to a conference to learn, that is mostly supported. I haven't ever heard anyone say they weren't allowed to get more education. In fact, it's almost the opposite— because there is no one saying no, people tend to be very frugal with their requests, as if it's their own money they are spending.

- The physical environment plays an important role in the day-to-day outcome of the business. Creating a welcoming, safe, and technology-driven atmosphere can cost more but reaps numerous intangible rewards.

- People are super friendly to visitors or anyone who looks like they have a question, and quickly learn names of new people, include them in things, learn about their families, and ask how they are doing.

- There's never a question of priorities; if someone has a sick family member, they are expected to attend to their family first.

- If people in support functions find out that you're struggling with something, they will insist on helping you. This has happened to me personally on a number of occasions.

- There is plenty of consideration to helping people get what they want out of work and life.

- At CSM, we take a shaping approach and utilize coaching to instill positive reinforcement to help and support personal growth.

- People are allowed to try new things, are encouraged to pilot ideas, collect data, and fail fast or expand, depending on the results.

However, he added that:

> With all this positivity, it would be easy to assume that nurturance simply means creating a positive environment by being ridiculously nice to each other, but one of the keys to making this work is also having accountability. Accountability and responsibility is valued at the company and CSM Group is on the journey toward getting better at it, just like every other complex skill.

The company's nurturance extends to its relationships with the contractors and suppliers who work with it. They strive to infuse these collaborating organizations not only with the safety standards they maintain but with their approach to nurturing workers. CSM Group has unique relationships with its contractors and suppliers. They do not build buildings themselves as much as they organize and hire contractors who do the work, which gives them leverage to select companies that meet their standards. East told me the company rates its collaborators on a monthly basis on the technical aspects of their work, their safety efforts, and whether they are "nice to work with." They select better practices among collaborators by sharing their ratings of six hundred local contractors, choosing them on the basis of those ratings, and sharing the ratings with the contractors. And they turn away clients who do not fit with their values.

CSM Group president and CEO Jim Feltch added:

> Being "nice to work with" is the emotional context of not just what we do but how we do it. The intention one has to inspire others to achieve greatness outperforms the "do as I say" obedience model that can plague a worksite. Our teams have learned that positive outcomes are not just more achievable, but relationally sustainable through a communication channel that harnesses emotional connectivity. When you talk to site teams and ask "What did you see in your rearview mirror when you left home this morning?", their response varies from my home, my family, my life...devoting ourselves to providing a physically and emotionally safe project site allows them to return to that at the end of the day. My position at CSM Group is not to chase perfection, but to strategically and collaboratively pursue greatness in the relationships so vital in building safe projects.

Mandy Backler, chief administrative officer, pointed out that it was also relevant for me to know that, as of December 31, 2016, women made up a mere 9.1 percent of the construction industry in the United States. She added:

> In stark contrast, CSM Group's (construction) leadership team comprises 50 percent women! In my opinion, this fact alone embodies a nurturing environment where employees, and specifically women in construction, thrive. As a member of the leadership team, I am proud to say I have a seat at the table in a male-dominated workforce but also a very healthy work/life balance, where being a mother is fully embraced. For example, I am able to get my daughters on and off the school bus every day without the aid of before or after childcare, due to flexibility in my schedule. Additionally, due to accountability and responsibility being so valued at the company, I am able to work remotely several days a week. This gives me more time with my family, without the commute to the office, while still being highly valued at the company and advancing my career. I strongly believe these two factors alone are impacting the lives of the next generation in the workforce by changing the face of what construction, leadership, and nurturing business can truly look like.

I asked East whether they ever forgo profits that would require them to deviate from their values. The answer was yes: "[We] separate from (fire) clients who do not fit our culture. We have done this with some very large clients because of their actions, specifically as it relates to bullying, coercion, non-fair play, deception, etc. I will simply not tolerate giving our best to organizations who do not represent our values."

I asked how he felt about regulation. He said, "Absolutely, yes! We need to clearly articulate what is acceptable and what is not. We are a society of laws and I believe we all need to respect that foundation. Does it ever get out of hand? Occasionally. But that is expected and most generally it is rationally dealt with."

CSM Group is certainly an example of a business organized to benefit all five of the parties a business can affect. And while its survival provides some evidence that businesses don't have to be rapacious and ignore the harm they may do in their quest for profits, I found myself pondering the question of profitability.

I asked East whether there are situations in which they must make a choice between actions that might increase their profits but also have externalities, and actions that might reduce externalities but also profits. His answer:

> Absolutely, we make choices each and every day that have potential to affect our profits. As previously stated, we simply do not tolerate any actions that would compromise safety on our job sites. As in traditional "corner-cutting" tactics to expedite work. We rigorously vet our trade partners to verify they comply with all safety, insurance, financial and quality requirements. We invest heavily in safety training, coaching, personal development, and accountability.

The dominant vision of capitalism, as it is currently practiced, is that companies must maximize their profits at all costs. By this standard, every company's performance must be measured by how profitable it is *relative to other companies*. I submit that this fundamental value and goal has led many business interests to do anything they can to eliminate any laws and regulations that would reduce their profits. If Company A is making 5 percent on its investment and Company B is making 10 percent, then obviously we need to invest in Company B.

If I claim that CSM Group is a model for the kind of corporation we need to evolve, don't I need to show that it is more profitable than companies that ignore the well-being of employees, customers, suppliers, and the community at large?

I think not. To accept that as the criterion for saying all companies should emulate CSM Group's practices would be to accept the argument that capitalism must maximize profits to the exclusion of any other consideration. That is the principle that has gotten us into the mess we are in today.

Nonetheless, for any company to survive, it must make enough money to pay its employees and investors. If we are seeking to evolve a society in which companies that benefit society make enough to ensure their prosperity and the prosperity of others in the society, we need to show that such a result is possible.

With respect to CSM Group, it appears that it is. Feltch stated that CSM Group has consistently achieved its financial goals in the past ten years. They aimed to have a 10 percent increase in their investment each year, and their investment doubled from 2010 through 2019. Their return on equity since 2010 has been between 2 percent and 3 percent. And projected revenue has more than doubled since 2010.

I submit that this is a matter of values. CSM adopted a set of values that give priority to the well-being of every person they touch. This is a choice. It may be that they could make more money by not firing a client that is harming its employees or otherwise acting for its benefit at a cost to others. But they choose not to.

As the above comments show, however, they are convinced that the nurturing environment they create for their employees and partners is good for business; it results in fewer accidents, better communication, more cooperation, and greater employee commitment to the values the company maintains.

East also wrote the following about his view of leadership:

> I would describe the culture of CSM Group of Companies as based on stewards and servants in all respects. I believe in servant leadership as it relates to the well-being of our employees, customers, and our community. My goal is to encourage and support those around me so they can reach their full potential whether in our office, in someone else's or in our community. I also believe in inclusion, awareness, and consideration of all perspectives.

My experience working with Austin and East was striking for one other reason. It lines up so well with what Steven Hayes has been teaching about self-compassion and what David Sloan Wilson has been teaching about the evolutionary value of cooperation. In my contacts with thousands of people that resulted from publishing *The Nurture Effect*, I have found so many different groups who are often unaware of other groups that are working on creating nurturing environments—another basis for the grand coalition I am advocating.

B Corporations—a Nurturing Variant of Corporations

The B Corporation ("B Corp") movement directly addresses the issue I laid out at the beginning of this chapter about the well-being of a broader group of stakeholders. It is an excellent example of a coalition forming to advance these values. B Corps are "certified by the nonprofit B Lab to meet rigorous standards of social and environmental performance, accountability, and transparency." You can find more information about B Corps on the Internet. The rationale for B Corps is articulated in their declaration of interdependence (which, ironically, I read for the first time on the Fourth of July).

> We envision a global economy that uses business as a force for good.
>
> This economy is comprised of a new type of corporation—the B Corporation—which is purpose-driven and creates benefit for all stakeholders, not just shareholders.
>
> As B Corporations and leaders of this emerging economy, we believe:
>
> - That we must be the change we seek in the world
>
> - That all business ought to be conducted as if people and place mattered
>
> - That, through their products, practices, and profits, businesses should aspire to do no harm and benefit all
>
> - To do so requires that we act with the understanding that we are each dependent upon another and thus responsible for each other and future generations

B Lab, which does the certifying, is a nonprofit company that aspires to create societies in which "all companies compete not only to be the best in the world, but the Best for the World." They are explicitly trying to align the interests of business with those of society. To be certified, a company must provide information about the governance of the company, as well as its impact on employees, the community, and the environment. B Lab indicates that it has certified 3,243 corporations worldwide in seventy-one countries and 150 industries.[2]

In discussing B Corps, Wilson notes that at the level of small groups, humans have evolved mechanisms to monitor whether group members are acting in the interests of the group, and to correct their behavior if they are not. At the level of corporations, however, we lack mechanisms for monitoring and influencing whether they are benefiting or harming society. Wilson argues that B Corp certification enables people to monitor whether a company is acting in the interest of the society and thereby facilitating prosocial actions. Wilson cites a study by Xiujian Chen and Thomas F. Kelly at Binghamton University's School of Management that compared a sample of B Corps with a matched sample of companies in the same business and localities.[3] They found that B Corps were no less profitable and were sometimes more profitable.

Conscious Capitalism

Conscious capitalism is a movement that promotes purpose-driven business, wherein the purpose includes the well-being of all the people who may be affected by the activity of the company—investors, customers, and any third parties that might be harmed or benefit.

My work on this chapter was well along before I learned of this movement. Ebba Karlsson, a Swedish political psychologist, forwarded me a link to ConsciousCapitalism.org. Just reading the blurb on the website got me excited: a network of people who believe, as I do, that capitalism needs to function within a framework of values, beliefs, and goals that ensures that many benefit and few are harmed.

Yet, I found myself cautious. So many companies are promising so much to so many these days, with few examples of those promises being kept. It makes me wonder if this will turn out to be mostly a new twist on how to become fabulously wealthy.

The movement was begun by John Mackey, the founder of Whole Foods. Mackey led Whole Foods to expand to 460 stores nationwide. The company was sold to Amazon for more than $13 billion. If you read much business news, you probably expect me to report that Mackey is now a billionaire. He is not; he is said to be worth $75 million. So far, so good. The guy appears to be living what he believes, and he appears to have just the kinds of values I think are needed to repair our country.

Mackey and Rak Sosodia have written a book titled *Conscious Capitalism,* which lays out the conscious capitalism framework.[4] They advocate that companies define their purpose and organize everything they do in light of it. They define purpose in terms of four qualities. Profits are pursued within the context of these values:

- **The Good:** This is pretty much what I mean by prosociality, nurturance, and compassion. They argue that "the most common way this ideal manifests itself in business is through service to others." They go on to say that "genuine empathy leads to the development, growth, and expression of love, care, and compassion."

- **The True:** Here, they are concerned with "discovery and furthering human knowledge." I hope they mean furthering human knowledge that will contribute to the well-being of the population. In retrospect, nuclear weapons don't seem like such a good idea. They cite Google, Wikipedia, Genentech, and Intel as organizations organized around this purpose (see, however, my discussion of Google in chapter 9).

- **The Beautiful:** They define this as "excellence and the creation of beauty." They cite Apple, Four Seasons, and BMW as companies that exemplify the pursuit of this purpose.

- **The Heroic:** Mackey and Sosodia borrow the first three categories from Plato. They add one, which they define as "courage to do what is right to change and improve the world." They offer as an example a set of higher purposes that the Whole Foods leadership came up with in 2011. These include (1) influencing the world's agricultural system to make it more efficient and more sustainable, (2) raising the public's awareness about the principles of healthy eating, (3) ending poverty around the world, and (4) making conscious capitalism the dominant economic and business paradigm in the world.

The conscious capitalism framework is guiding many companies to change the way they do business. The process begins with the company leaders, and, ultimately, all the members of the organization, defining the company's purpose. They are encouraged to enumerate the stakeholders in their business and articulate how the business creates value for each stakeholder. The stakeholders include not only the employees, investors, and customers but also the communities in which they operate and all the organizations affected by what they do.

Mackey and Sosodia cite a study of fifty U.S. and fifteen non-U.S. companies following this framework.[5] The companies were assessed for the degree to which they are pursuing conscious capitalism. They were classified as highly conscious, conscious, or becoming conscious. The study showed that the financial performance of all these companies was higher than the market during a period of ten to fifteen years. This was especially the case for the highly conscious organizations.

Business Reform through Reform of the Rest of Society

The B Corp and conscious capitalism movements are one facet of growing efforts to bring about more nurturing societies. Convincing all of our corporations to adopt B Corp or conscious capitalism standards is a tall order. B Corp has reached 2,100 companies worldwide. But there are 1.6 million corporations in the United States alone.[6]

This is why all the other reforms I have described are so important. Acting alone, the B Corp movement will surely make progress. But consider how the other changes I advocate would help.

- If business schools and economics programs taught students about the basic conditions people need to thrive and fostered students' consideration of the impact of business on all of society, support for the selection of nurturing companies would grow as these students entered the work force.

- If schools, human services, and health-care providers fostered prosocial behavior and values through school programs such as Positive Action, the PAX Good Behavior Game, Cooperative Learning, and Positive Behavioral Intervention and Support, as well as family programs such as the Positive Parenting Program, the next generation of students would be more inclined toward cooperation, empathy, and prosociality. This, too, would support the evolution of more-nurturing capitalism.

- If a new generation of lawyers were educated about behavioral science and what it tells us about human well-being, we would have more lawyers who are willing to work for laws and legal rulings that favor businesses that minimize harm to society.

In subsequent chapters, I elaborate on how we can achieve these changes.

Contingencies That Prevent Harmful Corporate Behavior

One thing to consider about any effort to evolve nurturing businesses is that no person or company will always do the right thing. Companies make mistakes. They may drift away from the kind of prosocial purposes that the conscious capitalism and B Corp movements are trying to promote. I think that individually, as citizens, and collectively, through the formal and informal instruments of the governance of society, we need clear and measurable standards for the performance of companies. When a company's actions are inconsistent with these standards, we need to call it out and require compensation for acts that harm.

Setting up contingencies that effectively deter harmful actions may not be as complicated as it might seem. I have already described some of the penalties imposed on companies that have violated the law or otherwise harmed people. In many cases, the penalties seemed huge in comparison with the scale of finances that non-wealthy people deal with. However, in most cases, the fines that were levied (e.g., in the pharmaceutical, tobacco, and financial industries) were far less than the profits the companies reaped from their practices. The fines were simply the cost of doing business.

The most egregious example was in the cigarette industry. In *U.S. v. Philip Morris,* the industry was found to have (1) caused 20 million deaths due to smoking, despite the fact that they knew as early as the 1950s that cigarettes cause cancer; (2) knowingly marketed low tar and nicotine cigarettes as safer, when the companies knew they weren't safer; and (3) marketed cigarettes to young people while denying they were doing so. Yet they paid no fines whatsoever for a half century of extraordinarily harmful behavior.

Thus, my simple solution is the *no-profit principle:* require that a company engaging in a business practice that does harm be fined more than the total profit the company makes in engaging in the practice. Although the contingency I propose is simple in concept, establishing it as a standard policy will only happen when we reform the other sectors of society so that they also function in the interests of everyone, not just the very wealthy.

Business as an Engine of Well-Being

David Leonhardt of *The New York Times* reminds us that there was once a "culture of financial restraint" in the United States.[7] For example, George Romney, the president of American Motors (and father of Mitt Romney), refused several substantial bonuses, saying he didn't think anyone should make more than $250,000 a year ($2 million in today's currency). This was in the early 1960s, when CEOs made twenty times what the average worker made, rather than 271 times more, as is currently the case.

A key component of a movement to make our society more nurturing is the return to a set of norms and values that consider huge wealth aggrandizement something to be ashamed of, and contributions to the well-being of society the measure of good business. In chapter 8, I discuss how higher education can contribute to a return to these values.

Action Implications

Personal

Be an effective consumer. One important way you can influence the evolution of nurturing businesses is through the actions you take as a consumer.

- Consider what you buy in a typical month. Food, maybe some clothing, gasoline, Internet access, entertainment, eating out, vacations. From an evolutionary perspective, you are one of the people who is setting the contingencies that select the practices of every organization you pay or give money to.

- A variety of organizations have organized ratings or rankings of companies with the best employment practices. You can find a list on the Cornell University website. You may be able to find out how the companies you pay money to (e.g., your bank, Internet provider, organizations that service things you do on the Internet, the companies that make the brands you buy) treat their employees.

- I would call the relationship between consumers and companies a *macro-contingency*. By that, I mean a contingency in which the proportion of the population that buys from a company can affect its practices. Well, of course, that is obvious in a sense. But you can play a part in selecting the kind of society you want by scrutinizing the practices of every company you have any type of contact with. The B Corp movement is an important step in facilitating this.

Be an effective investor.

You can have an effect through your investment choices. Even people of fairly modest means often have at least a small retirement account. You can make a difference by investing in companies, industries, and mutual funds that adhere to the principles I lay out in this chapter.

If you work in the media...

Look for ways to get others to "buy a better society," so to speak. Identify the best ranking systems from the standpoint of companies' impact on well-being. Send people to these companies and show people how they can affect company practices by spending on those that meet high standards, as well as by praising companies' good works.

If you own a business...

Consider formally or informally adopting the standards of the B Corps and conscious capitalism movements.

If you work for a company...

Look for ways you can be more involved in the governance of the organization.

- Examine how your organization stacks up against the B Corp standards.

- Examine the management structure of your organization and explore whether it could become more participatory. It is possible to build participatory approaches to management, whereby people are given a lot of say in how things get done in the company. Participatory governance is preferred by employees and it benefits companies. People who participate in decision making help companies make better decisions and be more committed to planned actions. For example, I work at Oregon Research Institute. In the 1980s, we hired an organizational consultant, Susie Phillips, who helped us reorganize into two councils: the scientist council and the science support council. We created a set of committees to make policy for the various facets of the organization (e.g., human resources, information technology, building maintenance). The science support council elected two-thirds of the members to each committee and the scientist council elected the other third. Each council also elected four members to the board of directors. With minor modifications, this governance system has been in place ever since, and our organization has been both financially successful and repeatedly voted one of the best places to work in Oregon.

- You might also learn more about employee stock ownership plans. According to the National Center for Employee Ownership, 6,600 employee stock ownership plans cover more than 14 million participants.[8]

Policy

Support laws and regulations that encourage B Corp formation or otherwise encourage the practices and standards articulated by B Lab.

Advocate for laws that require companies to assess and report to the public their impact on all stakeholders: employees, investors, suppliers, customers, and society as a whole.

Organizations

Join the Values to Action Network on business reform (valuestoaction.com/ business).

We are building a network of people and organizations who are actively working on the reform of business. You can get support for your efforts at the same time as you contribute to others' efforts by sharing your knowledge and experience.

Join or attend a meeting of the conscious capitalism movement.

CHAPTER 6:

Nurturing the Health of Every Person

We have a medical (that is, sick) care system—a system that waits until we become ill before it kicks into action—instead of a health-care system focused on helping us stay healthy. We give lip service to prevention [but] spend only about 1 to 3 percent of our $2 trillion in medical expenditures on public health.

— Stephen C. Schimpff, M.D.

THE UNITED STATES has the worst health-care system of any developed nation. Our current capitalist system is not the only reason for this but it is a major factor. An enormous amount of the money that goes into our inefficient and ineffective health-care system pays for activities that are highly profitable to companies but useless or even harmful to people. In this chapter, I provide a very brief summary of the problems with the system we have evolved and then focus on the reforms we need to improve the health of Americans while reducing the cost of health care. For a more detailed discussion of the problems with our system, I recommend Robert Kaplan's *More than Medicine: The Broken Promise of American Health.*[1]

The principles needed to reform the health-care system are the same as for all other facets of our economic and political system: (1) regulate it for the purpose of maximizing the well-being of the population and (2) do this by making profits contingent on achieving efficient and effective outcomes.

A Broken System

The United States has the most expensive health-care system of any developed country. In 2014, we spent \$2.6 trillion on health care.[2] That was 17 percent of our gross domestic product and nearly \$10,000 per person.[3] Our spending on health care is higher than that of any of the other thirty-five members of the Organisation for Economic Co-operation and Development; it was more than double the mean expenditure of those other countries in 2016.[4]

However, our higher expenditures do not deliver better health care than is found in other countries. The United States has "the worst life expectancy at birth of similar countries."[5] Thirty countries have a longer life expectancy than the United States. And while life expectancy has been increasing, it is not increasing as quickly in the United States as in other countries. Moreover, we have huge disparities in longevity. White men with sixteen years of education are living, on average, 14.2 years longer than black men with less than twelve years of education; the difference between white and black women is 10.3 years.[6] In addition, our infant mortality rate is worse than that of thirty-four other countries.[7]

Managing for Profit with Little Interest in Outcomes

In the context of free market advocacy, the health-care system has evolved in recent years to maximize profits, and those profits have not been aligned with health outcomes. Many facets of the health-care industry have lobbied to ensure that their businesses are profitable, but neither the government nor the businesses attend to whether the practices efficiently result in better health.

In an essay for the Evolution Institute, I describe the corruption in the pharmaceutical industry, where drug companies have made enormous profits by promoting opioids, anti-depressive medication, antibiotics, and psychostimulants.[8]

In 2009, Atul Gawande, a surgeon and public health researcher, published a piece in *The New Yorker* about the high cost of medical care in McAllen, Texas.[9] McAllen had the highest Medicare costs of any community in the nation. Compared with El Paso, a community similar in size, location, ethnic composition, and average income, McAllen had twice the rate of health-care costs: \$14,946 per person vs. \$7,504 in El

Paso. Gawande ultimately concluded that costs were higher because the medical community in McAllen evolved a culture in which physicians pursued a business model that maximized their revenue.

Gawande reviewed many explanations for the high costs, which simply don't hold water. For example, were doctors practicing defensive medicine because there were so many malpractice lawsuits? Couldn't be that because Texas capped the amount that can be awarded in such lawsuits, and the rates of lawsuits were the same in McAllen and El Paso. Did people get better care in McAllen? No, their outcomes were no better than in other communities.

However, physicians in McAllen were doing more tests, surgeries, and other treatments because it increased their revenue. Gallstones can usually be resolved through pain medication and changes in diet. Surgery is needed only in a small number of recalcitrant cases. However, McAllen surgeons routinely did surgery for first-time gallstone attacks. In general, people in McAllen were getting a lot more treatment than in most other places—more visits to specialists, bone-density studies, stress tests with echocardiography, nerve-conduction studies; 550 percent more urine-flow studies to diagnose prostate troubles, more gallbladder operations, knee replacements, breast biopsies, and bladder scopes. Medicare paid for five times as many home-nurse visits. Gawande concluded, "The primary cause of McAllen's extreme costs was, very simply, the across-the-board overuse of medicine."[10] But the benefit was far more to the providers than to the patients.

Gawande went on to explain that studies have shown that areas of the country with higher Medicare spending provide more services, but their health outcomes are no better than areas spending less. Gawande argued that if we brought the more expensive places into line with those that spend the average amount, "Medicare's [cost] problems (indeed, almost all the federal government's budget problems for the next fifty years) would be solved."[11] He also pointed out that all these extra, unnecessary interventions are themselves a risk. For example, a hundred thousand people die each year in this country due to complications of surgery.

The Highly Profitable Health Insurance Industry

Then there is the insurance industry. In the creation of Obamacare, the Obama administration probably rightly calculated that, at that time, they would get nowhere if they proposed a single-payer system. Too many big and wealthy health insurance companies would oppose a law that put them out of business.

In the first quarter of 2017, the five largest insurance companies had profits totaling $4.5 billion.[12] That was much higher than in the previous four years. In 2016, the salaries of the CEOs of the eight largest for-profit insurers ranged from $9.3 million to $22 million.[13]

The CEO making $22 million was Michael Neidorff, who happened to be the head of Centene, my insurer in 2017. Let me tell you a story about Centene. In May 2017, I fainted in a hotel room in Connecticut, hit my head, and ended up in an emergency room at Middlesex Hospital. They found no apparent cause of the fainting and released me. The visit cost about $5,000.

My understanding was that my insurer, Centene, would cover all but a small co-pay and that the hospital would bill them for it. However, I received repeated mailings from Centene about the charges from Middlesex Hospital. Each mailing listed all the charges, and, in the next column, the amount Centene was paying: $0 in every case. During about a four-month period, starting in the summer of 2017, I made repeated calls to Centene to try to find out why they had not paid the Connecticut bill. I got inconsistent answers from different people and was eventually given the address to which I could send an appeal of their decision to not pay these charges.

Although the company drove their customers to use their website for virtually every other type of communication with the company, to appeal their actions, I had to write an old-fashioned letter and mail it to them. I dutifully sent a letter, and a couple of weeks later, received a letter telling me I had sent my letter to the wrong address. I had not made a mistake; I had sent the letter to the address their representative had given me. I then sent the letter to the right address. Several weeks later, I got a voicemail from a polite man in the appeals department. When we finally connected by phone, he told me Middlesex Hospital had made mistakes in their billing of Centene, but when they corrected their errors, the bill was paid.

Here's what I said to this gentleman:

> It turned out there was nothing seriously wrong with me in Connecticut. But I'm 73 years old and it could have been a heart attack. And further suppose I was very poor. Receiving repeated letters from you telling me the $5,000 I owed the hospital would not be paid by Centene could have caused a heart attack that killed me. I know you are not the CEO and don't make the rules, but your procedures cause considerable stress, and stress causes heart attacks.

In my view, Centene's practice of delaying paying bills, like those of many other companies, are shaped by the profits it produces. If the company had a billion dollars in outstanding bills at any given time and could delay paying by a month, they would make money. If they made even 0.5 percent income on $1 billion for a month, that would amount to $5 million. Their delays in paying are not accidental; this is a profitable business practice. It just happens to be stressful to their customers.

Now, you might argue that these delays are not intentional and the company could not possibly have calculated that it could make money like this. That may be the case, but I submit that if there were profits to be made in paying these bills quickly, they would have teams of executives working hard to figure out how their rapid payment system could be improved.

I haven't been able to find research on the effects of stressful encounters with the health-care bureaucracy, but I suspect that if we studied it, we would find that it contributes to illness and even death.

The Conservative Obsession with Destroying Obamacare

Obamacare, as the Affordable Care Act came to be called, has increased the number of people with health insurance by 20 million.[14] Yet Republicans in Congress have voted more than sixty times to replace it.[15] And the Koch Brothers have made the repeal of Obamacare their highest priority.[16] Indeed, they are so opposed to Obamacare that they opposed the bill Republicans in Congress voted on in the summer of 2017 because it did not repeal every facet of Obamacare.[17] Why are conservatives so obsessed with Obamacare?

Reihan Salam, executive editor of *National Review*, explained conservative opposition to it in an article in *Slate*.[18] It violates the principle of free market ideology. It reduces the cost of insurance to poorer people by raising taxes on wealthier people. This is anathema to conservatives because it redistributes money from the wealthy to the poor and replaces free market exchanges with the heavy hand of government.

Or to put it more simply, it takes money away from wealthy conservatives and gives it to poor people. In a so-called free market (ignoring for the moment all the ways in which government contributes to the ability of business to make money, such as roads, airports, education, defense, and the rule of law), the value of a person is determined by what he or she can command in the marketplace. If poor people can't afford health insurance because they don't make enough money to do so and premiums are too high for them, it must be because they don't have enough to offer in the free market and so are not paid very much. And a wealthy person (ignoring, for the moment, inheritance, tax subsidies, such as the oil depletion allowance, etc.) has lots of money, which must be because he or she has valuable things to offer in the marketplace. To confiscate wealth through taxation is viewed as theft.

A second reason for conservative opposition to Obamacare, according to Salam, is that it will increase the federal deficit. (Let's pause to consider the tax cut for corporations and the wealthy that was passed by the Republican Congress and signed into law by Donald Trump, which added more than $1 trillion to the deficit.)

Third, Salam claims a market-based system of health-care reform "will be cheaper, less coercive, and less prescriptive than Obamacare."[19] Based on what we had before Obamacare, this market-based system will also be unaffordable to millions of Americans, though it will not oppress those poor people by forcing them to buy insurance they can't afford.

At base, the seven-year war against Obamacare and the failure over the previous fifty years to create a system that provides health care for every American are very much due to free market ideology.

The Social Determinants of Health

There is another aspect of the health of Americans that explains why we lag so far behind other countries. It is critical to improving Americans' health. At first glance, it may not seem at all related to free market capitalism. But bear with me, and I think you will see that it is very much related.

In chapter 3, I present a chart that estimates the causes of premature death in the United States. The chart was published by Steven Schroeder in the *New England Journal of Medicine* in 2007.[20] The largest proportion of premature deaths is due to unhealthful behaviors. Ali Mokdad et al. estimated the number of deaths in the United States each year due to risky health behaviors. The biggest is smoking (435,000 deaths, 18.1 percent of all deaths). Poor diet and physical inactivity account for another 365,000 deaths (15.2 percent). Alcohol consumption contributes another 85,000; motor vehicle crashes, 43,000; firearms, 29,000; risky sexual behavior, 20,000; and illicit drug use, 17,000. The only items on the list of major causes that aren't necessarily due to unhealthful behavior are microbial agents (75,000) and toxic agents (55,000).[21] In sum, if we want to prevent premature deaths, our number one priority needs to be to prevent unhealthful behaviors.

Notice that this has *nothing to do with treating illness*. People who engage in these behaviors may eventually end up seeking treatment—for example, for lung cancer. But that is long after the person begins to engage in the behavior that eventually takes his or her life.

J. Michael McGinnis and his colleagues estimated that 95 percent of health-care spending goes to direct medical care.[22] Yet, every one of these deadly behaviors can be prevented by influencing people's behavior—not with perfect reliability, of course, but enough that we could vastly improve Americans' health and longevity. And it will have far more benefit than we will ever get by providing the very best treatment for every American. (I am not saying we shouldn't make excellent and affordable care available to every American; I'm saying that even if we do, we will make a tiny impact on their health if we fail to prevent all these behaviors.)

But there is more. Shroeder's figure also shows that 15 percent of premature deaths are due to "social circumstances."[23] Schroeder includes in this category socioeconomic status, which he sees as a matter of income, education, employment, and neighborhood residence. Shroeder goes on to acknowledge that one of the reasons poorer people have higher rates of death is that they have higher rates of unhealthful behavior. However, even when you control for differences in unhealthful behaviors, poorer people have higher rates of death.[24]

I have been studying these issues for the past several years. Stressful social environments are at the root of most of our health problems. They make unhealthful behavior more likely,[25] and they directly affect people's physiology in ways that contribute to ill health.

Given the evidence, you would think a huge proportion of federal expenditures on health-related research would go to addressing the social determinants of health. However, if you read Robert Kaplan's analysis of the health-care system we have,[26] you will see that the majority of funds go to research on how we can change human biology to treat or prevent illness—through genetic research, the development of new drugs, or precision medicine that supposedly allows physicians to pinpoint exactly how a particular patient needs to be treated. Sadly, despite huge expenditures in these areas, very little progress has been made in reducing the major causes of premature death.

The impact of stressful social environments on unhealthful behavior. First, let's consider what influences young people to develop unhealthful behaviors. Research shows that child poverty is associated with high rates of cigarette smoking, juvenile delinquency, depression, academic failure, and obesity.[27] Among the reasons are the fact that families living in poverty are more likely than wealthier families to have coercive interactions that lead to children failing to develop self-regulation, becoming uncooperative and aggressive, failing in school, and developing friendships with other aggressive young people.[28] These deviant peer groups become a training ground for delinquency, risky sexual behavior, and substance use.[29] Of course, poverty isn't the only factor leading to unhealthful behavior. Smoking, unhealthful eating, and youth alcohol use are also the results of marketing to children.

The direct impact of stressful environments on health. In addition to these difficult social environments resulting in unhealthful behavior, it is clear that such environments directly affect our physiology.[30] Psychologist Greg Miller has been a leader in figuring out how stressful childhood environments get under our skin and change our physiology well into adulthood.[31] Research had shown that people who grow up in poverty or are maltreated as children have a higher likelihood of cardiovascular disease as adults. Figure 6.1 comes from a paper that Miller, Edith Chen, and Karen J. Parker published in 2011.[32] It summarizes the ways stress affects our physiology. In essence, stress compromises children's immune systems and drives inflammatory processes that contribute to obesity, diabetes, and, ultimately, cardiovascular disease.

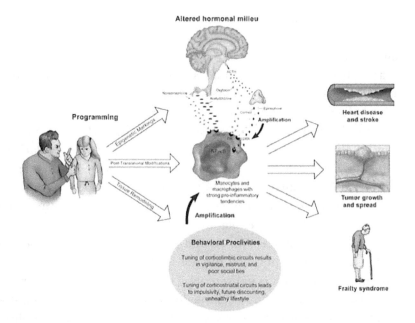

Altered hormonal milieu

Programming

Amplification

Heart disease
and stroke

Amplification

Monocytes and
macrophages with
strong pro-inflammatory
tendencies

Tumor growth
and spread

Behavioral Proclivities

Tuning of corticolimbic circuits results
in vigilance, mistrust, and
poor social ties

Tuning of corticostriatal circuits leads
to impulsivity, future discounting,
unhealthy lifestyle

Frailty syndrome

FIGURE 6.1

These effects are not due to people continuing to live in poverty. Miller et al.[33] found that even when young people who were raised in poverty escape from it as adults, they still have higher rates of cardiovascular disease than people who grew up in wealthier families. The only exception is that if people raised in poverty say their mother was nurturing, the effect goes away—they don't have higher rates of cardiovascular disease.[34] I submit that the impact of poverty on health is due to the fact that poverty makes family life more stressful.

Discrimination is also a major influence on health. Why do college-educated white men in America live, on average, more than fourteen years longer than less-educated black men?[35] One of the reasons is almost certainly that black men experience more stress. According to the Pew Research Center, 71 percent of black people report experiencing discrimination regularly or occasionally.[36] Jules P. Harrell, Sadiki Hall, and James Taliaferro reviewed research on the effects of discrimination on physiology.[37] People exposed to discrimination react with classic stress responses: elevated blood pressure, increased heart rate, changes in skin conductance, and greater arterial pressure. This was true for a wide variety of aspects of discrimination. Whether people were asked to describe discrimination they had experienced, were exposed to discrimination in a laboratory setting, were asked to discuss discrimination, or simply listened to a debate about it, they had these stress reactions. And, as Miller's work shows, chronic stress contributes to inflammatory processes that lead to obesity, diabetes, and cardiovascular disease.[38]

It is not just African Americans who experience discrimination. The Pew Research Center also reported that 52 percent of Hispanics and 30 percent of Caucasians report experiencing discrimination regularly or occasionally. Forty-two percent of homosexual or bisexual adults report experiencing discrimination.[39] I can't find similar data on Muslims, but Pew reports that the number of assaults on Muslims in 2016 surpassed the level in 2001.[40] Poor people are also discriminated against, especially if they are homeless. We should therefore not be surprised to learn that they have higher rates of poor health.[41]

And since our interest is in promoting the well-being of *every* person, consider other groups we don't normally think of as experiencing discrimination. In the divisive society we currently have, how many police, white males, poor white people, Republicans, and religious fundamentalists experience discrimination? You may not have much sympathy for the latter two groups. But if we are truly committed to having everyone feel safe and cared for, will we advance this value by insisting that any discrimination such groups experience is well deserved, or at least "not our problem"? You may be right that members of some of these groups have harmed members of the other groups. But is the child of a white police officer who is picked on because his father is a cop deserving of that treatment? Indeed, is every police officer deserving of our approbation because of the behavior of those who do harm?

I am in no way implying that disparities in police behavior toward black people aren't a serious public health problem. I share the distress of millions of Americans about the police shootings that continue to occur. I only ask that we consider what will work. The evidence suggests that it is unlikely we will get people to be more compassionate toward groups they have ill-treated if the only thing we do is punish their acts. We will not achieve a nurturing society if the only thing we do is punish unacceptable behavior.

Why Are People in Other Developed Countries Healthier?

You might think that people in other countries are healthier than Americans because they have health care for everyone. But the evidence I just reviewed shows that, by itself, health care plays a fairly small role in people's health and longevity. The quality of one's social environment is far more important. Health is better in other countries because they have less poverty, inequality, and discrimination, and greater social cohesion.

With about 21 percent of America's children being raised in poverty,[42] all the evidence of the impact of poverty on ill health pretty much guarantees we will have higher rates of premature death than other developed countries, where a much smaller proportion of children are raised in poverty.

And then there is economic inequality. It is a major cause of our poor health. The United States has the highest rate of economic inequality of any developed nation.[43] We're number one! The richest 10 percent own 77 percent of the nation's wealth. The bottom 80 percent have 22.6 percent of the wealth.[44]

This is a direct result of the success of free market advocacy in convincing so many Americans that small government, unregulated business, and low taxes will benefit everyone. In chapter 1, I show how much the wealthy increased their share of America's wealth until 2013. But it has gotten even worse since Trump and the Republican Congress passed the 2017 tax cut, which reduced the taxes of those making more than $200,000 a year far more than for those in lower tax brackets.

Inequality is doing great harm to Americans. The leading experts on this issue are Richard Wilkinson and Kate Pickett.[45] They reviewed hundreds of studies that show that economically unequal countries have higher rates of crime, substance use, depression, obesity, and premature death than do countries with greater equality. Children in unequal countries have lower levels of academic achievement, high drop-out rates, and higher levels of teenage pregnancy. Unequal countries also have lower levels of trust, social cohesion, and participation in civic activities.

Wilkinson and Pickett thoroughly explored why countries with high levels of inequality have so many more problems. They concluded that it is because life in countries like ours is much more stressful. We are constantly reminded of our status and have many more interactions with people that remind us of our status.

Now, what would be a good strategy to make your way in an unequal society? Well, you'd better be deferent toward those who have the power to take things away from you; you don't want to piss them off. On the other hand, you don't need to worry about the people below you. If your servants or subordinates at work do something you don't like, you can fire them, criticize them, demote them, or ridicule them, and get others to ridicule them. To the extent that the country you live in is more hierarchical, you are likely to have a lot more experiences of people pushing you around. Think, for example, of the many communities in the United States where poor people have been fined for minor violations, to the extent that they are continuously in debt to the municipality and are often jailed.[46]

But you don't have to be poor to experience stress. Even if you have a good job, your fortunes could sour quickly if your boss turns against you. For example, when Wells Fargo was discovered to have pressured employees to create more than 1.5 million "ghost" accounts for customers that customers did not know about, the company simply blamed the low-level employees. Wells Fargo fired more than five thousand of them, while the leadership who had promoted this fraud did just fine. True, the CEO lost his job over this, but he left with nearly $84 million, thanks to stock options and deferred payments.[47]

Economically unequal countries also have much more emphasis on materialism, compared with more equal countries. They have more advertising. Because status is more important, people are prone to buy things they don't need in an effort to keep up with those around them. And as our materialistic focus on having as much or more than the people around us has escalated in recent years, it has made us slaves to jobs we don't like and work schedules that undermine the quality of our lives. Americans work more hours per week than do people in twenty-eight other countries, according to the Organisation for Economic Co-operation and Development—eight hours a week more than Germans. And according to a Gallup poll in 2017, 85 percent of Americans hate their job.[48]

On the other hand, in a more economically equal society, you have far fewer challenges. Wilkinson and Pickett tell a story from Oliver James about how in Denmark, a much more economically equal country than the United States, when a new luxury item comes on the market, nobody buys it because people don't want to be ostentatious. But when the price comes down, within eighteen months, 70 percent of the population buys the product.[49]

All this affects our health. People in unequal countries die earlier than those in more equal countries. This is not just the case for the poorest people. Up and down the hierarchy in an unequal country, people are rubbing up against higher-status people who may be condescending, hurtful, or rude. You may also encounter people who have less than you and are angry and irritated about the slights they have experienced in this materialistic and competitive society.

Think about road rage. That guy who cut you off and flipped you the bird may be poorer than you, but he just raised your stress level. The desperate efforts to maintain our status in such a competitive and materialistic world exact a toll in terms of increased stress levels that directly contribute to higher levels of cardiovascular disease.

One of the reasons we have allowed such extraordinary income inequality is that most people don't realize how bad it is. As Chris Rock put it, "If poor people knew how rich rich people are, there would be riots in the streets."[50]

Michael Norton of Harvest Business School and Dan Ariely at Duke University asked a nationally representative sample of Americans how they thought wealth in the United States is distributed and how it should be distributed.[51] This graph (Figure 6.2) from their paper tells the story. The top bar shows how wealth is actually distributed—84 percent of wealth was owned by the top 20 percent of Americans at the time of the study (2005). The bottom 40 percent had no wealth at all. Americans of all political persuasions thought it was more evenly distributed—the middle bar. Their ideal of how it should be distributed is shown in the bottom bar—a little more than 32 percent would be owned by the wealthiest, and the bottom 20 percent of people would have more than 10 percent instead of nothing.[52]

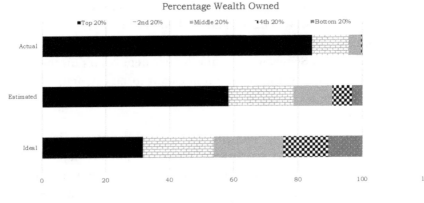

FIGURE 6.2

Economic inequality is both a product of our economic policies and a contributor to them. As I show in chapter 1, inequality has risen steadily with the increasing control of policy making by conservatives. At the same time, inequality increases people's experience of threat, which makes them even more susceptible to materialism and more likely to attack anyone they perceive as an outsider.

In conclusion, reducing economic inequality should be a high priority in our efforts to make American society healthier.

Values in the Health-Care System

Let's return to Gawande's article on the cost of health care in McAllen, Texas. Two things stand out about the culture he describes. First, the main players in the system—physicians and administrators—keep careful track of their costs and profits, and, as a result, these consequences shape their behavior. Second, they haven't a clue about whether their practices are maximizing the health of the people in their community, and so it is unlikely that these consequences will ever shape their behavior. As Gawande puts it:

> Local executives for hospitals and clinics and home-health agencies understand their growth rate and their market share; they know whether they are losing money or making money. They know that if their doctors bring in enough business—surgery, imaging, home-nursing referrals—they make money; and if they get the doctors to bring in more, they

make more. But they have only the vaguest notion of whether the doctors are making their communities as healthy as they can, or whether they are more or less efficient than their counterparts elsewhere.[53]

Gawande cites evidence that the areas in which physicians run up the bills are those where the treatments of choice are not well defined. For problems where the appropriate course of treatment is well defined, physicians in both high-expense and low-expense communities do the same thing. But for other problems, doctors differ with respect to how many tests and treatments they do.

Gawande reviews the various schemes that economists and policy makers have argued over for delivering lower-cost medicine with better health outcomes: single-payer systems, making patients pay a larger share of their care, and so on. He argues that none of them get to root of the problem. In the end, Gawande sees the problem as a matter of whether the medical community has as its foundational value the "needs of the patient" or the maximization of revenue.

Given the emphasis in current American society on accumulated wealth as the measure of a person's worth, we should not be surprised that many people in health care focus on maximizing revenue. Even in payment models and systems that emphasize cost savings and more utilitarian metrics, such as return on investment, the saved money and returns are rarely invested in addressing the social factors that result in the stress so many people are experiencing.

In the context of the culture of financial self-aggrandizement that has been promoted over the past forty-five years, we should not be surprised that physicians' salaries have gone up faster than the rate of inflation. Between 2011 and 2017, physicians' salaries rose nearly 50 percent, from $206,000 to $294,000. If they had only kept up with inflation, they would have risen to $230,000.[54]

In addition, physicians' salaries are far higher in the United States than in other countries—many of which have better health than we have in this country. Here is a chart of the average salary of general practitioners (generally the lowest-paid doctors) in different countries. These numbers are adjusted for the cost of living in different countries. As you can see, physicians in the United States are making much more money than those in other countries.[55]

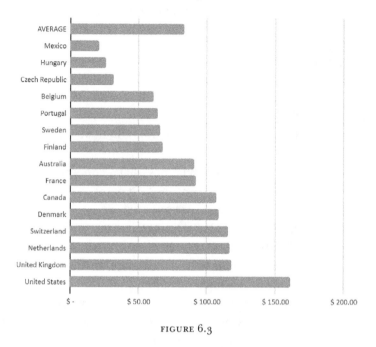

General Practitioner's Pay

FIGURE 6.3

Salaries of CEOs in the pharmaceutical industry are gargantuan. According to *USA Today*, the top fourteen CEO salaries' ranged from $8.7 million to $47.5 million in 2015.[56] Taking a longer time span, the CEO of Gilead Sciences made $863 million since the Affordable Care Act was passed.[57]

What should we make of this evidence? Can we reasonably expect to drive down the cost of health care or improve the health of the population by forcing physicians to take a pay cut? It seems unlikely that we could do so even if we wanted to. Instead, I would ask you to consider this situation in the context of a society that has come to measure the worth of every person literally in terms of how much money he or she makes.

We must adjust our values throughout society such that the well-being of every person is our foundational value and CEOs receive very generous compensation only if they are making significant contributions to the general well-being. If we do not do this, our health-care system, like every other facet of our society, will continue to deliver great wealth to a small proportion of the population and harm a large proportion of the rest of the population—or at least fail to benefit many people to the extent that it could.

Here, as in other sectors of society, we need to align our practices with the consequences we are trying to achieve. In medicine, this begins by specifying the health of the population as our ultimate criterion for selecting our practices. The sad fact is that in most places in this country, what we do in the name of health is horribly misaligned with what we need to do, because we put the vast bulk of our money into treating problems that could have been prevented.

The Reforms We Need

We need to do at least four things to improve the health of Americans. First, we need to focus on improving the health of the entire population. Second, we need to address the social determinants of health. Third, we can better address these first two points if we move from traditional fee-for-service health-care providers to accountable care organizations. Fourth, we need to make better use of the wealth of behavioral science knowledge that can contribute to addressing social determinants, promoting healthful behavior, and preventing unhealthful behavior.

Managing for Public Health

I think Gawande is right that the specifics of the system created to pay for health care (e.g., single payer, multiple insurers) are not the key to improving health care. Other countries that have better health and lower costs include countries with single-payer systems and private insurers. What is far more important is that provider practices be aligned with outcomes we are seeking so that practices that affect those outcomes are selected and maintained.

Thus, the reform of the health-care system needs to be organized around the ultimate goal—namely, that every member of the population lives a long and healthy life. We are quite capable of measuring these outcomes. At the national level, we do a good job of monitoring the incidence and prevalence of physical illnesses, as well as of psychological and behavioral problems, which make such a significant contribution to physical illness and premature death.

However, we need data on the health of the population at the level of the community. The physicians in McAllen, Texas, had no idea how the entire population was doing. They simply treated the diseases of the people who showed up on their doorstep. And when they treated them, they ran up the bill.

Gawande does a good job of pinpointing the practices in McAllen that make health care there so costly. However, like the majority of physicians, he overlooks our failure to address the social determinants of health.

If we are going to improve the health of the population, we need to stop putting all our money into treating problems that could have been prevented. Instead, we need to build a world-class prevention system. Such a system will track the prevalence of all the psychological and behavioral problems of children and adolescents, which result in most of the physical illnesses we pay so much money to treat. The system will implement effective family and school interventions that can prevent the development of all the unhealthful behaviors I describe above and that can convert stressful social environments into much more nurturing places. The system will require changes in public policies to ensure that fewer children are living in poverty and fewer people are being exposed to stressful discrimination.

Ironically, the McAllen area is launching an effort along these lines. By coincidence, I have consulted with the University of Texas Rio Grande Valley School of Medicine, helping them to strengthen their efforts to affect the health of the entire population. They are creating a system with outreach to underserved communities, those that have many poor people and little health care. They are developing a system of integrated behavioral health; instead of simply treating sick people, they will assess health behaviors and social circumstances and intervene to affect these determinants of health.

Ultimately, these are empirical matters. Once we begin to assess the health-care system in a given community—or in the nation as a whole—in terms of its impact on the incidence and prevalence of disease, we will be in a position to implement policies and practices that reduce disease and abandon those that are not contributing to optimal outcomes. This can be done not only at the level of evaluating a specific treatment for a specific disease but at the level of a policy's or program's effect on the incidence of multiple risk factors or diseases. For example, raising the tax on tobacco can discourage cigarette smoking, which contributes to two of the biggest causes of premature death: cancer and heart disease.[58]

The Social Determinants of Health (Again)

The idea that addressing the social determinants of health is the most important thing we can do to improve public health is so overlooked by the leadership of our current health-care system that I feel I should take one more crack at illustrating the surprising role of social stress in affecting physical health.

Gene Brody and his colleagues developed a program to help rural African American families in Georgia.[59] The program helps parents adopt a parenting style that involves staying warmly involved with their children; helping them understand the realities of racial discrimination "while emphasizing the possibility of achieving success in the face of these obstacles" and making expectations about alcohol use and early sexual behavior explicit. A randomized trial evaluating the impact of the program showed that it significantly improved the quality of the parent-child relationship. This, in turn, was associated with changes in the children's attitudes toward alcohol use and early sex.

What was more interesting was the fact that these kids, who were eleven at the time of the program, had lower levels of physiologically measured stress nine years later.[60] Specifically, the youth in the families who participated in the program had significantly lower levels of two of the major hormones that affect cardiovascular health: epinephrine and norepinephrine. Recall that high levels of these stress hormones drive the inflammatory process that can cause cardiovascular disease and shorten the lives of African Americans.

The limitation in my argument is that, although there is a tremendous amount of evidence that we can reduce stressful social interactions in families and schools by implementing the kinds of programs developed in the past forty years,[61] the Brody study is one of the few that documents actual changes in stress processes. This is another example of how our health-care research and treatment system is paying far too little attention to the social determinants of health and the benefits of prevention.

Accountable Care Organizations

One encouraging development is the creation of accountable care organizations. Oregon, for example, has created a system of accountable care organizations that provide health care for people whose income is at 158 percent of poverty or lower. A little more than a quarter of the population of Oregon receives health care through these coordinated care organizations.

The organizations are charged not only with paying for the treatment of illnesses but for improving the overall health of the population through preventive interventions. For example, the Yamhill Community Care Organization asked me to advise them about preventive interventions that could improve the health of children. One thing I suggested was that they implement the PAX Good Behavior Game in elementary schools. They began by introducing it in three schools, and I am happy to report that they have seen significant improvements in children's behavior and in the happiness of children and adults in the schools. Because of these results, the organization is in the process of rolling it out to the rest of the elementary schools in the county.

If this seems far afield from physical health, it is not. For example, long-term studies of the impact of the Good Behavior Game in elementary schools showed that it significantly reduced rates of substance abuse, antisocial behavior, suicidality, and academic failure (all of which contribute to premature death) in young adults.[62]

Contributions That Behavioral Science Can Make to Public Health

The success of efforts to influence social determinants of health depend on considerable expansion of behavioral science research and practice. Behavioral scientists hold the keys to this kingdom.

We are just beginning to translate what we know into widespread benefit. Family interventions, such as Parent Management Training Oregon, the Incredible Years, and the Family Check-Up, are being implemented around the nation and the world.[63] Tested and effective programs for improving prosocial behavior in schools are being widely adopted. Positive Action, a program that has proven benefit in reducing problem behavior and improving academic performance in elementary schools, is in twenty thousand schools around the country.[64] The PAX Good Behavior Game[65] is being implemented in Manitoba, Estonia, Ireland, and Sweden, as well as many schools in Ohio, New Mexico, and Oregon. More than twenty-five thousand schools have instituted Positive Behavioral Interventions and Supports.[66]

Therapists around the world are adopting recent advances in clinical psychology, such as acceptance and commitment therapy. In the field of behavioral medicine, clinics around the country and the world are adopting tested and effective methods to promote healthy behaviors such as increasing exercise, quitting smoking, and losing weight.[67]

We are hearing more about the contributions behavioral economists and decision researchers have been making. Richard Thaler won the 2017 Nobel Prize in economics for his work on decision making and human motivation in public policy making. He has shown that it is possible to influence people to make healthier choices simply by making the default choice the beneficial one and requiring people to take action if they want to choose a less healthy alternative.

We even have evidence that communitywide interventions can benefit an entire population. For example, a group randomized trial of a program called Communities That Care helped reduce levels of adolescent antisocial behavior and substance use by selecting specific interventions tailored to communities' risk and protective factors.[68]

And empirical evidence is beginning to guide public policy making. My friend Kelli Komro and her colleagues have been systematically searching the literature to identify policies whose effectiveness is supported by empirical evidence. See her paper in *BMC Pediatrics* for a list of forty-six policies that met stringent scientific criteria, showing their efficacy for consistently producing positive outcomes.[69]

Overall, we are steadily increasing the well-being of people by adopting many interventions and public policies that benefit people. Many of the most common and costly psychological and behavioral problems people have can be prevented or treated, thanks to the knowledge we've accumulated. We can have less crime, delinquency, depression, and suicide; fewer children failing in school; and less obesity, diabetes, marital discord, child abuse, cardiovascular disease, and cancer.[70]

However, I cannot claim that we have made much progress in changing the behaviors related to climate change, and I do not think our science has made much progress in areas such as the prevention of terrorism. But the main reason we haven't made much progress in these areas is that we haven't funded the research needed. The task force on climate change research I have been leading has searched the world literature and found that less than 1 percent of the studies we could find tested a strategy for getting a policy adopted that would reduce greenhouse gas emissions. In a piece I published in *The New York Times,* I describe a similar dearth of research on how to prevent people from joining terrorist organizations.[71] The absence of experimental evaluations of strategies for addressing these problems is, in my view, the biggest failure of behavioral science.

Finally, we need much more investment in behavioral science research. If Schroeder is correct, as many as 55 percent of premature deaths are due to the social determinants of health and the unhealthful behaviors that result from them.[72] However, federal investment in behavioral science research is far from what it needs to be, given the potential of such research to improve the human condition. The Office of Disease Prevention at the National Institutes of Health (NIH) analyzed the proportion of NIH-funded projects focused on the prevention of the ten leading causes of death or on the ten most important risk factors for death.[73] Despite the fact that the ten leading causes of death accounted for 74 percent of deaths, only 25.9 percent of research projects focused on preventing these causes of death. Similarly, although the top ten risk factors for death accounted for 57.3 percent of deaths, only 34 percent of NIH research projects focused on the prevention of one or more of those risk factors. In other words, the NIH portfolio of research is not focusing as much on preventing these risk factors and causes of death as seems justified by their importance.

Moreover, if we measure the ultimate benefit to society in terms of the impact of our work on the incidence and prevalence of psychological, behavioral, and health problems, we would have to conclude that our research investments are not well organized to improve the health and well-being of Americans.[74] Consider, for example, that for major aspects of Americans' health, we are going in the wrong direction. According to the CDC, the suicide rate in the United States rose 24 percent between 1999 and 2014.[75] Despite decades of research on substance abuse, the rate of deaths from drug overdoses has increased 137 percent since 2000, including a 200 percent increase in the rate of overdose deaths involving opioids (opioid pain relievers and heroin).[76] According to a 2014 report by the Substance Abuse and Mental Health Services Administration, the rates of serious mental illness in the United States have generally remained unchanged since 2008, except that the rate in 2014 was significantly higher for those aged eighteen to twenty-five than it was in 2008 through 2013.[77] According to the most rigorous study of the rates of mental, emotional, and behavioral disorders among children and adolescents in the United States, "The overall prevalence of disorders with severe impairment and/or distress was 22.2 percent."[78]

Unfortunately, data for all disorders are not available from earlier periods. However, an annual survey of adolescents found that the prevalence of depression increased from 8.7 percent in 2005 to 11.3 percent in 2014.[79]

These statistics do not indicate that the current priorities of the NIH are contributing as much as they could to preventing many of the health outcomes they are charged with affecting. NIH needs to increase its investment in research on the social determinants of ill health and the prevention and amelioration of social determinants.

Building a Healthier Society

America's health-care system is expensive and ineffective because it is organized to generate profits for key players. Of course, profitable activities can be quite beneficial. I think, for example, of the walks I took in Paris with my wife six months after her second hip replacement surgery. However, far too many activities are not particularly beneficial, and others are quite harmful.

We can readily define and measure harmful practices. There are all the people who have died of drug overdoses because they became addicted to opioids that were prescribed too heavily. There are the people who died due to cigarette smoking, both because we allow the tobacco industry to market its products and because health-care providers don't intervene to influence people to quit smoking. And so on. We can tighten regulations so that these harmful outcomes are more quickly detected. We can increase penalties for harmful practices such that no company will profit from harmful practices.

It is, of course, easy to say these things, but much harder to achieve them, given that lawmaking and regulations are almost completely in the hands of a network of individuals and companies organized to maximize profits and little motivated to detect and prevent harm.

We can and should work within the health-care system to get the kinds regulations needed. However, we will be much more likely to create the system we need if behavioral science becomes more influential, business generally moves toward values-based practices, higher education instills values that promote the well-being of every person, the criminal justice system adopts less-punitive and more-effective practices, the media report accurately about the reforms needed, and our political system works for the well-being of everyone. And given the social disruptions and health consequences that our rapidly deteriorating climate will create, we must take radical action to address this problem. On that note, let's move on to the reforms needed in higher education.

Action Implications

Personal

Join the Social Determinants Network on Health-Care Reform (valuestoaction.com/healthcare).

You can become a member of a network of people around the nation who want to see our health-care system move in the direction I am describing. My colleague Shaylor Murray and I hope to create a large network of people who will work together to make the facts widely available. If we get enough people (and enough money), we will invest in conferences organized to advance the reforms needed. We can evolve a healthy society that science shows can be created.

Read Robert Kaplan's excellent book *More Than Medicine: The Broken Promise of American Health.*

It documents how the health-care system is failing Americans.

Advocate for the reforms needed in the health-care system.

Speak up at every opportunity about what is needed to improve health in this country. Here is your elevator speech about health care:

> We spend virtually all our health-care dollars on the treatment of diseases that could have been prevented. The causes of premature death are unhealthful behaviors and stressful social conditions, and these can be prevented. There are numerous tested and effective ways of reducing these social stressors and preventing problems such as cardiovascular disease and cancer. All over the country, interventions to prevent obesity, cigarette smoking, substance abuse, and criminal behavior are being implemented. If we invest more in these solutions, we can reduce our health-care costs while greatly improving people's health.

Learn more about how you can improve your health and the health of those around you by increasing your kindness and compassion.

- Check out the work of Barbara Fredrickson from the University of North Carolina.[80] She studies how you can improve your well-being and that of people around you through kindness meditation.

- Read Doug Carnine's book *How Love Wins: The Power of Mindful Kindness.*[81]

Policy

Advocate for policies that:

- Reduce poverty, inequality, homelessness, and discrimination

- Make evidence-based family interventions available to every family who would benefit

- Ensure that evidence-based teaching practices are in every school

- Create systems for monitoring the well-being of the population in your community, county, and state

  ○ When Toyota builds a car, they monitor the quality of work very carefully *for each car.* Why should we not monitor the well-being of the people in our communities with the same precision and care?

  ○ Systems for monitoring the psychological and behavioral problems of children and adolescents are well developed. If these assessments were done annually in every school, the community would have fairly precise estimates of how well it is ensuring the proper development of the next generation.

  ○ Evaluate each sector of health care in terms of its success in reducing the incidence and prevalence of the disorders it is responsible for. For example, is a community's health-care system achieving a steady decline in deaths due to cardiovascular disease? Is it reducing consumption of sugar-sweetened beverages? (Yes, I propose to hold the health-care system—among other systems—accountable for this problem.)

Organizations

Join the American Public Health Association.

It is the premier American organization working to advance the health of the entire population.

Join the Values to Action Network (valuestoaction.com).

Create a committee in your community to work for improved health.

Most improvement we can achieve will come not from treatment but from prevention—much of which needs to be delivered outside the traditional health-care system.

Support the Robert Wood Johnson Foundation's Culture of Health.

The foundation recognizes that improving the health of the population and reducing disparities in health among subgroups requires that communities make health and well-being a foundational value. The foundation is funding efforts to help communities change the social conditions that contribute to poor health.

You can also explore other organizations. I am sure many others are working to improve public health. Getting them to work together can advance the goals of each organization. If you are aware of an organization you think should be part of a coalition to advance public health, go to valuestoaction.com/healthcare and add it to our list.

CHAPTER 7:

Higher Education: The Incubator of a New Society

They have an almost unbelievable ability to earnestly present themselves as the solution to problems they have helped to cause.

— Duff McDonald, writing about Harvard Business School

I N HIS 1971 memo, Lewis Powell argued that the "single most dynamic source" of the "assault on the enterprise system" was universities. He cited a poll of twelve campuses that found that "almost half of the students favored socialization of basic U.S. industries." So Powell's first recommendation was that business make a concerted effort to influence universities to be more favorable to business.

Conservatives heeded his advice. Over nearly half a century, they succeeded in getting major universities to promote free market theories and values. They rightly believed that if they worked *for an indefinite period of time,* they could move higher education toward the promotion of their ideas, and thereby populate all the other sectors of society with people steeped in free market theory and working to advance its values, beliefs, and goals. Their success provides a lesson about what we need to do. If we are going to evolve a society that makes the well-being of every person a foundational value, then influencing higher education is essential for our success.

Imagine that twenty years from now, higher education has become a major force for constructing the kind of society we aspire to. What would it be like? To begin with, in evaluating themselves, colleges and universities would place far more weight on the degree to which they foster the well-being of the population. The behavioral sciences (psychology, sociology, anthropology, and economics) would have strong programs focused on the application of knowledge to assisting communities, states, and the nation in making families, schools, workplaces, and governments more nurturing, both at the level of day-to-day interaction between people and at the level of the impact organizations have on the general well-being. Strong programs would train practitioners and applied researchers in schools of public health and prevention science programs. Law schools would have programs of law and behavioral science. Schools of education would do a better job of training teachers not only to advance students' academic success but to instill values and skills vital to their social success.

Medical schools would train physicians to address the social determinants of health; they would have a much greater emphasis on public health and prevention. Business schools would do what Harvard Business School has failed to do for more than a century—instill ethical standards in graduates such that these people become a force for the kind of conscious capitalism I describe in chapter 5. The physical sciences would monitor the degree to which the products of their sciences contribute to harm or well-being. High-technology programs would have a well-developed code of ethics for data science and major research and training initiatives focused on how technology can enhance human cooperation and advance prosociality.

Before I go into detail on what needs to be done, I should address an argument many have made about universities being full of liberals and hostile to conservatives. There is some truth to this accusation. A study by Neil Gross and Solon Simmons found that although only 20 percent of people describe themselves as liberal, half of the university faculty they surveyed did.[1]

In part, these criticisms serve to weaken the credibility of faculty who are doing research that undermines support for policies conservatives want. For example, the criticisms are intended to get people to believe that faculty who have progressive views on issues are producing research that is biased by their progressive politics. Then, when such faculty members produce research showing that climate change is happening and is human caused, their findings can be labeled as simply a result of their liberal biases.

More than likely, however, the opposite is true. University faculty favor policies to reduce carbon emissions or to increase the income of poorer people because they are persuaded by evidence that shows these policies will improve human well-being.

In any case, the issue I would ask you to focus on is whether our universities are training students and doing research that is contributing to addressing the problems of our current economic and political system. This is not as much a question of political bias as one of pragmatism. Whose purposes are universities serving? How well are they working to advance a society that values everyone's well-being?

Reforming Higher Education to Increase Well-Being

In this section, I enumerate ways in which major areas of higher education can be reformed. I only scratch the surface. I have no doubt that university personnel and others who embrace prosocial, communitarian values and goals will be able to find many other ways they can advance those values and goals.

Increasing Universities' Focus on Societal Benefit

Universities have a long tradition of partnering with business and government to do research that benefits society. Soon after I became a graduate student at the University of Illinois at Urbana-Champaign, I went to the library. I discovered that next to the library was the oldest experimental corn field in the nation. When the university built an extension of the library a year or so later, they put it underground so it would not shade the cornfield. Illini were proud that the university played a major role in the enormous increase in agricultural yields—the so-called green revolution of the mid-twentieth century.

America's universities have played a similar role in most of the ways in which the United States has become a world leader in agriculture, medicine, technology, physics, chemistry, and defense. Our productivity is indicated by the number of Americans who have received the Nobel Prize: ninety-six in physics, seventy-two in chemistry, and ninety-four in physiology or medicine.

What would happen if our major universities put their considerable talents to work on addressing the most important problems we face as a nation? Our universities helped us win the Second World War and maintain a strong defense during the Cold War. They made extraordinary discoveries in medicine, physics, chemistry, and computers. However, further progress in these fields cannot solve the problems we currently confront. Physics, chemistry, and medicine can't tell us how to prevent drug addiction, crime, or intergroup conflict. They can't tell us how to redirect our values away from materialism and toward compassion and support for the well-being of every person. They can't tell us how to get individuals, corporations, and governments to take the steps needed to prevent catastrophic climate change. (Indeed, some advances, such as those in artificial intelligence and biology, could further imperil our well-being.) It is the behavioral sciences that hold the key to solving the problems that currently endanger our nation and the world.

Our funding priorities are wildly inconsistent with our needs as a nation. The top ten universities receiving federal funding for social and behavioral science research received a total of about $486 million in 2017.[2] That may seem like a lot, but consider that the total amount of federal funding for research going to the ten most heavily funded universities was about $8.135 billion in 2011.[3] An admittedly crude estimate is that less than 6 percent of total federal research funding went to behavioral and social science research.

We need the nation's universities to turn to the question of how they can conduct research that reduces all the psychological, behavioral, and health problems that harm our young people, and, ultimately, the nation. The health of the nation depends on universities recognizing that the highest priority in biomedical research needs to be addressing the social determinants of health, not the impaired physiology that results from these social influences.[4] The well-being of our cities and isolated rural areas requires comprehensive efforts as big and bold as the University of Oregon's new billion-dollar initiative in physical science. With respect to climate change, our universities need to invest heavily in behavioral science research on how to get our communities to adopt climate-friendly policies to an unprecedented extent.

Expanding Behavioral Science in Universities

A network of behavioral science specialties and university programs is already contributing to the spread of research-based strategies for increasing nurturance. Among the specialties are prevention science, behavior analysis, contextual behavioral science,[5] developmental psychology, educational psychology, behavioral economics, community psychology, and neuroscience. Each of these specialties has contributed to the development of strategies that reduce stress in environments and promote nurturance.

One of the key features of these specialties is their pragmatic orientation, which integrates basic and applied research around the goal of *prediction-and-influence* of behavior.[6] This may seem like an inside-baseball point, of interest only to philosophers and psychologists, but it is actually quite important for determining whether behavioral science delivers the benefits I have outlined. Much research can be successful at predicting behavior but not tell us how to influence it. Science working within the pragmatic framework I am describing focuses on identifying *malleable* influences on behavior that can be exploited to promote beneficial behavior.

Universities are beginning to develop programs that train scientist-practitioners—professionals who use empirically supported practices and continuously evaluate the impact of what they do, so that the efficacy of their work continues to increase. Programs to train prevention scientists have been created at a number of universities, including the University of Oregon, Pennsylvania State University, and Arizona State University. These programs are training masters-level people who can work in states and communities to get evidence-based prevention programs more widely adopted. They are training doctoral-level people, who are accelerating the rate at which tested and effective interventions are being developed, refined, and disseminated.

However, these efforts are tiny and underfunded compared with the money that has poured into academic programs designed to promote free market ideology. Just as Lewis Powell advised the conservative business community to develop its skills and capacity to advocate for its interests, we need many wealthy progressive individuals to invest in the behavioral science research and advocacy that is foundational for the society we aspire to.

Here are three specific areas in which investment in the expansion of behavioral science in higher education would accelerate the evolution of a more nurturing society.

Law and behavioral science. Just as the conservative billionaire coalition created law and economics programs in the nation's law schools, we need programs on law and behavioral science. As a behavioral scientist with great respect for the legal profession (my father was a lawyer, my sister is a lawyer, and I was president of the American Civil Liberties Union of Oregon), I have often been struck by the fact that the profession that dominates the making and administration of our laws has very little training in the science of human behavior. The law is ultimately a system for guiding human behavior. It has evolved over centuries as societies grappled with how to prevent egregious and harmful behaviors and resolve conflicts. There are some programs on law and behavioral science, such as the one at Arizona State University. And there are some journals on behavioral science and law, such as *Law and Human Behavior*. However, most of their focus is on the existing criminal justice system.

Perusing recent literature in relevant journals, I could find nothing on how laws might be rewritten to increase the use of prevention science and prevent crime in the first place. In the next chapter, I discuss the problems with our punitive criminal justice system. What we need in law and behavioral science programs is not minor, piecemeal modifications of an existing punitive system that evolved long before we understood the power of positive reinforcement or the harm that coercion does to people.[7] We need programs that, in a sense, start from scratch and ask, "Knowing what we know about human behavior, how can we construct a system of laws that minimizes coercive human relationships and richly reinforces all the diverse forms of prosocial behavior societies need to thrive?" It would be a system with a strong emphasis on creating laws that promote positive behavior, rather than one that waits until people offend and then punishes them.

Law and behavioral science programs would correct the mistakes that law and economics programs have promulgated, such as the notion that privatizing prisons would produce a better prison system. These programs would train a generation of lawyers to analyze the consequences that select individual behavior and corporate practices and to create laws that select beneficial practices and deter harmful ones by aligning consequences with desired outcomes.

Evonomics. If we want the economics profession to contribute to correcting public understanding of how economies work, we need major universities to develop programs in evonomics. As I noted earlier, this word connotes a version of economics that is firmly rooted in evolutionary thinking. It refers to a large and growing movement to understand economic systems in terms of the principles of variation and selection. Evolutionary theory provides a better account of economics than does free market theory.

Free market advocates insist that the individual pursuit of personal gain will necessarily benefit the wider society—as though there were an invisible hand. An evolutionary analysis of economics is founded on evidence about multilevel selection. An individual's actions may or may not benefit the group he or she is in—whether that individual is a cell, a member of a group, a corporation in a country, or a nation in the world. The cooperative actions of a group member that contribute to the success of the group may enable the group to succeed. To the extent that it does, the group is more likely to survive, and, with it, the cooperative behavior of the group members.

For example, a supervisor who recognizes the contributions of the people she supervises may contribute to the success of the company—in part, by reinforcing other behaviors that benefit the company. On the other hand, a group member or supervisor may act in ways that harm the group. A supervisor who berates employees may drive valuable workers from the company and undermine the company's productivity. (Last night, my Lyft driver told me she used to work decorating cakes, but the woman who owned the bakery was so critical that she left the job.)

Or consider the same process at the level of corporations and society. A corporation may make great contributions to human well-being by marketing an inexpensive way to generate electricity in rural areas, and thereby increase the ability of farm families to grow crops as well as learn (because they have electricity for lights to read by and televisions to watch). On the other hand, a company may garner great profits by marketing opioids but cause the death of thousands of people.

Evonomics analysis is in line with the fact that markets sometimes benefit others and sometimes do not. Moreover, it provides an explanation of how and why we can set contingencies to select practices that benefit the larger society, up to and including the world as a whole.

Robert Frank has pointed to some additional ways that evolutionary thinking can help us evolve a more nurturing society.[8] In a series of books and papers, he argues that people do not choose actions on the basis of their absolute value but on the basis of that value relative to alternatives. For example, your decision to buy a $40,000 car is not simply a matter of your valuing that particular car, it is also a matter of how it makes you feel relative to the cars that others own.

Frank makes the case that humans are influenced by their status in a group, that many of our purchases are made in order to have things that are better than what others have—or, at least, equivalent: "Keeping up with the Joneses." He argues that this is what has accelerated materialism. As the very wealthiest have escalated their spending, people just below them in wealth are motivated to escalate their spending. The size of the average American house went from 1,660 square feet in 1973 to 2,687 square feet in 2015.[9] In a similar way, the average cost of weddings rose from $16,000 to $28,000 in the past ten years.[10] As young people see their friends spend a lot on weddings, they are motivated to do so, too.

Is this good for society? Neither Frank nor I think so. What is the value added to society if we build bigger homes, buy big, gas-guzzling cars, and go into debt to have our children marry? Keep in mind that one of the things that led to the crash of 2008 was the desire of people to have more and more. People took out loans they could not repay to have money to buy bigger houses, bigger cars, more things.[11]

Frank has been advocating for a number of years that we change the tax system so that this runaway inflation of materialism is discouraged. He proposes that people report how much they made and how much they saved, and then pay taxes on the difference. Functionally, this would be a consumption tax. If you make $40,000 and save $5,000, you pay tax on $35,000. However, if your neighbor makes $40,000 and saves nothing, he or she pays tax on $40,000. These are contingencies that favor saving by putting an added cost on spending. (Of course, if we are going to be consistent empiricists, we need to empirically evaluate whether this is true.)

What would be the effect of this? Presumably, people would spend less and save more. Increased savings would reduce the number of people who arrive at retirement without the funds to live comfortably for the rest of their life. Currently, 50 percent of Americans think they don't have enough saved for retirement.[12]

For more information about this field, go to evonomics.com.

This book is inspired by the evonomics movement. I do not deny that market forces are a powerful influence on the selection of improved products and services. But the evidence tells us that the behavior of actors in a market will be selected by the contingencies that are legally allowed. If great wealth is the socially constructed outcome most actors have been socialized to pursue, and if such wealth can be attained by influencing the legal system to allow the creation of products that are harmful yet extremely profitable (e.g., collateralized debt obligations, automatic weapons, or cigarettes), then these are the products that will be produced. I seek a capitalist system organized by contingencies that favor health and well-being for all people participating in the market.

Such a system will never allow a harmful practice to be fined less than the profits the company receives from the practice. It will require companies to assess the impacts of its practices on customers and the community as well as on its profits. It will organize the political system to routinely assess the well-being of the entire population and evaluate the impact of laws and regulations on the population's well-being.

People working within the evonomics framework also provide a counterpoint to the free market argument that government is bad because it interferes with efficient market exchanges. According to this antigovernment view, most functions of society will be better provided by markets than by government because governments will not be motivated to spend wisely. June Sekera wrote a critique of this view:

> Marketization and its confederate, privatization, have led, sometimes
> intentionally, to the evisceration of governmental capacity, the
> downsizing of democracy and the dismantling of traditions of responsible
> public administration that are grounded in law and the Constitution.[13]

Sekera argued that under the thrall of free market ideology, economists have failed to develop a "coherent comprehensive theory of the public economy." She proposed that we view the "public goods and services" that governments provide as the result of collective choices we make as a society. Of course, thanks to forty years of relentless criticism of government, the collective choices we have been making of late are often the wrong ones from the standpoint of our future well-being. Sekera's work begins to create a sector of economic theory and research that can help rebuild a public sector that is in tatters due to free market advocacy.

Another counterpoint to the antigovernment perspective comes from Michael Lewis, who wrote an excellent description of the many ways the federal government benefits the well-being of Americans.[14]

For example, it provides the benefits of an excellent system of weather forecasting, government control of nuclear weapons, the Agriculture Department's funding of rural community development, and the prevention of terrorism.

In short, universities will improve their contribution to the problems we face by creating evonomics programs organized to develop empirically supported analyses of economic practices and study how to minimize the harm of capitalism while retaining the benefits of a market-based economy.

Business schools. Do a Google search for "business ethics at business schools" and you will discover widespread concern and recognition that our business schools are not cultivating business leaders who value benefiting society. Business schools have simply failed to instill ethical values that would prevent the myopic pursuit of short-term returns and the ignorance of the egregious harm that often results.[15]

Duff McDonald has written a thorough history of Harvard Business School (HBS) that documents this failure.[16] HBS is the largest and most prestigious school of business. It has trained many of the most prominent corporate leaders, including Jamie Dimon, CEO of JP Morgan Chase; Sheryl Sandberg, CEO of Facebook; Jeff Immelt, CEO of General Electric; Michael Bloomberg; Wilbur Ross, the current Secretary of Commerce; and billionaire hedge fund managers Bill Ackman, Ray Dalio, and John Paulson. In the 1990s, HBS graduates got 60 percent more job offers than did the average of the top twenty business schools and had starting salaries 40 percent higher than average.

McDonald explains how HBS played a key role in the rise of economic inequality. *Harvard Business Review,* a publication of HBS, published a study in 1951 that documented how hourly employees' pay had doubled between 1939 and 1950, while that of upper management had risen only 35 percent. Thus began great attention to executive pay by *Harvard Business Review.* McDonald argues that increased attention to and advocacy for increased executive pay was one reason the ratio of executive pay to that of other employees rose from 20 to 1 to 354 to 1 during a fifty-year period.

In my essay on the Great Recession, I describe how the free market delusion led the leaders of the financial industry to believe markets couldn't fail.[17] HBS played a significant role in this debacle. Ironically, the hundredth anniversary of the creation of HBS was in 2008, the year of the great crash. McDonald quotes one of HBS's own graduates, Philip Delves Broughten, who criticized the failure of HBS to see what was coming: "It should be a profound embarrassment to the faculty of the Harvard Business School that for the second time in less than a decade, it failed to identify an economic catastrophe in which its alumni played a starring role." McDonald went on to list HBS graduates who played a role in the crisis: George W. Bush; Henry Paulson, the secretary of the Treasury; Christopher Cox, chairman of the Securities and Exchange Commission; Stan O'Neal, CEO of Merrill Lynch; John Thain, subsequent CEO of Merrill Lynch; Jamie Dimon, CEO of JP Morgan Chase; and numerous others who worked for McKinsey and Company, which advised most of the companies involved in the crash of 2008.

McDonald reviewed the tortured history of efforts to integrate business ethics into the HBS curriculum. At the outset of its creation, its founder, Professor A. Lawrence Lowell, spoke of "inculcating good morals." However, courses on business ethics came and went. They weren't required, and few students subscribed to them.

In 1987, HBS alumnus John Shad donated $30 million to the school to endow a program in business leadership and ethics. Shad had been appointed chair of the Securities and Exchange Commission. Despite initial moves to pare back SEC regulatory activity, he eventually became concerned about the extent of fraud when he found himself dealing with a huge insider trading scandal in which Ivan Boesky and Michael Milken were using advance information about favorable developments of companies that allowed them to buy their stock before the stock rose in value.

However, when one of HBS's own, Jeff Skilling, was convicted on insider trading and securities fraud in connection with the bankruptcy of Enron, the HSB leadership essentially threw up its hands and concluded that it was not possible to affect the ethics of young adults because ethical values were inculcated at an earlier age. (As a student of human behavior for fifty years, I can tell you this is nonsense.)

The fundamental problem, as McDonald sees it, is that it is hard to "marry free market capitalism with an egalitarian democracy." The culture of HBS—like the culture of much of business, which HBS has influenced so heavily—is massively focused on material success. CEOs nowadays are rewarded for increasing the price of a company's stock.

The well-being of those who might be harmed by a company's activities is simply not very high on the list of management's priorities.

McDonald cites one voice at HBS that has called for the kind of attention I think business ethics requires if our society is going to evolve a more nurturing capitalism. Rakesh Khurana wrote:

> Business will not be part of the solution if it is populated by individuals who have a very narrow conception of what their role is, who have a very narrow view about how business fits into the larger institutions of society. I believe that what we need to do is to begin that conversation among our students and to make that conversation not something that is circumscribed to an ethics course or a single course in organizational behavior, but to be part of a conversation that runs through every single course we have for our students, so that they are socialized, just like you take a doctor, that at the end of the day, the most important thing is that the role of the corporation is to improve the general welfare of the society.

There is no reason business schools could not inculcate prosocial values in their students. But the history of HBS and the advocacy for free market economics shows it would require considerable investment in programs that advance these values and ethics. That won't happen unless foundations and wealthy progressive individuals invest in changing these root influences on society. They need to fund progressive business schools and the integration of ethics into moderate and conservative business schools. Rather than investing in more narrowly defined problems, such as the marketing of cigarettes or unhealthful foods, we need to recognize that all these problems stem from our underlying failure to promote ethics and practices that are consistent with prosocial values.

Higher Education Can Be the Cutting Edge of Reform

If we succeed in making our society more nurturing, it will be because people working in every sector of society are skilled in cultivating the prosocial values and behaviors of everyone they contact. Many more teachers will be skilled in cultivating their students' prosocial behavior through practices they learned in implementing evidence-based programs, such as the PAX Good Behavior Game, Positive Behavioral Intervention and

Support, Positive Action, and Promoting Alternative Thinking Strategies, which teach and richly reinforce emotional regulation and cooperative, caring behaviors.[18] Health-care providers will have skilled behavioral health specialists who treat and prevent all the most common and costly psychological, behavioral, and health problems. Public health specialists will monitor the well-being of the population and develop, test, and implement policies that prevent problem development. People working in the criminal justice system will focus on the prevention of crime and on evidence-based programs for rehabilitating offenders and minimizing the harm to families that results from incarceration.

We can move toward this society if universities train cadres of masters- and doctoral-level people who have the skills to help each sector of society—human services, health care, juvenile justice, and education—adopt more effective treatment and prevention programs. These efforts are also being advanced by the leading organizations of behavioral science, which are convening a growing number of highly skilled scientist-practitioners dedicated to the kinds of values we are discussing. These organizations include the American Psychological Association, the Association for Behavior Analysis International, the Association for Contextual Behavioral Science, the Association for Positive Behavioral Intervention and Support, the Behavioral Science and Policy Association, the Society for Behavioral Medicine, and the Society for Prevention Research.

Every state would benefit from having an endowed university center that is organized to translate what is known into effective policies, programs, and practices. Such endowed centers would have as their mission increasing the prevalence of families, schools, workplaces, and neighborhoods that nurture people's well-being. They would advance the monitoring of well-being so that ultimately every community would have accurate and timely data about how people in the community are faring on measures of psychological, behavioral, and health problems. Such centers would be advocates for policies, programs, and practices to improve well-being. They would train people to work in education, health care, human services, and criminal justice. They would work collaboratively with the public health, human services, and health-care systems to conduct applied research on the implementation and impact of evidence-based interventions.

Just as Lewis Powell influenced a generation of scholars to embrace and promote free market ideology, we need higher education to embrace the goal of evolving a society in which most people are living caring and productive lives. Major reforms in higher education could significantly alter the direction of the nation. A much greater investment in applied behavioral science research is needed. Programs in law, medicine, economics, business, and computer science will be particularly valuable.

Action Implications

Personal

Join the Values to Action Higher Education Network (valuestoaction.com/education).

We are creating a network of people and organizations to flesh out a plan for the reform of higher education and advocate for its adoption throughout the nation.

If you are a behavioral scientist...

- Invest more in educating the public and policy makers about the need for more research and training of behavioral scientists focused on the solution to our major social and behavioral problems.

- Create programs on comprehensive approaches to increasing well-being in communities and neighborhoods of concentrated disadvantage.

If you are a lawyer...

- Study behavioral science.

- Begin to reconstruct law schools so that lawmaking is better guided by behavioral science knowledge and the use of empirical methods to evaluate the impact of our laws on the population's well-being.

If you teach at a business school...

Act on the advice of Rakesh Khurana at HBS and make business part of the solution to the corruption of our current capitalist system.

In information technology...

- If you teach software development or data science, include ethics in your curriculum.

- If you work in software development or data science, does your organization have a code of ethics? If not, work to create one and get it put into practice.

- As an investor, invest in companies with strong codes of ethics and technologies that accelerate prosocial behavior.

Policy

Develop laws and policies that favor colleges and universities assessing how well they are contributing to societal well-being.

An interdisciplinary program on law, behavioral, science, and higher education could translate the ideas presented here into concrete policies.

Organizations

I did an Internet search for "organizations working reform of higher education" and found a long list. I have not thoroughly vetted these organizations, but in just reading their names, I did not see any focused on the kinds of reform I have described in this chapter. The first step of the higher education reform effort will be to crowdsource an analysis of these organizations to see if any of them could be allies in the reforms we seek. The second step will be to convene a conference to further map out the reforms that are needed and what we can do to promote them.

Reforming Criminal Justice

*The statistics documenting the failure of our system are
unrivaled in human history.*

— Craig DeRoche, the Prison Fellowship,
a Christian ministry

THE CRIMINAL JUSTICE system is one of the most important ways in which our society undermines the well-being of millions of people. Our capitalist economy is not the only reason we have such a harmful criminal justice system, but it is a major factor. As the belief was spread by the conservative billionaire coalition that the private sector could do things better than government—that is, get better results at a lower cost—entrepreneurs began a movement to privatize prisons. As the business of running private prisons, providing services to prisons, and renting out prison labor has grown, a network of business interests (including unionized prison employees) has evolved. This network has an enormous financial stake in continuing its work and expanding the number of people trapped in the criminal justice system. These developments are simply another example of the way in which, in the absence of regulation to reduce harmful effects of its practice, any business will naturally look for ways to expand its operations and prevent any policies that might impinge on its profits.

I begin this chapter by summarizing the harm that the existing system is doing. Then I describe the reforms that are needed.

Our Harmful Criminal Justice System

The United States incarcerates 2.2 million people. Among 223 nations in the world, we have the second highest rate of incarceration; 655 per 100,000 people, compared with 140 per 100,000 in the United Kingdom, 104 per 100,000 in France, and 59 per 100,000 in Sweden.[1]

Our astronomical rates of incarceration are a relatively new phenomenon. They were comparable to rates in countries such as the United Kingdom in 1970.[2] What changed things in this country was the massive incarceration of black men that began in the 1980s. The difference between U.S. rates of incarceration and rates in other nations is almost entirely the result of the huge number of black men in prison. About a million of the 2.3 million people in prison are black.[3] In other words, about 43 percent of the people in prison are black, though blacks make up only 13.3 percent of the U.S. population. (More than 90 percent of those in prison are men.)

Michelle Alexander's book *The New Jim Crow* provides a history of how this happened.[4] Alexander makes a compelling case that we have evolved a new form of Jim Crow. *Jim Crow* is a pejorative term for black people that arose in the early nineteenth century.[5] Following the Civil War, Southern states implemented laws requiring racial segregation in schools, trains, and public accommodations. These laws came to be called Jim Crow laws.

Alexander shows that the criminal justice system we evolved in the past forty-five years disenfranchises and stigmatizes black men as effectively as Jim Crow laws did in the post–Civil War era. Not only does it lock people up for unnecessarily long sentences, it prohibits them from voting.[6] In Florida, Kentucky, Tennessee, and Virginia, more than 20 percent of black people cannot vote for this reason. Moreover, the system often restricts where formerly incarcerated people may live and makes it difficult to get a job, which frequently results in their returning to jail. And in recent years, as governments have strained to pay for their bloated system of incarceration and parole, the system has imposed fines and fees on prisoners and rented their services to businesses to defer some of its costs.[7]

(Lest you think these injustices are due solely to historic mistakes policy makers who are no longer with us, let me tell you about In November 2018, the citizens of Florida passed a ballot

rity

Leik

have writte

on children.

has a parent who

ceration—regardless of

than for white children

ciated with higher rates of s

ing disabilities and attention de

asthma, depression, post-traumatic

Morsy and Rothstein point out that t

ation probably account for much of t

between African American children

ger-term harm to children includes th

will be arrested, which harms not on

These costs to society should be inclu

benefits of the existing system.

The Prison-Industrial Comp

Although corporate America did not s

ment, it quickly found ways to profit

increasingly popular sentiment that private con

inefficient and ineffective. The governm

formerly provided only by the governm

has revenues of $5 billion annually.[13]

corporations is in place, they will wor

to their business opportunities. Thus,

In addition to incarceration separating parents from their children, a number of federal laws contribute to family breakup and poverty.[11] Federal welfare laws require states to seek termination of parental rights if a child has been in foster care for fifteen of the last twenty-two months. Thus, any single parent serving more than twenty-two months is at risk of losing his or her parental rights. Another federal law prohibits anyone convicted of a drug-related felony from *ever* receiving cash assistance or food stamps during his or her lifetime. Another law prohibits those who violate their parole from receiving Temporary Assistance for Needy Families (TANF), food stamps, or Supplemental Security Income.

Leila Morsy and Richard Rothstein of the Economic Policy Institute have written a thorough review of the impact of parental incarceration on children.[12] They report that one in four African American children has a parent who is or has been incarcerated. That is six times higher than for white children. Morsy and Rothstein found that parental incarceration—regardless of the reasons or the race of the parent—is associated with higher rates of school dropout, the development of learning disabilities and attention deficit hyperactivity disorder, migraines, asthma, depression, post-traumatic stress disorder, and homelessness. Morsy and Rothstein point out that these harmful effects of incarceration probably account for much of the disparity in academic success between African American children and white children. The longer-term harm to children includes the likelihood that they themselves will be arrested, which harms not only them but those around them. These costs to society should be included when we weigh the risks and benefits of the existing system.

The Prison-Industrial Complex

Although corporate America did not start the mass incarceration movement, it quickly found ways to profit from it. Taking advantage of the increasingly popular sentiment that public agencies were necessarily inefficient and ineffective, private companies rushed in to offer services formerly provided only by the government. The private prison system now has revenues of $5 billion annually.[13] Of course, once a set of profitable corporations is in place, they will work very hard to prevent any threats to their business opportunities. Thus, we now have an entrenched lobby gave felons the right to vote. It would affect 1.5 million people in the state. However, since the majority of these people are black and black people are more likely to vote for Democrats, the Republican-dominated legislature passed a bill in 2019 that required convicted felons to pay back all fines and fees to the court before they could be allowed to register.)[8]

Alexander shows that the increase in rates of black incarceration occurred in conjunction with the war on drugs that began in the 1980s. However, despite the fact that black people's use and sale of illegal drugs is no higher than use and sales by whites, arrest, conviction, and imprisonment rates skyrocketed only in communities of disadvantaged black people. (At each of these three stages in the criminal justice system—arrest, conviction, and imprisonment—the rates are higher for black people than for white people.)

While the worst impacts have been felt by black communities, Alexander acknowledges that the system also harms other groups—both other minority groups and poor white people. This is an important point to remember in our effort to build a movement that brings people together around reforming this system.

Deterrence is often cited as the goal of increasingly punitive approaches to sentencing and incarceration. It is certainly not in the long-term interest of the offender or anyone else if the offender reoffends. However, our system is doing a terrible job of preventing further offenses. The recidivism rate in the United States is 76.6 percent, compared with 20 percent in Norway.[9]

Our concern should not be restricted to the 2.3 million people who are themselves imprisoned. The emphasis on punishment that is so fundamental to our current system harms millions who are not imprisoned. Incarceration reduces family income, increases the likelihood of divorce, and often traumatizes and stigmatizes children of offenders.

Consider the experience of Charlene and Samuel Holly of Chicago.[10] They and their six grandchildren, ages eleven months to thirteen years, were held at gunpoint for half an hour while the police ransacked their home. According to a lawsuit the Hollys subsequently filed, the police made them lie on the floor and repeatedly shouted "motherfuckers" at the children. It doesn't take a psychologist to know that these children are likely to have significant problems with anxiety and distrust.

Our Harmful Criminal Justice System

The United States incarcerates 2.2 million people. Among 223 nations in the world, we have the second highest rate of incarceration; 655 per 100,000 people, compared with 140 per 100,000 in the United Kingdom, 104 per 100,000 in France, and 59 per 100,000 in Sweden.[1]

Our astronomical rates of incarceration are a relatively new phenomenon. They were comparable to rates in countries such as the United Kingdom in 1970.[2] What changed things in this country was the massive incarceration of black men that began in the 1980s. The difference between U.S. rates of incarceration and rates in other nations is almost entirely the result of the huge number of black men in prison. About a million of the 2.3 million people in prison are black.[3] In other words, about 43 percent of the people in prison are black, though blacks make up only 13.3 percent of the U.S. population. (More than 90 percent of those in prison are men.)

Michelle Alexander's book *The New Jim Crow* provides a history of how this happened.[4] Alexander makes a compelling case that we have evolved a new form of Jim Crow. *Jim Crow* is a pejorative term for black people that arose in the early nineteenth century.[5] Following the Civil War, Southern states implemented laws requiring racial segregation in schools, trains, and public accommodations. These laws came to be called Jim Crow laws.

Alexander shows that the criminal justice system we evolved in the past forty-five years disenfranchises and stigmatizes black men as effectively as Jim Crow laws did in the post–Civil War era. Not only does it lock people up for unnecessarily long sentences, it prohibits them from voting.[6] In Florida, Kentucky, Tennessee, and Virginia, more than 20 percent of black people cannot vote for this reason. Moreover, the system often restricts where formerly incarcerated people may live and makes it difficult to get a job, which frequently results in their returning to jail. And in recent years, as governments have strained to pay for their bloated system of incarceration and parole, the system has imposed fines and fees on prisoners and rented their services to businesses to defer some of its costs.[7]

(Lest you think these injustices are due solely to historic mistakes of policy makers who are no longer with us, let me tell you about Florida. In November 2018, the citizens of Florida passed a ballot initiative that

CHAPTER 8:

Reforming Criminal Justice

*The statistics documenting the failure of our system are
unrivaled in human history.*

— Craig DeRoche, the Prison Fellowship,
a Christian ministry

T HE CRIMINAL JUSTICE system is one of the most important
ways in which our society undermines the well-being of millions of people. Our capitalist economy is not the only reason we have such a harmful criminal justice system, but it is
a major factor. As the belief was spread by the conservative billionaire
coalition that the private sector could do things better than government—that is, get better results at a lower cost—entrepreneurs began
a movement to privatize prisons. As the business of running private
prisons, providing services to prisons, and renting out prison labor has
grown, a network of business interests (including unionized prison employees) has evolved. This network has an enormous financial stake in
continuing its work and expanding the number of people trapped in
the criminal justice system. These developments are simply another
example of the way in which, in the absence of regulation to reduce
harmful effects of its practice, any business will naturally look for ways
to expand its operations and prevent any policies that might impinge
on its profits.

I begin this chapter by summarizing the harm that the existing system
is doing. Then I describe the reforms that are needed.

of companies (and unions) whose earnings depend on having a large prison population.

Privatization came about thanks to the belief in the untested theory that it would have benefits (beyond the profits to the companies involved). Whether this is true is an empirical question. Unfortunately, very little rigorous research has been conducted on this subject. A study by the Bureau of Prisons, which runs the federal prison system, compared fourteen private prisons managed for the bureau with fourteen the bureau runs. The populations of the two sets of prisons are different, with the private ones mostly housing "adult male inmates who are undocumented immigrants and are nearing the end of their sentences," and this difference makes any comparison more difficult.[14] However, the study did find that the private prisons had significantly higher rates of contraband; reports of incidents, such as assaults; lockdowns; inmate discipline; and grievances.

All prisons should be evaluated in terms of the degree to which they prevent further offending and succeed in preparing former inmates for life as healthy, productive members of society. Given the impact of stress on human health and well-being, we should also be asking how well prisons do at minimizing stress on inmates and guards alike.

According to free market theory, having competition among private companies motivates each company to deliver better results, thereby steadily improving the efficiency and effectiveness of the service. But in our current highly corrupt political system, market competition does not seem to be selecting better and better outcomes. Companies are motivated to invest in ensuring that they get and keep contracts with the state by paying for the election of policy makers who will ensure that they get those contracts. Yet actual research on the impact of privatization on outcomes is lacking.

Goals for Reform

If we are to achieve our goal of increasing the proportion of people who live caring and productive lives, the criminal justice system needs to be reformed in numerous ways. Evolving a criminal justice system that rehabilitates offenders and, better yet, prevents crime in the first place, should be a major aim of a coalition that seeks to advance everyone's well-being. In this section, I outline what needs to be done.

Rehabilitation

Mark Lipsey, a research professor at the Department of Human and Organizational Development at Vanderbilt University, has done meta-analyses to examine what works to reduce prison recidivism. He found that interventions based on punishment and deterrence increased *recidivism*.[15] On the other hand, cognitive behavior therapy interventions significantly reduced recidivism. Cognitive behavior therapy helps offenders develop specific behavioral and cognitive skills for handling situations that might lead them to reoffend. For example, an offender might have problems holding a job because he or she is quick to get angry and get in fights with supervisors. That person could get help from a therapist who encourage him or her to notice thoughts that may push him or her to react to criticism with anger. By noticing these thoughts, the offender can become better able to control behavior rather than simply act on anger without thinking about the consequences. Through coaching and practice, offenders can be helped to develop new skills for handling situations in ways that avoid confrontation and improve their relationships with their supervisors.

Lipsey found that cognitive behavior therapy reduced recidivism for both juvenile and adult offenders. It worked whether it was provided to offenders in prison, in residential facilities, or while on parole or probation.[16] It even worked for high-risk offenders. Consistent with Lipsey's findings, countries that focus on rehabilitation rather than punishment have lower rates of recidivism.[17] Among the rehabilitative practices that seem to work to reduce recidivism are financial literacy programs, allowing prisoners to work outside the prison, education to prepare prisoners to join the workforce, paying a minimum wage, and providing supervised Internet access so prisoners can keep up with technology developments while in prison.[18]

Prevention

In *The Nurture Effect,* I describe numerous family, school, and community interventions that can prevent delinquency and crime. The Good Behavior Game, which helps elementary school children develop cooperation and social skills, led to significantly fewer adolescents and young adults committing crimes compared with children who didn't participate in the game. A review of family intervention programs by Leslie et al. identified sixteen programs with proven benefit in reducing antisocial behavior and crime.[19] The Nurse Family Partnership, which helps high-risk pregnant moms through pregnancy and the first two years of the baby's life, cut the rate of arrests at age fifteen in half, compared with arrests for children not in the program. The systematic implementation of Communities that Care—a communitywide effort to implement family and school programs, was associated with a reduction in delinquency in Pennsylvania of 44 percent.[20] Taken together, these programs and others like them show us how we can set young people up to succeed in life.

Changing Public Policy

These rehabilitation and prevention programs can vastly improve the system. However, they are unlikely to be widely adopted without changes in public policy.

The foundation for reform of public policy involves a change in the goals of the system. The primary goal of the system in the past fifty years has been to catch and punish offenders. Virtually all the just-discussed reforms will require that the goals and mindsets of policy makers and administrators shift from punishment to prevention and rehabilitation. When we have achieved this embrace of prevention and rehabilitation, here are some of the policies that are needed.

First, we need to reduce overall rates of incarceration and the racial disparities in incarceration. Federal and state laws are needed that require the system to report on the numbers of people incarcerated, their race and economic status, and the steps each component of the system is taking to reduce incarceration and achieve equity. One way to reduce incarceration rates is to require that imprisonment not be allowed for any crimes for which it can be shown that incarceration leads to greater recidivism than do less-restrictive alternatives.

Second, we need laws that require that evidence-based rehabilitation be widely and effectively implemented. This will only happen if recidivism rates are tracked and the efficacy of interventions is tracked. There is no reason state and federal prison systems could not routinely evaluate their interventions through experimental studies that compare the impact of different interventions.

Third, we should eliminate post-incarceration restrictions on people, such as limitations on voting, where people can live, and what jobs or professions they are entitled to work in. Rather than stigmatize people, implying that they are not to be trusted and must be punished for the rest of their lives, we should send them into the community with the skills they need and the expectation that they will be successful in moving forward with their lives. An excellent analysis of what is needed was provided by the Urban Institute.[21] Whereas it has been common to simply release prisoners without much planning or support for their new life, a good reentry program would provide the following:

- **Transportation.** People released from prison need to get from prison to the community they will be living in, and once they get there, they need transportation to get to and from work.

- **Clothing, food, and furnishings.** Released prisoners need the basics before they can begin to look for work, attend school, make friends, and reconnect with family.

- **Financial resources.** Released prisoners need enough money to live on until they can get a job.

- **Documentation.** Upon release, people need some form of identification. Someone who has been incarcerated for several years won't have a valid driver's license.

- **Housing.** Released prisoners need a safe and affordable place to live.

- **Education and employment.** People coming out of prison need help enhancing their skills and finding work.

- **Health care.** Released prisoners need health insurance and a connection with a health-care provider. Leaving people to fend for themselves makes it more likely that they will not get mental and physical health care.

- **Support systems.** Released prisoners need a list of community resources. They may need help contacting family members or finding other forms of social support, such as a community or faith-based organization. They may also need treatment and recovery services for substance-use disorders.

In my hometown, Eugene, Oregon, we have an organization, Sponsors, that has been developing these types of support for more than forty years. Sponsors reported, "A 2018 analysis conducted by the Oregon Criminal Justice Commission found a 60 percent reduction in three-year recidivism rates among individuals who participated in Sponsors Long-

Term Housing programs as compared with the Lane County baseline for people releasing from state prison."[22]

Fourth, improving the criminal justice system requires far more empirical work. Putting in place systems for monitoring outcomes makes it possible to experimentally evaluate the impact of every program, practice, and policy. Just as experimental evaluation has produced an increasingly effective set of family and school interventions,[23] stepped-up use of experimental methods will produce a steadily more effective system of prevention and rehabilitation. This is essential to test the free market theory that privatization of prisons is beneficial. Given the growth of for-profit prisons and the existing evidence that suggests they may be harmful, the U.S. Department of Justice should fund systematic research, including experimental evaluations of the impact of privatizing prisons.

We also need to adopt effective policies for reducing the rates of all offenses. And the system should be judged by how well it is reducing the crime rate. This, of course, has not been the criterion by which we have judged our criminal justice system. Unfortunately, we have not managed our communities with this outcome in the forefront of our discussion. As a result, the criminal justice system does little to prevent crime. Indeed, many of the system's most common practices (e.g., congregating delinquent adolescents) are increasing offending, and, not coincidentally, the profits of, for-profit prisons.

The success of the criminal justice system in reducing crime requires an effective alliance with other sectors of society. We will prevent crime if the educational system is more effective in preventing academic failure and promoting prosocial development. We will prevent much crime if we have more effective treatment for substance use disorders. We need higher education to train a new generation of specialists skilled in evidence-based approaches to prevention, treatment, and rehabilitation. Crime will be prevented if the human service and health-care systems are more effective in delivering evidence-based family interventions to families at risk to raise antisocial children. We will prevent it if businesses drop hiring policies that screen out people with a criminal record. In short, we will prevent crime and enhance the lives of millions of Americans if all the people and sectors of society that are committed to enhancing everyone's well-being come together to push for policies and programs that commit to prevention and treatment and end America's obsession with the punishment of our fellow Americans.

The Benefits of Criminal Justice Reform

Consider who would benefit from a reformed system. First there are all the people who will not be crime victims. There were 5 million victims of violent crime in 2015, a more than 75 percent decrease since 1993.[24] However, that is little consolation to those who were victims in 2015. As the system does a better job of preventing crime and reducing recidivism, these numbers will go down even more. (One of the challenges to promoting prevention is that if you prevent something from happening, no one will notice it. That is why systematic experimental evaluations of the impact of preventive interventions are so important.)

Children will also benefit. As fewer children are traumatized by their parents' involvement in the criminal justice system—including by seeing their parents violently arrested or even killed—more children will develop normally. Based on the statistics I cite above, we should see fewer students dropping out of school and fewer with learning disabilities, attention deficit hyperactivity disorder, migraines, asthma, depression, post-traumatic stress disorder, and homelessness. And as we shift from a system that waits for people to offend and then punishes them to a system that prevents crime, we will have fewer young people committing delinquent acts. And because many of the most effective family and school programs that prevent crime also prevent substance use, depression, and academic failure,[25] we will see lower rates of most child and adolescent problems.

Finally, there are all the people who have already been harmed by the system, including those who have been locked up too long and have lost contact with their families. Under the existing system, people caught up in our highly punitive system have had their own lives ruined as well as the lives of family members. With the reforms we are pursuing, we can expect to see ex-offenders voting, getting jobs, rebuilding relationships with friends and families, and making significant contributions to their communities. We should see reductions in the racial disparities in incarceration, and improvement in the well-being of black and Hispanic children. As these reforms spread, think of how many people will escape the fate that so many have experienced in the existing system.

Action Implications

Personal

Join the Values to Action Criminal Justice Reform Network (valuestoaction. com/criminaljustice).

We are building a network of people who want to be better informed about the problems with the current systems and more effective alternatives, and who want to bring about the reforms needed. You do not have to be working in criminal justice or be one of the many people who has been harmed by the system. We need you if you are in one of those groups, but we also need people who have not paid much attention to the problem. We can help you address the problem.

Bring the problems with our criminal justice system up in conversations at least once a week.

Imagine that everyone who understands this problem mentioned it to another person just once a week. How many more people would become sensitized to the problem? How much more support would there be for changing our ways?

If you work in the criminal justice system...

Advocate for the use of the least punitive and most effective strategies for reducing recidivism and for the continuing monitoring of the rate of recidivism, rate of incarceration, and disparities in treatment among racial and economic groups. By encouraging the use of more nurturing rehabilitative practices, you can not only help offenders but lessen the stress experienced by people working in the system.

If you are in a position to hire people...

Be open to hiring ex-offenders. See Jails to Jobs, Unicor, and Hope for Prisoners.[26]

Policy

Advance reform by advocating for policies that:

- Require that every jurisdiction annually report the rate of crimes, rate of recidivism, and disparities in these measures due to race and income

- Require the use of evidence-based rehabilitation practices

- Require law enforcement to report annually on the status of prevention efforts in each community and the role law enforcement is playing in supporting effective preventive interventions

- Reduce or eliminate the use of imprisonment for offenses or offenders when empirical evidence indicates that alternatives to incarceration are more effective in reducing recidivism

- Require that post-incarceration services be provided when evidence indicates that they contribute to reducing recidivism

- Eliminate laws that impede effective adjustment following incarceration

Create a policy clearinghouse.

Given the need for all these policy changes, a clearinghouse needs to be created that can conduct a systematic analysis of what policies are in place in every jurisdiction. This would provide a baseline and guide reformers to focus on advancing needed policies in specific places.

Systematically research the impact of policy changes.

This needs to be funded by the Department of Justice. Research on how to get policies adopted is also needed.

Experimentally compare the outcomes from for-profit and government-run prisons.

Let there be a competition. If for-profit prisons are more effective, we should have them. I am doubtful, but I am an empiricist.

Organizations

Explore the numerous organizations working on prison reform.

See the Namaste website, which has an essay by Matthew Monahan that profiles two dozen inspiring nonprofits working toward positive change in the criminal justice system.[27]

CHAPTER 9:

Evolving Social and News Media to Promote Prosocial Values

This technology that you have invented has been amazing.
But now, it's a crime scene.

—Carole Cadwalladr,
speaking in Silicon Valley about social media

P ERHAPS THE BIGGEST challenge we face in evolving an economic and political system that works for everyone is reaching
and persuading millions of people to embrace prosocial values. If anything, the task is more challenging than it was even
twenty years ago, thanks to the development of social media and the
decline of local newspapers. Large swaths of the American public have
beliefs that are contrary to facts, attitudes, and values that are neither in
their best interests nor in the interests of society as a whole.[1] And as you
will see, social media is largely responsible for the divisiveness in society.

In this chapter, I explain how our media evolved to its current state
and what we can do to evolve media that promote communitarian values
and outcomes. I describe how we can move toward a society in which a
larger proportion of the population is being influenced by facts, supportive of the society we are aspiring too, and taking actions needed to
move us in the right direction.

In the 1950s, Americans were more united. In that decade, we went
from 3 million homes having TVs to 55 million. There were only three TV
networks: CBS, NBC, and ABC. All of them reported the news in roughly
the same way, at the same time. As a result, most Americans got the same

news. With the advent of cable TV, we have gone from having three or four channels to hundreds. The diversity of media has continued to grow. In addition to TV, we have the Internet, providing thousands of options for people to not only get their news but actively promote stories—including many that are untrue.

And so, like a cup of mercury spilled on the floor, our society has dissolved into tiny droplets of groups coalesced around issues and activities as diverse as quilting, basketball, genealogy, religion, and preventing Sharia law from taking over whole states. Thanks to these developments, we not only have a diversity of interests, we have a diversity of "facts." The question is whether we can understand the current state of media in a way that allows us to counter the harmful impact of individual and state actors in order to bring people together around social values and efforts to reform our economic and political systems.

The problem is enormously challenging, but we'd better get to work on solving it. If we don't, we will be subjected to ongoing division, conflict, and intergroup aggression, hurtling toward living on a planet on which, if human life is not extinguished, will be much more difficult.

I first discuss how social media is contributing to our divisions, then examine the role of three Internet monopolies that have evolved in the past twenty years and contribute to the problems we face. I argue that the principles I propose to regulate other corporations are just as relevant to these behemoths of the Internet age: Facebook, Google, and Amazon. Finally, I discuss what we can do to forge a network of people actively working to promote the values, behaviors, and policies needed to reform society.

Problems with the Current Media Landscape

I see two ways in which various media are undermining the solidarity needed to reform capitalism. First, social media has created a huge community of mostly white Americans who have congealed around the belief that white people, and therefore America, are doomed. The Trump presidency is as much the result of this community as the cause of it. Second, numerous organizations are using highly sophisticated methods to influence beliefs, attitudes, and behaviors in ways that benefit them but undermine our democracy.

The Internet of Hate

Until I read Andrew Marantz's book *Antisocial,* I did not realize how thoroughly the right wing has created a parallel universe on the Internet.[2] Marantz describes a loose network of right-wing leaders who have a huge following. The Internet has enabled people who had no connection to the major opinion-leading newspapers, TV networks, and magazines to reach millions of people with messages far outside the scope of beliefs, values, and goals that traditional media allowed.

Here are some of the examples of the kind of claims and opinions that are widely and frequently reaching a huge proportion of Americans, according to Marantz:

- Mike Cernovich, "a self-employed lawyer and motivational blogger" started blogging that "Hillary Clinton was suffering from a grave neurological condition and that the traditional media was covering it up. He turned this conjecture into a meme, which gathered momentum on Twitter, then leaped to the Drudge Report, then to Fox News, and then into Donald Trump's mouth."

- Jim Hoft runs a far-right website called The Gateway Pundit. During the 2016 presidential campaign, it had 1 million page views per day.

- At a right-wing rally on the steps of the Lincoln Memorial, one speaker, Chris Cantwell, promoted the views of Hans-Hermann Hoppe, a "hard right political philosopher whose work seemed to justify preemptive murder." Cantwell said "At what point do we begin physically removing Democrats and Communists to establish and maintain the libertarian social order necessary for our desired meritocracy? Non-white immigration and breeding alone are rapidly diminishing what electoral majorities we have remaining. Jewish influence disarms us."

- Following the death of Heather Heyer, who was run down by a neo-Nazi at the Charlottesville demonstration, a SubReddit site that claims to be "The #1 place to go on the internet to discuss Hans-Hermann Hoppe's idea of physical removal" posted the following: "Details still remain to be known, as well as motives, but we have at least one dead antifa and 19 others injured. This is a good thing. They are mockeries of life and need to fucking go."

- The Fourteen Words, a meme widely circulated among right-wing adherents, states: "We must secure the existence of our people and a future for white children."

- Andrew Anglin, the publisher of the neo-Nazi website the Daily Stormer, urged his followers to harass Tanya Gersh, a Whitefish, Montana, realtor who is Jewish, because she allegedly insulted the mother of white nationalist Richard Spencer. Anglin provided his followers with phone numbers, addresses, and links to social media for Gersh, her family, and friends. As a result, she and her husband and son received more than seven hundred "anti-Semitic and homophobic emails, phone calls, texts, social media comments, letters, postcards and Christmas cards."[3] Among the messages:

  - "Rat-faced criminals who play with fire tend to get thrown in the oven"

  - "Merry Christmas, you Christ-killer"

  - "Worthless f—— k—."

  - "It's time for you to take a one way ticket to Tel Aviv."

  - "You have no idea what you are doing, six million are only the beginning."

  - One message had a photoshopped picture of Gersh's twelve-year-old son being crushed by a Nazi truck.[4]

This network of right-wing illuminati insists on free speech. They often imply they are joking when they raise topics such as the "Jewish question" (e.g., "Why are Jews overrepresented in media, academia, and banking?" "What should we do about the Jews?") But then they argue that no speech should be suppressed. Yet one of the things that such speech has contributed to is murder. *The New York Times* (an outlet the right-wing illuminati revile) has documented how recent mass shootings were inspired via the Internet by previous shooters.[5] For example, the Christchurch shooter said he was inspired by the Norwegian man who killed seventy-seven people, as were three other mass shooters. The *Times* analysis identified at least fifteen instances in which mass shooters indicated their admiration for an earlier shooter.

Think about this in evolutionary terms. A technology was created that allowed anyone with a computer or cell phone to engage in public discussion without the need to reach people through the existing channels—newspapers, magazines, TV. This enabled advocates for white nationalism, anti-Semitism, anti-immigration, and all kinds of other anti-social ideas to reach many more people than could ever have been reached through a mainstream media that would not allow such racist and anti-Semitic material.

It turns out that many people are quite open to these views. The result is that this willing audience has richly rewarded the advocates of antisocial views. Thanks to the fact that everyone can actively participate in the discussion by liking and sharing such views, the advocates for extreme views are reinforced at rates rivaling slot machines. Indeed, Marantz describes how the right-wing deplorables are active online at virtually every waking hour. (Hillary Clinton called them deplorables and they immediately embraced it.) Each tweet, Facebook post, podcast, Reddit post, YouTube video, and periscope feed can be immediately assessed in terms of the shares and likes it produces. Posts that don't work are dropped and those that get attention are refined—an evolutionary process, if there ever was one. For at least the past ten years, Americans have been shaping the behavior of right-wing trolls, and this has shaped and spread views and actions that would have been unimaginable before social media came into being.

In chapter 3, I describe Tom Dishion's research on the growing problem of socially rejected young men forming deviant peer groups. Traditionally, these small groups have supported each other in criminal acts and social aggression. However, thanks to the Internet, it is now possible for young, socially rejected males to join with thousands of similarly marginalized young men who bond around one or another ideology that justifies and amplifies their hatred of groups they blame for their plight. Tom pointed out that whether the ideology is jihadist, racist, anti-Muslim, or anti-immigrant is less relevant than the fact that marginalized young men are forming worldwide networks that result in hate crimes and terrorism.

However, I am not saying the leadership of the current right wing is uneducated. Many of the people Marantz describes are educated and well read. They have a number of things in common, however. They all seem to have a contrarian view and resist every facet of what they see as the "establishment," which includes both the Democratic and Republican parties. They believe most people are living inside the establishment narrative, not unlike the world depicted in the movie *The Matrix*.

They have taken the blue pill that makes them feel comfortable but blinds them to the truth. From their frame of reference, all mainstream media are part of the blue-pill narrative. And their views on this have been strengthened not only by the thousands of likes and shares they achieve but by the advertising revenue they receive.

The evolution of the Internet was touted as something that would bring us together and strengthen our democracy. It is currently doing just the opposite. We have to find ways to counter the use of the Internet to foster hate, division, and authoritarianism.

Disinformation

Our media are flooded with messages designed to influence people's beliefs and attitudes in ways that benefit the messenger but harm society.

Over the past twenty years, we have seen Fox News convince a couple of million people of things that simply aren't true.[6] Climate change is a hoax; more children drowned in bathtubs than were killed by guns; second-hand smoke does not kill people; if you make $250,000 a year, you only take home about $125,000. (You can read more examples on the PolitiFact website.)

We thought it could not get worse than Fox News, but it did, thanks to the Internet. In Great Britain, the campaign for Britain to leave the European Union (EU) used sophisticated microtargeting to get a majority of Brits to support leaving, a move that may result in the dissolution of Britain.

Journalist Carole Cadwalladr described a community in Wales, Ebbw Vale, that voted 62 percent in favor of leaving the EU. Yet the community, which had been devastated by the demise of the coal and steel industries, was recovering, thanks to considerable investment from the EU. She discovered that those who voted to leave felt the EU had done nothing for them, despite the big new sports center and several other buildings paid for by the EU. They said they were fed up with the immigrants and refugees. Yet the community had very few immigrants. The good citizens of Ebbw Vale had been influenced by a flood of Facebook ads, such as the lie that Turkey was joining the EU and would soon be sending immigrants to Britain.[7]

In the United States, it is now clear that Russian trolls reached and influenced millions of Americans during the 2016 election.[8] They released stolen emails from the Democratic National Committee that were designed to discredit the Democrats and alienate supporters of Bernie Sanders from supporting Hillary Clinton. They flooded the nation with tweets and Facebook posts designed to heighten Americans' animosity toward Muslims and sow divisions among racial and ethnic groups.

The most complete account I have been able to find of the way in which social media was weaponized to sow discord is Christopher Wylie's book *Mind F**k*.[9] Wylie was a tech savant who ended up working for Cambridge Analytica in his early twenties. It was this organization that refined the techniques of artificial intelligence and microtargeting to affect the outcome of both the Brexit campaign in Great Britain and the 2016 American Presidential election.

Micro-targeting is a process of reaching individuals with messages that are finely tailored to influence them, based on precise information about their motivations. Political parties have long tried to influence voters by tailoring their messages to subgroups. A message about a woman's right to choose might work well with women but have little impact on men. Black people are more likely to be swayed by a message about civil rights than are white people.

Microtargeting takes persuasion to a whole new level. If we know that a person is female, never married, has two children, and dislikes immigrants, we can send a message about how immigrants are harming single mothers that will arouse her anger and motivate her to vote for anti-immigrant candidates.

However, knowing precisely which messages will work with which people requires analysis of the personal characteristics most predictive of a person's behavior—especially voting behavior. This is where artificial intelligence comes in. If you can get lots of data on thousands of people, you can analyze which characteristics of specific people will be most important in motivating them to believe what you want them to believe. Once you have that understanding, you need the data on millions of people so you can reach them with the messages most likely to persuade them. Cambridge Analytica got such data—the complete Facebook accounts of 87 million people, mostly Americans.

Once Cambridge Analytica came under the control of right-wing millionaire Robert Mercer and Steve Bannon, the former head of right-wing website Breitbart News, it used these principles to figure out how to intensify the anger of a small slice of the electorate to influence their voting. The result was the Brexit vote to leave the EU and the election of Donald Trump.

Through artificial intelligence techniques and experimental testing of the impact of its messages, Cambridge Analytica developed a way to reach and enrage a segment of the population. It identified people who were high in neuroticism (a trait involving high levels of fear and anxiety) and three traits known to predict resentment and antisocial behavior: narcissism, ruthless self-interest, and emotional detachment (psychopathy). The messaging was designed to inflame resentment toward more educated and affluent people and to engage them in a group that would continue to support their resentments. Initially, Cambridge Analytica reached individuals with these characteristics and drew them into Facebook groups with similarly motivated people. The group members then maintained the group motivations by mutually reinforcing each other's resentments.

Wylie indicated that one of the things Cambridge Analytica's research revealed was that once you get a person to identify with a group (e.g., being a Trump supporter), criticism of the group further strengthens the person's support of the group. (Recall Hornsey's research, discussed in chapter 2.) This is a major reason Trump's base has been so stable despite all the criticism Trump has received from so many quarters.

In the case of Brexit, these principles were used to inflame the passions of people, such as those in Wales, who were relatively poor and resentful of the more urban and educated. Provoking their anger and resentment not only motivated them to vote for Brexit, it immunized them against messages about the impact of Brexit on the economy. As Wylie put it, "Some people would *support* the economy suffering if it meant that out-groups like metropolitan liberals or immigrants would suffer in the process...in effect, their vote would be used as a form of punishment."

In the case of Trump's election, both the Trump campaign and the Russians appear to have influenced the election in two key ways. The first was to inflame and galvanize the anger of lower-middle-class white Americans against the elites, whom they saw as the cause of their own difficulties. The second was to dissuade black people and young supporters of Bernie Sanders from voting for Hillary Clinton.

In the first case, all the research Bannon did at Cambridge Analytica on stoking the rage of disaffected white people was put to work on behalf of the Trump campaign. It is unclear whether the campaign had access to the data Cambridge Analytica had on millions of Americans. But it is certainly the case that the campaign knew how to target less-educated white people about their resentment of immigrants and urban liberal elites.

It is also unclear whether Russian interference in the election was coordinated with the Trump campaign or Cambridge Analytica. However, Kathleen Hall Jamieson's analysis of the Russians' role in the election shows they had ample information about how and where to target key segments of the electorate. Based on her analysis and the Mueller Report, the Russians instigated numerous public events designed to promote tensions between immigrant groups and anti-immigrant groups. They reached 126 million Americans through Facebook and sent 130,000 messages through Twitter. Russian Facebook pages aimed at African Americans got 1.2 million followers. Their messaging was designed to discourage black people from voting for Hillary Clinton: "NO LIVES MATTER TO HILLARY CLINTON. ONLY VOTES MATTER TO HILLARY CLINTON." A message on November 3 added, "NOT VOTING is a way to exercise our rights."[10]

Keep in mind that because of the electoral college, only a small slice of the electorate needs to be influenced in order to win most elections. In 2016, Trump won Wisconsin by 27,000 votes, Michigan by 13,000 votes, and Pennsylvania by 68,000 votes.

Traditionally, when disinformation was put into mass media, false claims were countered by others who saw the claims and knew they were untrue. However, because we no longer have mass media reaching most people with the same information, it is possible to reach a segment of the population with disinformation without others even knowing it has happened. Even three years after the 2016 election, few people are aware of how intensively disinformation was used to influence the election. For example, it wasn't until 2018 that the *Milwaukee Journal Sentinel* identified hundreds of tweets sent by Russian trolls that were designed to alienate black voters in Wisconsin from the Democratic Party.[11]

The problem is continuing. TV stations routinely refuse to run patently false political ads. However, Facebook and YouTube will run them.[12] As I write this, Facebook is running ads from the Trump campaign claiming Joe Biden and his son acted corruptly in Ukraine—a claim that has been thoroughly debunked. As long as foreign and domestic actors can stealthily influence the electorate through disinformation, it will be possible to win elections by inflaming sectors of the electorate and impossible to have public discussions that move us toward solutions for our most pressing problems.

Of course, elections have always been affected by the lies candidates tell. But given the extent and sophistication of the latest Internet techniques, lack of public understanding of what is going on, and lack of regulation of Internet practices, we need far more scrutiny of these practices, their impacts, and what can be done to prevent them from further undermining our democracy.

The Internet Behemoth Monopolies

The Internet has enabled the development of unprecedented monopolies that are using highly sophisticated techniques to influence our behavior. Their practices are in their interests—and often in ours. But while we enjoy the immediate gratification of our material needs (Amazon), connections with our friends and family (Facebook), and the ability to find out in thirty seconds how old Jane Fonda is (Google), we need to seriously examine whether abandoning our privacy to these companies is an unparalleled good.

Jonathan Taplin's *Move Fast and Break Things* and Roger McNamee's *Zucked* document the harmful practices that major technology companies—Facebook, Amazon, and Google, in particular—have evolved.[13] These companies are the third, fourth, and fifth largest in the world.[14] (Microsoft and Apple are first and second.)

Like me, you may have thought mostly about the benefits these companies provide. I don't know how I could have written this book without Google searches. And most of the books I cite I purchased through Amazon. If you are reading this book, you may have learned about it from a Facebook ad and purchased it on Amazon.

However, over the past fifteen or so years, these companies have established monopolies that are enabling them to set prices for advertising, books, music, and movies. Facebook and Google are number 1 and number 2 in revenue from advertising, having diminished the advertising revenues of newspapers by more than 60 percent and thereby reducing the size and influence of newspapers dramatically. Amazon controlled 65 percent of book sales as of 2015.[15]

These companies have powers far beyond what any prior monopoly has had. They have enormous amounts of information about millions—even billions—of people, and an unprecedented capacity to use that information to influence our behavior. According to Facebook, more than 2.4 billion people use Facebook each month. Amazon has about 310 million active customers. And Google, which owns two hundred companies, processes 63,000 searches per second and has more than 2 billion people using active devices on Android.[16] Can you name another organization connected with a billion people? The Catholic Church is estimated to have 1.2 billion adherents,[17] but it doesn't have data on every one of its parishioners. These three companies have more information about you than probably all other organizations you have any contact with, including your family.

Writing for *The Guardian*, Dylan Curran describes the data Facebook and Google have on you.[18] Google has a complete record of your searches. Don't believe me? Google "my activity". Google has all kinds of information that is useful for targeting you with ads for things you are likely to want: your location, gender, age, hobbies, career, interests, relationship status, possible weight, and income, as well as a complete record of your use of apps. According to Curran, "They know who you talk to on Facebook, what countries you are speaking with, what time you go to sleep." Want to see what they have about you? Go to google.com/settings/ads/. Google also has your YouTube history. (They own YouTube.) If you want to see all the data Google has on you, go to google.com/takeout. Curran adds that they have "every Google ad I've ever viewed or clicked on, every app I've ever launched or used and when I did it, every website I've ever visited and what time I did it at, and every app I've ever installed or searched for."

Are you ready for Facebook? It has a record of everything you have ever done on Facebook. According to Curran, "This includes every message you've ever sent or been sent, every file you've ever sent or been sent, all the contacts in your phone, and all the audio messages you've ever sent or been sent." You can get this at https://www.facebook.com/help/131112897028467.

Like the tobacco, gun, financial, pharmaceutical, fossil fuel, and food industries, the practices of these companies have been shaped by financial consequences. The Internet provided the opportunity to reach a scale unlike anything ever achieved. As the number of people using these platforms grew, it was obvious that further growth was the key to fabulous profits. The more users, the more Amazon could reach customers, and the more Facebook and Google could advertise. Google has bought or proliferated numerous products that have brought more people, along with their data, to it. These include YouTube, Gmail, Google maps, and Google Docs. Facebook has acquired WhatsApp and Instagram.

In their quest for scale, these companies, like many others, have adopted whatever legal practices would contribute to their profits. However, the laws were written before anything remotely like these companies existed. And given that few people in government even understood these businesses, there has been very little scrutiny of their practices and little effort to bring the laws into line with what is needed to prevent their harmful actions while retaining their benefits. And, indeed, as lawmakers have begun to examine some of the problematic behaviors of these companies, the companies have gotten heavily involved in lobbying government to protect their interests.

The policies and practices of Facebook are an excellent example of the problem we have. McNamee describes how the company's singular focus has been on getting as many users as possible and getting those users to spend as much time as possible on Facebook.[19] With all the users it got in its first few years, Facebook was able to experimentally evaluate its strategies to an extent that would make any behavioral scientist drool. The company discovered that Facebook posts that aroused negative emotions were particularly good at keeping people engaged. In this way, even before groups such as Cambridge Analytica perfected ways to create groups of angry, disaffected users, Facebook was sowing division. I have lost count of the number of people I know who have complained about the arguments they get into on Facebook.

When reports emerged that Facebook had allowed Cambridge Analytica to obtain the Facebook data on at least 50 million people, the company said Cambridge Analytica had violated its policy.[20] However, according to Christopher Wylie, Cambridge Analytica simply followed Facebook policy. The company policy was that researchers could advertise on Facebook to users to fill out surveys and get paid small amounts for doing so. When a user downloaded Cambridge Analytica's app to get paid, the app would take the survey responses, plus all the user's Facebook data, as well as all the Facebook data on all the user's friends.

Why the data on friends? Because the default setting on Facebook allows it. The friends have to find and change that setting, which virtually no one does.

That setting is greatly to the benefit of Facebook. Why? For the same reason it was valuable to Cambridge Analytica—it enables the company to get more precise predictions about users by knowing not only what they like and do but what their friends like and do. You many think of yourself as a customer of Facebook, but you are not. You and your data are products offered to advertisers, who are the real customers of Facebook.

Thanks to the data Cambridge Analytica obtained, it was able to pursue Steve Bannon's goal of learning how to identify and motivate large numbers of disaffected men to join the alt-right. And although there is dispute as to whether or not the Cambridge Analytica data was subsequently used in the Trump campaign, there is no doubt that the techniques Bannon and Cambridge Analytica developed created fertile ground for Trump's campaign, and that these same techniques were used, and continue to be used, to create the base that has remained so devoted to Trump.

One would think a Harvard-educated billionaire who donated $992 million to Planned Parenthood and $100 million to the Newark, New Jersey, school system would be appalled at the evidence that Facebook was complicit in both Brexit and the Trump victory. But to paraphrase Upton Sinclair, it is difficult to get Mark Zuckerberg to understand the role of Facebook in undermining democracy when his profits depend on his not understanding it. When reports about the Cambridge Analytica data came out, Zuckerberg initially said the idea that fake news on Facebook affected the election was "crazy."[21]

Roger McNamee, a mentor to Zuckerberg early in the development of the company, enumerates the many ways Facebook's singular focus on maximizing people's addiction to Facebook led it to do harm around the globe:

> Facebook's policy of allowing third-party app vendors to harvest
> friend lists, its tolerance of hate speech, its willingness to align with
> authoritarians, and its attempt to cover up its role in the Russian election
> interference are all symptoms of a business that prioritized growth
> metrics over all other factors.

McNamee describes how Facebook became virtually the only platform for public discussion in Myanmar, and thereby the vehicle promoting the Rohingya genocide.

Facebook has announced some policy changes. However, McNamee sees these as largely cosmetic and not likely to reduce the harm Facebook is facilitating. Facebook continues to engage in practices that allow the microtargeting of vulnerable people with false political ads designed to stoke their rage. It recently refused to take down political ads that contain lies. Facebook claims it is working to stop misinformation and false news. However, it makes an exception for political ads. This allows the Trump campaign to run an ad saying Joe Biden promised money to the Ukraine if it would fire its prosecutor. That ad is generating hundreds of millions of dollars in revenue for Facebook.[22] Trusting the company to regulate itself runs up against the fact that effective regulation will reduce its profits.

The Libertarian Ideology of Many of Our Internet Leaders

If you are appreciative of the unquestionable benefits the Internet giants have brought us, you may be disinclined to entertain any doubts about their leaders. But if you agree that we want to evolve societies committed to the well-being of every person, you should know there is a strong streak of libertarianism in the Silicon Valley community.[23] This is the same philosophy that has driven the advocacy of the Internet trolls Marantz describes. It argues that government should impose very few restrictions on what people or corporations can do and that society is best run by wealthy titans of industry who know better than government. In essence, it is a total repudiation of the idea that we are all in this together and have responsibility for the well-being of others. As a character in libertarian philosopher Ayn Rand's *Atlas Shrugged* put it, "I swear—by my life and my love of it—that I will never live for the sake of another man, nor ask another man to live for mine."[24]

Cross that with the enormous wealth and huge impact the leaders of Silicon Valley have had on the world, and you can imagine how easily they would fall into the belief that they—not political leaders—know what is best for the world. Peter Thiel, who created PayPal and was one of the earliest investors in Facebook, believes so strongly in his superiority to elected leaders that he has developed a project called *seasteading*.[25]

He wants to create floating cities that are outside the jurisdiction of any government so he can create a society on his own terms.

You can be sure these leaders will not view efforts to constrain their wealth and power warmly. And so, given that they have detailed data on virtually every American and the means to reach them with targeted advertising, they have the means to sway public opinion in their direction to an extent that the conservative billionaire coalition never dreamed of. And in addition, since they control the channels to everyone, they can, if they choose, prevent their opponents from ever reaching the electorate. Think there might be reasons to reign in their power? That is, if we still have the ability to do so.

Given the number of people who are connected to Facebook and Google, the amount of data these companies have on each of us, and the fact that they are the two biggest advertisers in the world, Facebook and Google are in an almost unprecedented position to influence people.

In Nazi Germany, Joseph Goebbels, the propaganda minister, saw to it that every household had a radio so the Nazis could use that new technology to influence the populace. Thanks to this and the fact that the state controlled all communications, the party achieved unprecedented control over the population. Now, I in no way suggest that the titans of the Internet have the goals and intents of the Nazis, but I do want to suggest that they are in a position to influence the population to a greater extent than the Nazis did. Why? Because they are able to reach just about everyone and they have far more sophisticated methods of persuasion, thanks to the data they have on each person and their ability to micro-target different people with messages tailored to those people's concerns and beliefs.

Regulating These Behemoths

Much could be done if we simply updated our laws on monopolies and applied them to these modern behemoths. Taplin describes how these companies got exempted from traditional concerns about monopolies (though these concerns have already dwindled in recent years, thanks to free market thinking). Collectively, Google, Facebook, and Amazon have 58.3 percent of expenditures on digital advertising.[26] Is it in the public interest to have three companies control that much advertising when it is contributing to the demise of journalism?

At the same time, we need to evolve new ways of addressing the threats that the Internet and the size and reach of these companies pose to the further evolution of society. Cadwalladr points out that it has been impossible to fully understand how Internet advertising affected the Brexit vote because Facebook has refused to share the ads that were run.[27] At a minimum, we should have access to what is currently stealth advertising. For example, when Elizabeth Warren proposes policies that threaten both the continued monopolies of these companies and the wealth of their owners, the public should have the right to know who is reaching whom with what ads.

In the 1980s, the United States abandoned two policies designed to ensure that people would hear diverse ideas. One was the equal time provision for political candidates. This required that if one candidate got air time on TV or radio, any opponents had to be allowed an equal amount of time. The other was the fairness doctrine, which required broadcasters to cover public policy in a way that gave groups for or against a policy the opportunity to put forth their views.

It could be required that people who are microtargeted with ads be sent ads about the other side of an issue or for a different candidate. Even if no provision required that they receive an equal number of messages from the "other side," simply requiring that the specifics of microtargeting be made public would enable opposing groups to know whom they might target—or how they might counter disinformation.

Furthermore, the government should fund research on the impact of Internet marketing. The NIH is the premier organization funding research on factors that affect human health. In what ways are people's involvement with the Internet affecting their health? Research is already being conducting on the effects of screen time, cyberbullying, and digital advertising on children's health and development.[28] But what about the way in which social media promotes antisocial behavior?[29] And given that much of the political advertising has been focused on arousing people's anger and resentment, what is its impact on problems such as depression, anxiety, and violence?

And then there is materialism. It is a safe bet that microtargeting by advertisers is effective in increasing people's motivation to buy things.[30] And it is likely that many fewer ads urge people to be more kind or prosocial. No profits are to be had from doing so. Earlier, I reviewed evidence that people become more materialistic when they feel threatened, and that such an orientation is associated with numerous psychological and behavioral problems. Yet Facebook has become adept at keeping people's eyes on Facebook through messages that raise their sense of threat and anger. It may seem un-American to suggest we would be better off if we reduced our buying. But if we are going to evolve a society that benefits us all, we may want to take a look at whether Internet advertising, as currently experienced by most people, is improving or diminishing the quality of our lives.

Regulating the Internet

The Internet has become the public square in which we enact our democracy. Our goals for that space should be the same as they have been throughout our history—to enable a free exchange of views, in the hopes that from our public discussion, good ideas and policies will gain ground and harmful policies and practices will be prevented. But in the Internet era, we have to face the fact that present practices are not enabling a free exchange of ideas. The primary answer to the problem is not, however, to suppress the massive amounts of loathsome speech that are currently occurring.

With respect to the corporations that currently control the Internet, the principles I enumerate in chapter 3 are just as applicable to Internet corporations. First, we need to do forensic epidemiology to assess the harms and benefits of the practices of each company. Second, we need to develop, implement, and evaluate regulations to see if we can reduce harm. This will require considerable research. Like nuclear weapons and climate change, the practices these Internet giants have evolved are something completely new in human history.

To see what we are up against, consider Yair Rosenberg, a Jewish journalist who was subjected to repeated harassment by supporters of Donald Trump. He took it lightly:

> They sent me threats, photoshopped me into gas chambers and hurled
> an uncreative array of anti-Semitic slurs my way. A study by the Anti-
> Defamation League found that I'd received the second-most abuse of any
> Jewish journalist on Twitter during the campaign cycle. My parents didn't
> raise me to be No. 2; fortunately, there's always 2020.[31]

Rosenberg decided to do something to combat hateful trolls on Twitter. He described how they have taken to assuming the identity of a well-known person and putting out messages that defame the person and pro-mote racist views. For example, someone posing as Herschel Silverstein tweeted that "Jews are so self-centered" and, after referring to a mother accused of strangling her infant, wrote "Black women: Please chill on the violence."[32]

Rosenberg enlisted the assistance of Neal Chandra, an Internet devel-oper, to identify these trolls on Twitter and out them. They created a crowd-sourced database of impersonator accounts and a program called Imposter Buster. Imposter Buster could detect whenever troll accounts inserted themselves into conversations and could intervene to alert any-one who might see the bogus post. It worked well.

Unfortunately, Twitter didn't see the beauty of it. Twitter said, "A large number of people have blocked you in response to high volumes of untargeted, unsolicited, or duplicative content or engagements from your account." Of course, the people doing the blocking were the neo-Nazi trolls.

Rosenberg points out that he was doing the work that Twitter should have been doing. As long as Twitter and other Internet companies fail to weed out imposters and counter trolling, the Internet will remain the wild, wild West.

Twitter's response to this situation meets the standards I articulate in chapter 3 for regulating capitalism. Twitter trolls are committing fraud. They are stealing people's identities. Twitter's policy of not allowing Rosenberg to out these trolls is doing direct harm to many people. If Twitter does not adopt policies to prevent such fraud, it is incumbent upon the government to create laws that prevent such criminal acts.

Some countries exercise considerably greater control than the United States. China blocks access to Google, Facebook, Twitter, and Instagram. Germany has an agreement with Facebook, Twitter, and Google "to remove hate speech from the Internet within 24 hours of it being reported."[33] The BBC reported that Google had complied with requests from a variety of nations to remove material the countries objected to. The materials ranged from videos the Thai government felt insulted the king to YouTube accounts American law enforcement authorities said were posting "threatening or harassing content." How-ever, in many other cases, Google refused to remove material that was simply critical of political figures.

The problems we face can be addressed in other ways. The Southern Poverty Law Center (SPLC) has shown that civil suits against hate groups that recover damages done to people these groups injure can diminish the resources and support for these groups. For example, SPLC won a $14 million judgment against Andrew Anglin and the Daily Stormer for the harm they did to Tanya Gersh.

In general, I think speech that results in measurable psychological harm should be deterred. It could be deterred by criminalizing it or by courts holding the speakers civilly liable for the harm they do. But I admit that this is a tricky issue. If you are reading this book, you have probably experienced stress over the last two years as a result of the outrageous things Donald Trump has done. Will we make it illegal to launch a critical attack against someone we disagree with? Where would we draw the line?

Perhaps the standard should be that we can prohibit or penalize speech that has the intent and likelihood of causing imminent violence. Could that standard be extended to psychological harm? It would have to be substantial and lasting harm, such as Tanya Gersh has suffered. Certainly, the law has standards for assessing emotional damage. However, I believe attempts to prohibit hateful speech will have limited value and do not address what is most needed.

A Better Way

Trying to suppress speech we don't like has at least three problems. First, the process of trying to suppress speech can simply make people shout all the louder. Second, attempts to suppress it can call attention to the speakers and gain them sympathy from others. Third, criticism of that speech is likely to further strengthen the speaker's support of their position. There is a good case to be made that one reason the alt-right developed is that many of its followers are attracted to the movement precisely because mainstream people are criticizing it. Indeed, Marantz tells us the Internet trolls he got to know loved it when people attacked their views. One woman, Cassandra Fairbanks, made her living by harassing establishment figures and livestreaming the process. Apparently, many people enjoy seeing people they view as "above them" taken down a peg. Every direct attack on racists makes them more attractive to people who feel that their own status in society is eroding.

I am not saying we should have no consequences for speech that causes harm, but we need to invest the greatest proportion of our time, money, and energy in building a movement of people who are working for the values that are antithetical to those of hate groups. There is a saying among civil libertarians that the answer to speech we don't like is not prohibition of that speech but more speech. If we are threatened or disagree with the positions that others are taking, the best antidote is to strengthen our ability to persuade people to accept the positions we value.

Numerous groups around the world promote the opposite of the network of hate. Many of these efforts grew out of the behavioral science research on the evolution of prosociality and its fundamental importance for evolving societies that work for everyone—on up to the level of the whole world. In my view, it is a race between these efforts and the forces for division and antisocial behavior. I believe the promotion of prosocial values and efforts is the most important antidote to the web-based spread of hate in the world. Here is a sampler of them.

Marco Polo. My son Mike's closest friend in high school was Michael Bortnik. He and his wife, Vlada, created Marco Polo, a website that enables friends and family members to send brief videos to each other. It has several million users. One thing they discovered was that people began to create groups around common interests. These "affinity groups" ranged from veterans to quilters to moms. Groups formed around a huge variety of interests: weight loss and fitness, marital infidelity Bible study, veteran support, eating disorders, truckers, military families, learning the guitar, and twelve-step programs such as AA and Al-Anon.

Laure, the research director at Marco Polo, gave me examples of the ways in which the site has helped nurture prosocial behavior:

- A veteran who, after connecting with his battle buddies on Marco Polo, and, as a result, no longer felt suicidal, began a nonprofit to help other vets

- A veteran whose Marco Polo groups of women veterans give members a way to provide support and hold one another accountable, such as by making sure they get out of bed

- A woman who said participating in a marriage counseling group on Marco Polo saved her marriage

- A woman who said using Marco Polo after being released from an inpatient mental health program helped her get her life back, with the support of family she could see and connect with

- A mother who reported that her autistic son was able to connect with friends on Marco Polo, where he didn't feel any pressure to read other people's faces while talking

Marco Polo is proof that you don't have to elicit negative emotions to bring people together. It may be true that Facebook's strategy of eliciting negative emotions gets people addicted to being on Facebook, even though it keeps them distressed. As McNamee has documented, the Facebook business model uses negative emotional content to keep people on Facebook but has no interest in the psychological harm this might do.

You may ask whether Marco Polo is sustainable. It certainly isn't the size of Facebook. And how does it generate revenue? When I asked Vlada about this, she gave me an answer that speaks to their values:

> Given what's happening in the world right now, people really crave a private place to connect with the most important people in their life. And we believe that the current ad-based business models don't allow for that place to exist. Moreover, we believe that private place is so valuable for people that they'd be willing to pay for it.
>
> So when we think of monetization, our priority is to make Marco Polo be a private, trusted place for you and your most important relationships. In other words, create something so meaningful and valuable that you'd be willing to pay for it :)

In essence, Marco Polo provides privacy, while Facebook sells everything about you to whomever will pay.

29K. In Sweden, Frederik Livheim and his colleagues at 29K are developing online materials that use acceptance and commitment principles to help small groups of strangers develop their skills in taking a more compassionate stance toward themselves and others. Key to this process is getting good at noticing and accepting difficult thoughts and feelings, without trying to do anything about them. Instead, people get good at focusing on their values and acting in the service of them.

29K is developing individual and group experiences to help people support their growth as a person and as a member of their community. For example, people connected via the Internet might be asked to share self-critical thoughts they have as a way of stepping back from such thoughts and also as a way of understanding that we all have such thoughts. They are then asked to discuss what a friend or family member who loves them deeply might say to them about their self-critical thoughts. The aim is to create self-compassion and compassion from others through this process.

29K has the resources to create, evaluate, and refine these tools. It has the potential to create connected groups throughout the world who, rather than bonding around hate of others, bond around building the kind of nurturing world we so badly need.

Prosocial. One of the efforts to promote prosociality comes out of the collaboration I helped promote between evolutionist David Sloan Wilson and the creator of acceptance and commitment therapy, Steven Hayes. Together with Paul Atkins, they developed an approach to helping groups work together cooperatively in the interest of achieving group goals.[34] Their approach is based on Elinor Ostrom's worldwide study of groups dealing with common pool resource problems (e.g., fisheries, resource extraction). She identified eight core design principles that characterize how effective groups work. She and Wilson subsequently showed how these principles are relevant to the effective functioning of any group.[35] Here are the principles:

1. Prosocial groups have assured identity and purpose. Atkins et al. describe a process by which group members can come to an agreement about their identity and purpose.[36]

2. Well-functioning groups need to have an equitable distribution of contributions to the group and benefits to those who contribute.

3. Decision making needs to include each member and be experienced as fair by group members.

4. The contributions of members need to be monitored to ensure that people are doing what they agreed to do.

5. Helpful behavior of group members needs to be rewarded, and unhelpful behavior needs to be addressed through graduated sanctions.

6. Conflicts need to be resolved quickly and fairly.

7. Groups need to have the authority to self-govern.

8. Groups need to have effective collaborative relations with other groups.

The prosocial movement is training people to work with groups around the world. Their goal is to help groups work more effectively and ultimately to facilitate cooperation of groups around prosociality, up to the level of the entire world. They think big.

Their online magazine describes numerous successes resulting from training of groups in the use of the prosocial principles.[37] They used the principles of prosociality to help villages in Sierra Leone reduce violence against women. They facilitated improvements in the way teams in the National Health Service in Scotland work together. They worked with Contemplative Life, a nonprofit focused on connecting people and communities with transformative spiritual practices. The prosocial principles have been used to improve the functioning of agencies of the Australian government. And they helped an organization of Kenyan citizen journalists use the prosocial principles to strengthen the trust and cooperation of their groups to work more effectively with citizen journalists and use the Ostrom principles in reporting on corruption.

They provide online and in-person training, as well as a recently published book, *Prosocial: Using Evolutionary Science to Build Productive, Equitable, and Collaborative Groups*.[38]

The kindness movement. In chapter 6, I mention Doug Carnine's book *How Love Wins: The Power of Mindful Kindness*. He is now turning it into a movement. With friends Steve Christiansen and Bruce Abel, he started a movement here in Eugene, Oregon, called Choose Kindness. They are organizing schools, churches, and business and civic organizations to become more aware of the ways in which people can be kind to each other. In part, they were inspired by a similar effort in Anaheim, California, which achieved a million acts of kindness in its schools.[39]

Evolving News Media That Support the Reform of Capitalism

If we are going to promote needed reforms of capitalism, we must rebuild journalism. The profession has been decimated by the Internet revolution of the past twenty years. Google and Facebook advertising has replaced much of the print advertising in newspapers. As a result, newspaper revenue has declined, thousands of journalists have been laid off, and local news coverage has declined.[40] And, as I document earlier, people are being flooded with disinformation. We must rebuild journalism so it reaches people and gives them accurate information about the problems with our current society and the things that can be done to enhance well-being. We need a compelling vision, a large, diverse, and effective coalition of organizations, the creation of a network of media channels, and increasing skill at reaching, persuading, and activating people who share our values.

I make the case for an overall coalition in chapter 2. One facet of this coalition needs to be a network of media organizations working in concert to advance the values, goals, and outcomes I have been articulating.

How do we define prosocial media organizations? Here are five features they should have:

- Their stated intention is to contribute to the well-being of people.

- They are fact based.

- They use behavioral science research to determine how to most effectively reach and influence people and educate their audiences about what humans need to thrive and how we can promote nurturance.

- They tell compelling stories about the growing number of successful efforts to reform business, higher education, health care, criminal justice, and other sectors of society so that they nurture everyone's well-being.

- They are B Corps or subscribe to the conscious capitalism framework. They may be nonprofits, publicly funded, or member supported.

Just as for reforms in other sectors of society, media organizations need to themselves be models of the kind of society we want. They must be organizations in which sexual harassment and other coercive behavior would be unlikely to occur. They need to be organizations in which the members or employees play a significant role in determining the policies and practices. (This has been true of Oregon Research Institute, where I work, for forty years.) They should have ethical journalistic standards that are explicit and monitored by a certifying organization.

Goals. As in any other facet of a pragmatic approach to cultural evolution, these media organizations need to be designed (or redesigned) to advance the value of ensuring everyone's well-being and the goals, policies, programs, and practices needed to create a more just economic and political system.

They need to have a strong grounding in behavioral science—far more than is currently found in most news organizations. They need to report on the well-being of people, the things affecting well-being, and the programs, policies, and practices that can enhance well-being. They need to use behavioral science principles to reach and persuade people. There is no reason microtargeting methods can't be used to reach people with news that promotes prosociality and support for prosocial policies.

One reaction you may have to this is that the marketplace tells us what works to get followers, and the evidence is that, based on rating share, people want sensation, conflict, and humor. People would be bored by news about improving people's health and well-being.

However, consider the possibility that many people's interest in conflict and sensation has been cultivated. The conservative billionaire coalition convinced a large audience to be receptive to their free market ideology. How much did that effort shape the tastes of Americans? The conservative billionaire coalition told people that government was bad. That reduced respect for politicians and built a receptive audience of people aggrieved by threats to their status in society, their economic well-being, or their religious beliefs. The current state of receptivity to news outlets that promote suspicion and division is, at least in part, due to the cultivation of people's grievances. (And, as I elaborate on in chapter 11, to the failure of progressive groups to speak to the needs of this segment of the population.)

Ongoing evaluation. Whatever the current state of audience receptivity may be, we are not helpless. We have scientific tools for steadily increasing the reach and effectiveness of our media efforts. Thus, one of the other functions of this network of organizations would be to do empirical work on how to reach and persuade a very broad audience. Yes, it is the case that evangelicals watch "these channels" and progressives (or Hispanics or women or football fans or any other group you can name) tend to watch "other channels." But if you are not building a network of media organizations that is reaching and persuading people in all these groups, you are never going to achieve the society we are trying to create.

Of course, there can be media segmentation. That is, some organizations may be good at reaching Hispanics, others at reaching working-class white people—each with reporting as interesting and compelling as possible—on how neighborhoods, communities, churches, civic organizations, government agencies, health-care providers, and businesses are making contributions to the well-being of everyone.

At the same time, we should have lots of stories about people of diverse backgrounds working together, playing together, and building a loving society. See Jonathon Taplin's book *Move Fast and Break Things*. He makes a compelling case for the value of movies, music, and art for influencing our culture.

Progress is already underway on how to make our media more effective. The Media Consortium is cooperating on research conducted by Gary King and his colleagues at Harvard University.[41] In a series of studies, they tested whether reporting by multiple outlets on the same day could influence the rate of tweets favorable to the viewpoint presented in the reporting. They found that if multiple outlets co-published and co-promoted a story, it had a significant impact—greater than would be expected from the reach of individual outlets. They observed a 63 percent increase in public discussion of topics on which multiple outlets published stories and an additional 13,166 posts during the week of publication, compared with other weeks.

Incidentally, in the process of getting all these organizations to cooperate in testing the impact of coordinated publishing, the Media Consortium discovered that the process increased the quality of reporting and contributed to the professional development of reporters and editors.[42]

Meanwhile in the tech sector, Roger McNamee has worked with Tristan Harris, a former Google employee who created the Center for Humane Technology. The mission of this organization is to move from technology controlling people for the benefit of technology companies to technologies designed to advance human well-being. This is very much what I am trying to do in all facets of society.

Reforming Social Media

My research for this chapter helped me understand how much our problems have been amplified by the way in which Internet technology has evolved. As Taplin and McNamee documented, it didn't have to happen this way, and there are things we can do to rectify the current domination of the Internet by groups peddling disinformation and hate speech. Belatedly, we are beginning to learn how social media is spreading disinformation and stoking anger and resentment. We need much more attention to how this is happening—research documenting harmful social-media practices, transparency regarding advertising and social-media policies and practices, and research on effective ways to reach people with accurate information that increases support for the reforms needed. The large and growing network of organizations promoting some form of prosocial norms and behavior needs to be expanded. Creating a coalition of these organizations will strengthen such efforts.

Action Implications

Personal

Use social media to promote our values.

The first thing that comes to mind as I try to write something that will get you to participate in and support prosocial media is Dr. Seuss. In *Horton Hears a Who,* Horton the elephant saves the tiny speck of dust that holds Whoville by getting the tiny people in Whoville to make as much noise as they can so the other animals won't crush Whoville. But the other animals can't hear it—not until, that is, the Mayor of Whoville discovers JoJo. Instead of yelling, he is playing with his Yoyo. When JoJo joins the other Who in yelling, Whoville is saved.

The message is that "a person's a person no matter how small." You may very well feel too small to make any difference in evolving a more nurturing society. But in this age of the Internet, you have more power than you realize. You can share stories and reports that promote prosocial behavior and values. With Marco Polo, a Twitter account, and a Facebook page, you can routinely and very easily nurture others and share good news about the movement promoting nurturance.

Imagine that just a thousand people began to forward one thing a week to their connections. About 69 million Americans have Twitter accounts.[43] According to the KickFactory blog, the average Twitter user has 707 followers. If 1,000 people tweeted to their followers, we would reach more than 700,000 people. And if just 10 percent of those 700,000 retweeted, we would be reaching another 49 million with retweets. These numbers don't reflect the fact that many of these people could be reached more than once. But that is not bad—it indicates social influence.

And that's just Twitter. About 151 million American adults use Facebook, and they average about 338 friends each.[44] Using the same assumptions as for Twitter, the first round of sharing an article or video reaches 338,000, and if 10 percent of those people subsequently share, it reaches another 11,424,400. If 5 percent of those share, it reaches another 193,072,360. It adds up.

Support news media companies that are promoting your values and policies you favor.

Patronize or subscribe to media outlets whose reporting is educating people about the kind of society we need and how we can get it. Your support could include subscriptions, donations, and suggestions to friends that they consume these media and promote them.

Help identify organizations working to promote prosocial, communitarian values.

I describe a number of efforts above. You can go to valuestoaction.com/progressive and help crowd-source a list of all the organizations we might invite into a coalition to promote the reform of capitalism.

Policies

Update laws on monopolies and enforce them.

Advocate for updating our laws on monopolies and applying them to the major Internet and social media companies.

Fund research on the influence of the Internet on well-being.

The NIH should organize research that obtains data on the effects of particular media practices on well-being. For example, are there communities on the Internet that promote prosocial behavior? What are the public health effects of hateful Internet communications? Are there methods that can discourage hate speech and the formation of hate groups?

Push for policies that:

- Regulate privacy protections, including restricting the collection and selling of data about individuals

- Regulate speech that has the intent and likelihood of causing imminent violence

Organizations

Nonprofit media organizations

Support nonprofit media organizations that report on positive efforts to promote prosociality.

Behavioral science organizations

Behavioral science organizations can devote more of their resources to widely publicizing the facts about how we can promote human well-being. They can also do more research on how to reach and persuade people to move in a prosocial direction.

Media literacy organizations

Check out the websites of these organizations working to promote youth understanding and the use of new media:

- The News Literacy Project
- Common Sense Media

Progressive businesses

Businesses that subscribe to progressive values can examine their own advertising policies and ensure that the programming they sponsor is consistent with their values.

Public health and health-care organizations

Such organizations, which account for 17 percent of the U.S. GDP, can encourage media organizations to report on what people can do to promote their health—including the much-overlooked fact that the quality of our social relations plays a huge role in our health.

Higher education

Colleges and universities can examine how well their schools of journalism and computer science are contributing to strengthening the influence of media on the evolution of a more nurturing society.

Organizations bridging the divide between religious and secular communities

Progressive religious and secular advocacy organizations can do more to publicize their agreement about a set of progressive values.

If you work in the criminal justice system...

Those who are promoting more nurturing ways to address crime can do more to get stories about their successes into the media.

A grand coalition

If we can create a grand coalition of progressive forces in all these sectors of society, think of how much more effective we will be in getting media attention for what we advocate.[45] Hopefully, you are connected with at least one organization working to reform our economic and political system. If you are, see if you can encourage it to form a coalition with other organizations. The very fact that such a diverse coalition is visible and working together can have a huge impact on public understanding. We can do this, people!

CHAPTER 10:

Climate Change

The point of no return is no longer over the horizon.

— U.N. Secretary-General António Guterres

T HE ULTIMATE NEGATIVE consequence of uncontrolled capitalism is the looming climate catastrophe. As news about the seriousness of climate change grows, we see where the evolution of this form of capitalism is taking us. We are getting more and more material gratification in the near term but seem unable to prevent our planet from becoming nearly uninhabitable.

Can our evolutionary principles help us with this problem? I believe they can. In this chapter, I begin by describing how our current capitalist system is profiting from climate change, sometimes in ways that will accelerate change. Then, I briefly review the bad news: climate change is worse than you thought.

But all the corporate, government, and nonprofit practices affecting our climate—for better or worse—are a function of the consequences to organizations and the individuals who run them. Our only hope is to eliminate the profits for practices that are contributing to global warming and make practices that reduce emissions more profitable.

Profiting While the World Burns

There is an old joke about a boy who was caught masturbating. His father told him, "You will go blind if you keep doing that." To which the boy replied, "Can I just do it until I need glasses?" The joke came to mind when I read *Windfall: The Booming Business of Global Warming*, by Mckenzie Funk, a journalist who grew up in Eugene.[1] He takes you around the world to places where companies are getting rich thanks to climate change. Israelis invented an ice machine that is now providing snow for increasingly bare Swiss ski slopes. There is a burgeoning business of private companies fighting wildfires on the U.S. West Coast. The U.S. Forest Service pays the bills. Other companies are offering to coat homes with a fire-retardant gel. Dutch engineers are selling their expertise in surviving below sea level to the many cities around the world that face steadily increasing flooding.

The most disturbing story is one about the oil companies bidding for the right to drill for ever more oil in a 45,900-square-mile area of the Chukchi Sea, north and west of Alaska. The possibility of drilling there became a reality thanks to the melting of sea ice. Despite the fact that not a single drop of that oil should ever be burned if we are going to prevent a climate catastrophe, companies are investing heavily in getting the oil. This reminds me of the observation that V. I. Lenin supposedly made that when there are only two capitalists left in the world, one will sell you the rope to hang the other.

How Bad Is It? Very Bad

If you've gotten this far in the book, you probably believe that climate change is real and human caused. I won't belabor the problem we face, other than to say that virtually all the predictions about the impact of greenhouse gas emissions on the planet are proving to be underestimates. Here are just two examples:

The Permafrost Meltdown

If the whole world stopped all fossil fuel use tomorrow, we could still be in for catastrophic changes. You see, a vast store of methane has been locked in the permafrost of the Northern Hemisphere for thousands of years. Permafrost is frozen soil, and it covers most of the northern parts of Alaska, Canada, Northern Europe, and Russia. It is believed to contain 1,500 billion tons of carbon, locked in the organic matter of plants and animals, which has been frozen for as long as a thousand years.[2] When it melts, it will release methane and carbon dioxide (CO_2). Although methane dissipates more rapidly than carbon dioxide, during the first five years it is emitted, it is estimated to produce nineteen times as much warming as carbon dioxide does.[3]

The result could be that the initial thawing caused by the carbon dioxide already in the air will release so much more methane and carbon dioxide that even a total halt in human emissions of greenhouse gases would be unable to prevent acceleration of warming, due to greenhouse gas levels far beyond anything seen in the last hundred thousand years. (Just today, I read that the Arctic Ocean hit a new high of 84 degrees Fahrenheit and carbon dioxide hit its highest level in human history, 415.26 ppm.[4])

Here is how a recent report published by the National Academy of Sciences puts it:

> We explore the risk that self-reinforcing feedbacks could push the Earth
> System toward a planetary threshold that, if crossed, could prevent
> stabilization of the climate at intermediate temperature rises and cause
> continued warming on a "Hothouse Earth" pathway even as human
> emissions are reduced. Crossing the threshold would lead to a much
> higher global average temperature than any interglacial in the past 1.2
> million years and to sea levels significantly higher than at any time in the
> Holocene... If the threshold is crossed, the resulting trajectory would
> likely cause serious disruptions to ecosystems, society, and economies.
> Collective human action is required to steer the Earth System away from
> a potential threshold and stabilize it in a habitable interglacial-like state.
> Such action entails stewardship of the entire Earth System—biosphere,
> climate, and societies—and could include decarbonization of the
> global economy, enhancement of biosphere carbon sinks, behavioral
> changes, technological innovations, new governance arrangements, and
> transformed social values.[5]

Unfortunately, there has been an appalling lack of research on how to accelerate behavioral change, values transformation, and the adoption of more-effective public policy.

The Latest Estimates on Sea-Level Rise

In a paper published in *Nature Communications*, Scott Kulp and Benjamin Strauss conclude that the increase in sea level is likely to be three times what was predicted by earlier analyses.[6] If further greenhouse gas emissions are limited, predictions are that 190 million people will be living below the high-tide level. With the highest level of greenhouse gas emissions, as many as 630 million people will be living below the annual flood level.

What we are experiencing is evolution on an incredibly faster time scale than any evolution that has taken place, at least since the dinosaurs were extinguished by a meteor that hit what is now Mexico 66 million years ago.[7]

Acting in Light of the Future

Our problem is that, although humans are far better at dealing with distant threats to our well-being than any other species, compared with the dangers we face as a species, we are lousy at it. Yes, we can consider the future, but we tend to focus on the short-term consequences of our behavior and ignore the longer-term consequences. And we tend to avoid things that are aversive, so we naturally ignore reports about the dangers of climate change, especially when we don't know what we can do about them. Moreover, our tendencies have been greatly reinforced by the efforts of the fossil fuel industry to plant doubts about the existence of climate change, the fact that humans are causing it, and our ability to take effective action.

Humans can plan ahead—including planning to avoid disaster. Consider engineering standards. The American Society of Mechanical Engineers indicates that there are approximately 600 codes that guide engineers in their work.[8] These codes provide the rules regarding the materials, procedures, products, and services that engineers need to comply with to build things.

If you are not an engineer, you take for granted that the bridge, elevator, airplane, train, or automobile you use will be safe. The standards have been shaped by experiences of engineers over the course of many years to ensure that failure of things they design and make will be exceedingly rare. In this sense, the standards are a form of planning ahead.

In the 1620s, when Sweden was still a warlike nation, King Gustavus Adolphus ordered the building of a warship to be used in Sweden's war with Poland and Lithuania. On August 11, 1628, the Vasa sailed into Stockholm Harbor on its maiden voyage. As soon as a moderate wind hit its sails, it listed, water flooded in through the lower gun ports, and it promptly sank. The sinking was due to the ship being too narrow, with too much weight on the upper decks. Ship building was not an exact science in those days. Subsequent ship builders have been careful to not make ships so top-heavy.

Many of the standards that engineers have adopted were created because of disasters such as the Vasa sinking. After an iceberg sank the Titanic, they created doubled hulls that would be more likely to survive such a collision.[9] Disasters persistently spur engineers to modify their standards. Earthquakes have driven repeated improvements in the design of buildings and lifeline systems, such as electric grids, so that they will withstand earthquakes.[10] Hurricanes have prompted improvements in building design that allow buildings to withstand higher winds. Similarly, floods, which account for 80 percent of declared disasters, prompted the construction of numerous dams, beginning in the 1930s. However, recently it has become clear that flooding can also be reduced and mitigated by *not* allowing natural barriers, such as coastal wetlands, to be destroyed.

So while humans are able to learn from their mistakes and plan a future that avoids catastrophes of the past, our future planning is mostly shaped by past catastrophes. The Covid-19 pandemic illustrates how bad we are at preparing for things that happen rarely. This is what makes ongoing climate change such a threat to human well-being. There is simply no precedent for humans dealing with the worldwide disaster we are now facing.

However, recent research on humans' relational abilities points to ways in which we can motivate people and organizations to act in light of the looming climate catastrophe.[11] Humans act in light of the future by relating their present situation to a verbally constructed description of the future. All the standards that engineers have developed are the result of their relating a recent disaster to the possibility of a future disaster, their ability to plan what could be done to prevent the disaster, and our ability to take the actions specified in the plan.

With respect to climate change, we need to bring the future into the present in ways that motivate actions that prevent further greenhouse gas emissions. For example, compelling movies that accurately depict the future we face from global warming could motivate millions of people to feel differently about engaging in behaviors that contribute to greenhouse gas emissions. We have not effectively motivated people on the scale needed.

The increasing evidence of the extent and seriousness of climate change is beginning to get people to see that a catastrophic future awaits us. That is motivating greater support for doing something about climate change. Our young people are rising! They have every reason to be angry with us. See Greta Thunberg's TED Talk on climate change.[12]

We can also promote a positive vision of the future that is possible if we begin to address climate change. The Green New Deal promotes a future with well-paying jobs for people working on reducing emissions. It is a good example of how we can create positive consequences for actions that reduce emissions.

We do not need to have everyone understand climate change to get enough people to take action. All the reforms I advocate in previous chapters can contribute to the changes needed. If we can foster a movement throughout society that advances the values of compassion, caring, and respect for others, it will naturally lead to a society focused on future well-being. Policies and practices in every sector of society will be adopted, modified, or discontinued in light of their impact on the entire population. Policies and practices that can be shown to produce future harm, such as ill health and premature death, will be abandoned, and those that demonstrably improve health, well-being, and longevity will be embraced. In such a culture, thinking about future well-being will become routine.

These reforms will also include greater regulation of corporations. They will include restrictions on emissions, of course, but also restrictions on the ability of companies to spread disinformation, as the fossil fuel industry has done.

Such a society will be less materialistic. As Tim Kasser has shown, people who embrace values of concern for others and their community are less materialistic than people without those values. They will consume less, and, as consumers, be mindful of the impact of their consumption on the environment.

It is in this context that people will more readily examine the impact of what we do for future generations. If schools, the health-care system, the human service system, churches, criminal justice, media, and business are all increasingly attending to the impact on families of what they do, we will have a generation of parents who are actively attending to their children's future well-being. In such a context, simply accurately laying out the threat of climate change will motivate the parenting generation to demand effective climate policy. In essence, I am arguing that efforts to make our society more nurturing will readily promote greater support for addressing climate change.

At the same time, direct efforts to get people to adopt climate-friendly policies and practices will create a context that furthers prosocial values in all sectors of society. A company that adopts climate-friendly policies will necessarily be acting in the interest of others. That will reinforce prosocial values generally.

Yet, much more is needed. Most people have very little understanding of the most important things they can do to reduce greenhouse gas emissions. And we have far too little understanding of the most effective strategies for influencing the adoption of effective policies or changes in the behavior of people and organizations.

The Dismal State of Behavioral Science Research on Climate Change

Given the catastrophe that looms ahead, you would think the nations of the world would be mobilizing to a greater extent than they did in any war. But they are not. The most obvious focus would be on doing everything we can to reduce—indeed, halt—greenhouse gas emissions. But it's not.

For the past year, I have been leading a task force on behavioral science research on climate change. It was created by the coalition of six behavioral science organizations that I describe in chapter 4. We have been studying what behavioral science research is being done to reduce greenhouse gas emissions. We have done extensive searches of the literature (more than ten thousand papers), looking for studies of efforts to get policies adopted that would reduce emissions or influence people, organizations, and communities to reduce their greenhouse gas emissions.

We found an appalling lack of research on how to affect emissions. An enormous amount of research has mapped the extent of emissions, the changes in global temperature, the melting of ice, the rise in sea levels, the extinction of species, and the health of the human population. We are precisely tracking the budding disaster. Yet research on how we can reduce the greenhouse gas emissions causing all these problems remains miniscule.

Of course, the research that gets done is selected by funding sources (yet again, selection by consequences). So we looked into U.S. funding of research on climate change. A Government Accountability Office report shows that the U.S. government has projects on technology relevant to climate change (e.g., better batteries, clean energy) and physical science research on climate change, but *nothing* on human behavior.[13]

We looked at research funded by the NIH. They are doing an increasing amount of research on the health effects of climate change, but nary a study on how to get people to reduce their carbon footprint or get governments to implement effective policies.

The situation is absurd. Here is the biggest threat to human well-being you will see in your lifetime—and the lifetimes of your children, grandchildren, and beyond—yet we are doing next to nothing to figure out how to affect the human behavior that is creating this growing catastrophe. This is despite the fact that the behavioral sciences have proven their ability to address most of the common and costly problems of human behavior. See *The Nurture Effect* for a summary of the power of this science.

What Do We Do?

Our task force has developed a set of recommendations we hope will accelerate research on this critical problem. We are attempting to engage a wide variety of organizations to promote the research needed.

Advocate for Massive Interdisciplinary Programs of Three Sorts

Following the principle of variation and selection, we need to fund multiple programs to create and test multiple strategies for reducing greenhouse gas emissions.

Policy adoption and implementation. Numerous policies have the potential to significantly reduce greenhouse gas emissions. Many have been shown to work, including carbon taxes and cap-and-trade systems.

Economists seem to have reached a consensus that putting a tax on carbon is the most efficient and effective way to lower greenhouse gas emissions. In August 2019, a group of 3,554 economists, including twenty-seven Nobel Prize winners, issued a statement advocating for the implementation of a gradually increasing tax on carbon.[14] Here is their entire statement:

Global climate change is a serious problem calling for immediate national action. Guided by sound economic principles, we are united in the following policy recommendations:

1. A carbon tax offers the most cost-effective lever to reduce carbon emissions at the scale and speed that is necessary. By correcting a well-known market failure, a carbon tax will send a powerful price signal that harnesses the invisible hand of the marketplace to steer economic actors towards a low-carbon future.

2. A carbon tax should increase every year until emissions reductions goals are met and be revenue neutral to avoid debates over the size of government. A consistently rising carbon price will encourage technological innovation and large-scale infrastructure development. It will also accelerate the diffusion of carbon-efficient goods and services.

3. A sufficiently robust and gradually rising carbon tax will replace the need for various carbon regulations that are less efficient. Substituting a price signal for cumbersome regulations will promote economic growth and provide the regulatory certainty companies need for long-term investment in clean-energy alternatives.

4. To prevent carbon leakage and to protect U.S. competitiveness, a border carbon adjustment system should be established. This system would enhance the competitiveness of American firms that are more energy-efficient than their global competitors. It would also create an incentive for other nations to adopt similar carbon pricing.

5. To maximize the fairness and political viability of a rising carbon tax, all the revenue should be returned directly to U.S. citizens through equal lump-sum rebates. The majority of American families, including the most vulnerable, will benefit financially by receiving more in "carbon dividends" than they pay in increased energy prices.

Of course, thanks to relentless advocacy by free market ideologists, the word *tax* is anathema to millions of Americans. As described, however, this is an unusual tax because the money would not go to the government but to citizens. It might better be called a *fee and dividend* system.

In a cap-and-trade system, a government puts a cap on the amount of carbon dioxide (and possibly other greenhouse gases) emitted. A cap could be set for an industry or all industries in a community or state. Each organization is allotted a certain amount of the total and must pay for the right to exceed its cap. Companies that can lower their emissions below the cap are able to sell the right to emit their remaining allotment to other companies. This creates a market for permits that motivates companies to reduce their emissions and enables those most able to reduce their emissions to start the process. Over time, the cap is gradually decreased. The knowledge that caps will be decreased motivates companies to plan ahead to reduce their emissions. Notice the contingency. Companies can protect or increase their profits by reducing greenhouse gas emissions. Selection by consequences.

In our literature search, we could not find any studies that developed and evaluated strategies for getting these valuable policies adopted. To me, this is a huge missing link in efforts to reduce emissions. If we know a policy works, we should be determining as quickly as possible how to get communities, states, and nations to adopt it. And by the way, research on how to get policies adopted would also allow us to measure how well a policy works when adopted.

The research programs we have in mind would invite research groups to propose experimental evaluations of strategies for getting policies adopted. I am confident the incentive of funding for research would lead to innovative studies. This, too, is a matter of selection by consequences. We are creating a market for ideas about how to get governments to adopt policies. If only 10 percent of them succeed, we will emerge in fairly short order with moreeffective ways to get policies adopted.

Influencing the carbon footprints of households and organizations. The second program of research we need to promote involves experimental research on how to get individuals and households to reduce their emissions.[15] Here, too, if we offer significant grants for such research, behavioral scientists will step up with a variety of ideas, and if we fund the most promising, we will rapidly accumulate more-effective ways to influence individuals and households to reduce their emissions.

For example, smart electricity usage meters that have the potential to give feedback to households are increasingly being installed. However, I am not aware of experimental evaluations of their effectiveness in reducing energy use—or of research that would strengthen their impact. If you outfit a large number of homes with smart electricity meters, you lay the groundwork for all kinds of experiments for reducing electricity consumption. You can randomize households to different conditions that you think will motivate reductions, such as:

- Monthly or weekly feedback to the household about its use

- Rebates for reductions

- Competition among neighborhoods, with public recognition as the reward

- Email with suggestions on how to reduce energy use

In a first round, you might find that one of these strategies is most effective. That would open the way to refine that strategy and come up with additional strategies. Across even three rounds of studies, you would have an increasingly effective strategy. Think of what a hundred studies could produce.

Community intervention. Communitywide intervention seems particularly promising to me. By intervening in an entire community, you can implement a wide variety of policies and programs, each of which could contribute to the success of other programs. For example, a school program in which children learn about climate change could, through homework assignments involving parents, increase parents' awareness of climate change and encourage them to support policy initiatives in the community as well as efforts in work organizations to reduce companies' greenhouse gas emissions.[16]

Certainly, many community efforts are underway. However, solid experimental research testing the impact of these interventions is hard to come by. Our review of the literature found a number of reports about efforts communities have undertaken to reduce greenhouse gas emissions. For example, the European Network for Community-Led Initiatives on Climate Change and Sustainability (ECOLISE) published a monograph describing efforts in communities throughout Europe. However, it does not provide information about the extent to which these efforts are reducing greenhouse gas emissions.

There are many examples of governments and communities doing things to address climate change.[17] However, few of these efforts are making use of experimental methods that could help pinpoint what works and what doesn't. Our task force is calling for many more interrupted-time-series experimental evaluations.

OK, so I lapsed into jargon... Here's what I mean. Let's say you have three communities of roughly equal size, economic well-being, and population diversity. And suppose you have measures of their greenhouse gas emissions for a number of years. You could then work in one community to bring about changes in emissions, perhaps by organizing neighborhoods to reduce household emissions. In my experience with this kind of research, we have often found significant challenges to getting a community organized to take action.[18] But after you learn how to work with the first community, you can bring your refined strategy to a second and third community. If you have an effect on an outcome such as emissions, you can try to replicate the effect in subsequent communities. Your confidence that it was the strategy that made the difference in emission reductions is increased to the extent that you see changes in the first community but not in the others—until, that is, they subsequently use the same strategy.

Figure 10.1 illustrates an example of how we evaluated willingness of stores to sell tobacco in four Oregon communities, using a multiple baseline design. It shows the percentage of stores willing to sell before and after we introduced a program to reward clerks for refusing to sell cigarettes to minors.

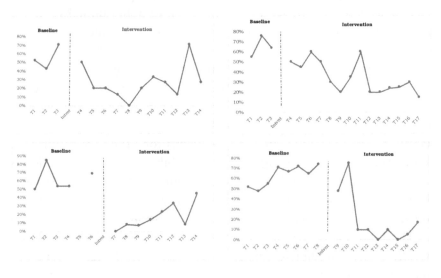

FIGURE 10.1

Studies using this type of experimental design are preferable to randomized trials at this stage of our knowledge. There is no sense in committing to testing an intervention in numerous communities until you have shown that it is working in the first few communities. And, for that matter, you may never need to do a randomized trial. On the basis of the results we got in Oregon, we replicated the benefit of this intervention in two entire states.

An Opportunity to Live Our Values

One last consideration is addressing the human tendency to avoid topics that are unpleasant or threatening. If you are worried about climate change and feel helpless to do anything about it, it may help to recall what we have learned about psychological flexibility. Cultivating the ability to step back from your worries and distress enables you to reduce their control over you and frees you to choose actions consistent with your values. We need not be sure our actions will work. We never can be. But we do not have to be deterred by our doubts and distress. If our planet is headed for a horrendous fate, which is nobler: do everything we can to avoid even thinking about the problem or make our lives about doing the best we can to address the problem?

I am acutely aware of how far we are from effectively addressing this problem. I do not get up every morning confident that what I am doing will make a difference, but I have chosen to make part of my life about trying to make a difference. And in the process, I have found myself working with many other people who are similarly committed to trying, while all the while not knowing how this will come out.

Action Implications

Personal

Lean into the problem.

Take small steps to move toward climate change involvement. Take ten minutes each day to think or read about the problem. If you feel distress, notice it. Accept it. Why? Because by accepting it, you are moving toward doing something about it. Read the *New York Times* article "How to Stop Freaking Out and Tackle Climate Change" by Emma Marris, who writes about ways to deal with your stress and become part of the solution.[19]

Learn more about what you can do.

Do an Internet search for "What you can do to stop climate change." You will find a treasure trove of things. Look for actions that will help you reduce your greenhouse gas emissions. The website drawdown.org provides a list of the top one hundred contributors to greenhouse gasses. Some things you can do may involve immediate action—using alternative transportation, reducing food waste, and adopting a plant-based diet. Others may be long term, such as buying an electric vehicle. You may not be ready for a big step, but you can begin planning to take that step in the future.

Talk to friends and family.

You may find that they don't want to talk about it. Be patient. Be a model for how to approach the topic with compassion and warmth. Make it fun.

Policy

Advocate for carbon fees and dividends.

I describe how this is generally believed to be the single most important thing we can do to reduce emissions. Find out how such a policy might be enacted in your state, community, or nation. The Citizens Climate Lobby has more than four hundred chapters in the United States and many more around the world. See if your community has one, and if so, join it.

Advocate for school policies that require teaching about climate change.

Every school should be teaching children about climate change.

- There is already a youth movement. Let's see if we can accelerate it. In the research my group did on tobacco use, we found that students could talk to their parents about it in a way that strengthened family norms against smoking. With more research, we should be able to find the most effective ways to make this strategy work.

- Find out if your state and local school district require teaching about climate change and whether they are actually doing so. If not, advocate for such a policy and its effective implementation.

Fund behavioral science research on reducing greenhouse gas emissions.

My colleagues and I were shocked to discover how little research is being funded to affect what is probably the most important behavior we need to influence. Demand that your legislators vote for more funding for this work.

Organizations

Support the Behavioral Science Coalition's effort to get more funding for behavioral science research.

If you are a behavioral scientist, lend your voice to this effort. Send me an email and I will connect you.

Visit the ClimateStore website for a list of nonprofit organizations working to fight climate change.[20]

Find an organization you like, join it, give it money, and work to advance its efforts.

Check out the websites of these organizations working to apply behavioral science to influencing climate-relevant behavior.

- Root Solutions

- EcoAmerica

- Center for Research on Environmental Decisions at Columbia University

- Citizens Climate Lobby

CHAPTER 11:

A Political System That Works for All

We can't undo decades of Republican maneuvering in just 18 months. It will take years of hard work, day in and day out.

— Amanda Litman, executive director, Run for Something

F OR MOST OF my life, I have been what might be called a moderate Democrat. As the fortunes of Democrats declined—thanks, to a great extent, to the success of the conservative movement—I accepted that the party needed to steer a prudent, moderate course if we wanted to have political power. I cheered the ascendancy of Bill Clinton; he knew how to get elected. I accepted that he had to veer to the right on free trade, law enforcement, and business regulation; it was the price we paid for his ability to be in the White House and advance liberal causes.

I was similarly inspired by the soaring rhetoric of Barack Obama. And here, too, I accepted that it was simply not politically feasible to take left-leaning positions on many issues in America at this time; we were, I was convinced, a right-of-center nation.

When Bernie Sanders ran against Hillary Clinton, I knew Sanders was right about the undue power that corporations have accumulated. I agreed that student debt was unconscionable, that health care should be available to all, that free-trade agreements had taken jobs from many Americans. But being a life-long student of politics, I knew better than all these young followers of Sanders. It was simply not possible to be elected president with such left-wing views.

Yet when I read Thomas Frank's book *Listen, Liberal,* the scales fell from my eyes. I realized that in my "wise" belief in the need for moderation, I have been part of a Democratic Party that abandoned its commitment to the working class. By abandoning traditional advocacy for the needs of working-class Americans and acquiescing to the conservative worldview, the Democratic Party deserves a large share of blame for the current political situation. In essence, Donald Trump is president because Democrats abandoned the working class.

An Upper-Middle-Class Leadership

Frank takes us through the history of the Clinton and Obama years using a different lens. I was aware of much of what he described but had not been willing to criticize it because I believed it was the Democrats' only option.

I was aware that the Democrats had joined with the Republicans in undermining laws and regulations that could have prevented the Great Recession of 2008. But I had not seen the situation for what it was: a full-scale embrace of Wall Street and a complete abandonment of policy goals that could have prevented much of the hollowing out of the middle class.

Recall that the conservative billionaire coalition chose not to directly confront liberals and overtly contest their influence in American politics. Instead, they chose to wage a stealthy campaign to advance acceptance of free market ideology: unfettered markets are what has made America great, governments are ineffective and harmful, governments take your money and waste it. Their stealth approach worked so well that it infected the thinking of Democrats. Bill Clinton got elected by embracing some of the ideology. In his State of the Union in 1996, he stated that "the era of big government is over."

Let me take you briefly through Frank's argument. He asks us to broaden our lens beyond the 1 percent. He argues that it is not just the 1 percent but at least the top 10 percent of earners who are complicit in the decline of the middle class. To be in the top 10 percent of earners, a household needed to make about $109,000 in 2017.[1]

Frank argues that a class of professionals has evolved in recent years who, on the basis of their education, are the experts who run most parts of society: health care, finance, law, education, economics, behavioral science, engineering, marketing, technology. He notes that the professional class has become more Democratic than it used to be and that it has surrendered any allegiance to the needs of the working class. The upper-middle class of professionals took control of Democratic Party policies and strategies. Their needs were no longer aligned with those of people making far less than they do.

This view is supported by Richard Reeves. In his book *Dream Hoarders,* he documents how a class system has developed in the United States in which the top 20 percent of earners (income above about $75,500) have separated themselves from people below this level.[2] If like me, you fall into this group, you not only make more than the lower 80 percent, your children go to better schools and are much more likely to attend college. You live in neighborhoods that, if not gated, are separated from those of poorer people. The tax structure favors you in many ways. Your connection to others in the same class—lawyers, accountants, physicians—give you advantages that people outside your class simply don't have.

The Clinton Years

Having read Frank's book and accepted the discomfort that came with his analysis, I now see things I knew about but had been ignoring. Here is a list of things Bill Clinton did as president that contributed to the demise of the middle class.

The Violent Crime Control and Law Enforcement Act of 1994. This act funded increases in prison building, harsh sentencing for nonviolent crimes, and a huge increase in incarceration rates. Among its poverty-increasing features were elimination of funding for higher education of prisoners, the creation of sixty new death penalty offenses, and the creation of "boot camps" for delinquent offenders. By Clinton's own admission, the bill led to a huge increase in the number of people imprisoned, and, as I detail in chapter 8, the result was the breakup of many families, more children living in single-parent households, more poor families, and much trauma for the children of those arrested and incarcerated.[3]

Lowering of the capital gains tax. The tax was lowered from 28 percent to 20 percent in 1996. This and subsequent reductions in the tax under George W. Bush have been identified as the single largest contributor to economic inequality.[4]

Telecom deregulation. Deregulation allowed the wholesale takeover of local radio stations by large networks. In many communities, local news is no longer broadcast, and seemingly local editorials are fed to local TV stations by the conglomerate that owns chains of stations. Our radio and TV stations are now dominated by conservative voices.[5]

Electricity deregulation. One result of deregulation was that Enron engineered power shortages in California that enabled it to run up the price of electricity.[6]

Financial deregulation. Clinton was as much under the thrall of free market ideology as were the Republicans. During his presidency, interstate banking was deregulated, so larger banks were able to take over smaller banks, and state-level regulation of banks was undermined. Banking regulation was virtually abandoned, thus allowing the creation of investment instruments such as collateralized debt obligation, which were hyped by rating agencies that were paid by the banks to inflate their value.

The North American Free Trade Agreement (NAFTA). There is a credible argument that reducing trade barriers benefits the nation. Doing so leads to each country doing the work it can do most efficiently. The result is cheaper goods for everyone, and, as a result, more trade. The analyses I have been able to find indicate that NAFTA did not result in an overall loss of jobs in the United States.

However, according to the Economic Policy Institute, an affiliate of the union movement, NAFTA led to the elimination of 682,900 jobs, mostly in manufacturing.[7] An estimated 61 percent of the jobs lost were higher-paying manufacturing jobs.

The Keystone Research Center in Pennsylvania analyzed the impact of NAFTA on jobs in that state.[8] They concluded that between 1993, when NAFTA was passed, and 2003, NAFTA resulted in the loss of 150,000 manufacturing jobs. Jobs in manufacturing in Pennsylvania averaged salaries of $42,852 in 2002, while jobs available in the service industries that laid off workers might have paid an average of $33,376.

There are clear benefits to NAFTA. We do, after all, get our TVs, computers, clothes, and cars more cheaply because they are made by cheaper labor in Mexico, China, and other Asian countries. However, the loss of manufacturing jobs in the United States has decimated many communities and left hundreds of thousands of Americans poorer than they were before.

Impact on the economy. Finally, not only did we lose manufacturing jobs, we didn't gain much in terms of our gross domestic product. In a 2003 report, the Congressional Budget Office wrote, "CBO estimates that the increased trade resulting from NAFTA has probably increased U.S. gross domestic product, but by a very small amount—probably a few billion dollars or less, or a few hundredths of a percent."[9]

The Obama Years

Frank is similarly critical of the Obama administration. Certainly, some accomplishments of the Obama era benefited working-class Americans. The Affordable Care Act resulted in 20 million more Americans having health insurance.[10] And the $800 billion stimulus program Obama initiated at the outset of his presidency saved about 3 million people from unemployment.[11] However, many other things could have been done to reduce economic inequality, increase the well-being of the less affluent, and, at the same time, assuage people's anger toward their government.

To begin with, the Obama administration wrongly sided with the deficit hawks at a time when greater government spending could have prevented the recession from being the most prolonged and worst in terms of employment recovery since the Great Depression. In 2011, Obama said, "Like parents with young children who know they have to start saving for the college years, America had to start borrowing less and saving more to prepare for the retirement of an entire generation."[12] That was certainly the popular wisdom spread by the conservative advocacy coalition, but as Nobel Laureate in economics Paul Krugman has so frequently indicated, it was simply not true.[13] With interest rates at historic lows, it was an excellent time for the federal government to borrow money to spend on things such as infrastructure repair and building. This would have stimulated the economy and put money in the pockets of millions of unemployed or underemployed Americans at the same time that it improved our roads, bridges, airports, ports, and Internet infrastructure.

I acknowledge—as did Krugman—that it would have been very hard to get a second stimulus package through Congress. But the very act of advocating for one would have been not only right on the economics but a statement on behalf of millions of Americans who were seething about bailouts for bankers and foreclosures for less-affluent Americans.

The program of bank bailouts established at the end of the Bush administration was pretty much continued by the Obama administration. No banks were closed or reorganized. No CEOs were fired. Indeed, bonuses went to the people who had major blame for the economic situation. The bonuses to AIG were particularly galling to Americans who got no help when their houses were being foreclosed on. AIG had received a taxpayer bailout in 2008 after posting a loss of $61.7 billion in the fourth quarter. In March 2009, AIG announced that it was giving bonuses of $218 million to employees of the financial services division and a total of $1.2 billion throughout the company.[14] The Obama administration not only did not try to stop these bonuses, they drafted changes in the Dodd-Frank bill that was being written to deal with the crises that allowed the AIG bonuses to go forward.

Nor were the many misdeeds of the banking industry prosecuted. Two examples: the fraud involved in the creation of complex collateralized debt obligations that received "A" ratings from the rating companies and the robo-signing of mortgage foreclosure documents that were never reviewed for accuracy. Indeed, the prosecution of white-collar crime hit a twenty-year low in 2015.[15]

Then there was the dithering on Dodd-Frank regulations. Six years after the Dodd-Frank bill to reform Wall Street was passed, 30 percent of its regulations had not been written, and many of the ones that were written were favorable to the banks.[16] While the working class watched banks being propped up, there was a huge failure to deal with foreclosures. According to Frank, Democrats proposed that judges be allowed to modify homeowners' mortgage debts when they filed for bankruptcy. The Obama administration did nothing to get the bill passed.

And there was the proposed Employee Free Choice Act, which would have made it easier for workers to bargain collectively. Obama had said he supported it, but the White House did nothing to get it passed.

Whatever you may think of these criticisms, America's failure to improve the well-being of working-class Americans during the eight years of the Obama administration is clear. Keep in mind that 8.7 million Americans lost jobs in the first two years of the recession; 1.2 million lost their homes; thousands died prematurely, either through stress-related illnesses or suicide; and a vast swath of the middle class saw that their children would not have—indeed, already did not have—the same opportunities they had.[17] It was not until five years after the recession ended (June 2009) that we returned to the level of employment we'd had when the recession began. According to the Pew Research Center, the net worth of households in the upper 7 percent of the wealth distribution rose about 28 percent two years into the economic recovery, while the net worth of the bottom 93 percent dropped 4 percent. For those in the top 5 percent of wealth in 2003, the decline in net worth as of 2011 was only .004 percent of what it had been. However, the net worth of those in the bottom 25 percent of wealth was more than 98 percent lower.[18]

Why didn't Democrats take stronger steps to ensure the well-being of the marginalized people in society? I submit that it was because they had lost touch with these people and had come to believe the free market theory that the success of business would benefit everyone. In the twenty years after the Second World War, lower-middle-class workers in manufacturing had made steady progress in income and wealth because they had political power. But in the ensuing years, they got left behind economically because they lost the attention of the Democratic Party.

In this context, I ask you to consider what happened to black people, in particular. I would argue that they have been loyal Democrats because the Republican Party has become increasingly hostile to them as it has sought the support of white working-class people through dog-whistle racism. For example, there was the Willie Horton ad that the George Bush campaign ran in 1988, which attacked his opponent, Michael Dukakis, for supporting a furlough program that enabled Horton to get out of prison. Horton was black, and the ad showed a picture of him; white people who were afraid of black people got the message.

How well has the Democratic Party served the interests of black people? In economic terms, not well at all. Between 2000 and 2016, the proportion of black families living in poverty remained essentially unchanged, hovering at 19 to 20 percent.[19] An analysis of wealth accumulation conducted by the Institute for Policy Studies found that between 1983 and 2013, the average wealth of black families rose from $67,000 to $85,000, while it rose from $355,000 to $656,000 for white families.[20]

Now, in the context of what I have just described, think about the election of Donald Trump. We have run out of adjectives to describe how terrible a president he is.

What are the two arguments Donald Trump relentlessly pursued in his campaign? Jobs being sent to other countries and building a wall between the United States and Mexico. These may not seem connected in your mind, but to people who know that the job they had a year or two ago is now held by someone in Mexico, hostility to Mexico should not be a surprise. Trump spoke to the anger of all the people whose communities have been devastated by the free trade policy. And the Democrats were as much to blame for that devastation as the Republicans.

How the Fortunes of Democratic Leaders Have Changed—Literally

Times have changed. When Harry Truman left the White House, he went back to his hometown of Independence, Missouri. He lived out his life as a middle-class citizen. When asked about the first thing he did when he came home, he said he took the grips up to the attic.

Fast forward to today. Whatever the background and origins of recent Democratic political leaders, the fact of the matter is that they have become solid members of the 1 percent. According to Forbes's analysis of the Clinton's tax returns, they made $240 million between 2001 and 2015.[21] Frank describes the economic success of many of the people in the Obama administration.

- Larry Summers, the secretary of the Treasury under Obama, earned $5.2 million working for the hedge fund D. E. Shaw. He worked one day a week, making about $52,000 a day.

- Rahm Emmanuel, Obama's first chief of staff, worked in investment banking, where he earned more than Summers.

- Jack Lew, who became Obama's secretary of the Treasury, managed a hedge fund at Citibank.

- Tim Geithner, Obama's first secretary of the Treasury, became president of Warburg Pincus, an equity firm.

- Peter Orzag left the leadership of the Office of Management and Budget for a job at Citibank, where he earned more than $3.1 million in 2013.[22]

- Gene Sperling, who headed the National Economic Council under Obama, took a job as a consultant on U.S. economic policy issues with PIMCO, a leading bond fund.

What Is Needed

What can we do to create a political party that works for the well-being of all of us—including all whose well-being has been undermined in the past forty years? We need a movement as big and effective as the ones that produced reforms in the Progressive era at the turn of the twentieth century, the New Deal in the 1930s, and the civil rights movement of the 1960s. It will require organizing, and it will require that we change some of the structural obstacles to change.

Organize!

Reforming our politics requires that we extend our ambitions beyond simply winning the next election. Keep in mind that the almost total capture of political power by the conservative billionaire coalition is the result of "careful long-range planning and implementation, in consistency of action over an indefinite period of years, in the scale of financing available only through joint effort."[23] A truly progressive coalition will have to do the same thing.

Lee Drutman is a senior fellow at New America, a think tank focused on increasing prosperity and promoting political reform. He published a study of eight thousand voters who were surveyed in December 2016. It provides useful insight on the differences between those who voted for Clinton and those who voted for Trump. However, Drutman's findings about the differences between Clinton voters and Sanders voters point to what progressives need to do if we are going to influence public policy. The survey showed that Clinton and Sanders supporters agreed on virtually all the issues—both those having to do with economics and those concerning social and moral issues. What they differed on was the view that "politics is a rigged game." On that, Sanders supporters were far more critical of the existing system.

In an op-ed in *The New York Times*, Drutman expanded on this issue. He argued that the leadership of the party sees themselves as hard-headed realists—my own view until very recently. Their focus has been on running campaigns, using sophisticated algorithms to identify and motivate those likely to vote. Local organizing of the party—something Howard Dean did when he headed the Democratic National Committee—was generally abandoned. The result has been that the party is not connected with people in ways that would engage them on a continuing basis in efforts to address the problems people are concerned about. Instead, he argued, people's "engagement with the party mostly consists of receiving fundraising emails intended to enforce programmatic conformity while activating fear of and resentment toward the other party."[24]

This is one of the mistakes that cost Clinton the 2016 election. The top-down, national-level organization was simply not in touch with people in communities that contained many more disaffected voters than the national party and the Clinton campaign realized.

But forget about losing the last election or even simply focusing on winning the next one. The party needs to rebuild the local organization around the immediate interests of people in those communities. It needs to become a vehicle for addressing the day-to-day concerns of people who have, in recent years, lost any sense of involvement in their communities or any faith that they could take collective action to make a difference in their community.

There is a theory in political science and social psychology called the *spiral of silence*. It refers to the tendency of people who hold minority views to not speak up for their views in settings in which majority views dominate public discussion. Imagine that you have just moved to a small rural town in the Midwest, where all the officeholders are Republicans and the local news media report almost every story with a right-leaning stance. They emphasize government mistakes and discuss government spending as though everyone agrees that the government wastes money. They report the actions of national Democratic leaders, such as Nancy Pelosi, with contempt.

You may say this would not affect you, but you say it in a context of interacting with many other people who see things the way you do. That is part of the reason you have the beliefs you have. One of the most important early studies of social influence demonstrated this. Solomon Asch, a social psychologist, put a naïve subject in a group of other people who were confederates of the experimenter.[25] He showed participants two cards: one showing a single line and another showing three lines of varying length, one of which matched the single line on the first card. He then asked each person to say which of the three lines was the same length as the single one. The naïve subject was the last to be asked. When the confederates all answered incorrectly, Asch found, the naïve subject was likely to do the same.

Humans are quite likely to follow the crowd. Think about all those small rural communities that the National Democratic Party abandoned. Without support from the party or any effort to organize advocacy for progressive views, those views perished in many places.

One result of the party's failure to organize locally is that we have had a very weak minor league of potential candidates. If progressives didn't even try to run for the school board, the city council, the state legislature, or the county commission, where would credible candidates for Congress or the Senate come from? In the process, communities would spiral into conservative worldviews that further undermine efforts to rein in the worst excesses of the current version of capitalism.

One organization addressing this problem is Run for Something.[26] It recruits young progressives to run for local office and works with them to get the training and financial support to run a campaign. In 2017, its first year, Run for Something helped seventy-two candidates across fourteen states, half of whom won. After the 2018 election, it claimed victory for two hundred of the candidates it helped. It is noteworthy that Run for Something was created outside the Democratic Party.

Even at the local level, it is important to bring together a greater diversity of views. For example, the Republican Party has skillfully co-opted the language of religion and morality, while the Democratic Party is dominated by secularists. But I am convinced that progressives share basic values with most religious groups. Religious and secular people need to work together on things they agree on.

Similarly, we need a party that is connected to all the local organizations working on addressing the many problems that face our communities—drug abuse, delinquency, school dropout, and so on. These efforts need to include behavioral scientists, who are a resource for the solutions to most of these problems but who have not been involved in addressing them. That is because few outside the behavioral science community are aware of their potential and because behavioral scientists have been reluctant to get involved in "politics."

In this context, we need to remember that long-term solutions to the selfishness, greed, and materialism of recent American culture require more than winning the next election. Indeed, we will have a hard time winning elections unless we more fundamentally reform all the sectors of society so that they are aligned with making the well-being of *every* person the fundamental value of our communities.

The Obstacles to Our Progress

I don't want to minimize the task before us. If our sole motivation is to win elections and policy victories, I fear we will not have enough motivation to make the protracted efforts required. Instead, we need to think about this in the way that acceptance and commitment therapy teaches. The meaning in our lives can come not simply from the successes we achieve but from the daily actions we take that are consistent with our values—even when our value-consistent behavior does not achieve everything we seek. The very process of working for policies we value is a noble thing that increases our solidarity with millions of other Americans who share our values.

With that mindset, I want to describe some of the obstacles to our effort—some of which we can change and some of which are built into the structure of government established by our nation's founders. The latter will be much harder to change.

The structure of our federal system. Our federal system of government is inherently conservative. First, we have two legislative chambers—the House of Representatives and the Senate—which makes it harder to enact laws than in countries that have a single parliament. Economists Alberto Alesina and Edward Glaeser argue that one of the primary reasons the United States redistributes wealth and income less than do most European countries is that parliamentary systems are more responsive to the demands of ordinary citizens.[27]

Second, our federal system guarantees that rural, less-populated states have more influence in decision making than other states. Senators John Barrasso and Mike Enzi each represent the 585,000 people of Wyoming. Senators Diane Feinstein and Kamala Harris each represent the 39 million Californians. In a sense, then, Wyoming voters have more than sixty times the influence of California voters. The analysis is also relevant to our system of electing presidents via the Electoral College. Each state is entitled to the same number of electoral votes as it has senators and representatives. Thus, the 585,000 people in Wyoming get three electoral votes, and the 39 million Californians get fifty-five. That means Wyoming has 189,000 people per elector while California has 678,000 per elector.[28] California's influence on the outcome of the election is diluted. Indeed, if California voters had as much weight as Wyoming voters, Hillary Clinton would be president.

To the extent that people in rural, more sparsely populated states are more conservative than people in other states, conservative views will be disproportionately more influential in lawmaking. However, rural voters are not inherently more conservative. In the populist era of the late nineteenth century, farmers were among the most militant opponents of large corporations. But in the current era, the most liberal views on most issues are found in our large cities.

Note what this analysis implies about the failure of the Democratic Party to compete in more rural states. It costs far less to run a campaign in Wyoming than in California. In a strictly cost-benefit analysis, the Democrats are crazy not to be competing in rural states.

Gerrymandering. This is the process through which a party in power redraws legislative or congressional districts to favor the party. If you have four legislators in four districts that have equal numbers of Republicans and Democrats, the winner of each election will tend to change from one election to the next. But suppose you create one district with many more Democrats? That will ensure that a Democrat wins that seat virtually every time. Sound good? Ah, but it will also mean you now have three districts in which a Republican will always win.

Gerrymandering is a long-standing practice by both parties. However, thanks to the Koch Brothers' conservative ascendancy, a large number of state legislatures and governorships were taken over by Republicans. Once in power, they redrew the state legislative and federal Congressional districts with a vengeance, thereby further solidifying their power. As a result, most Congressional districts are safe seats for them.

In most recent elections, as many as 90 percent of incumbents were reelected. Thanks to gerrymandering, when Republicans won control of the House of Representatives in 2012, they received a million fewer votes than Democrats did yet elected thirty-three more representatives.[29] In Wisconsin, the Republican-controlled legislature redistricted after the 2010 census, enabling the Republicans to achieve a sixty to thirty-nine seat advantage in the State Assembly, despite getting only 48.6 percent of the votes cast. And in the 2018 election, the Democrats won at least forty additional seats, but would have won many more if there had been less gerrymandering. According to *The Washington Post,* in North Carolina, Democrats got 50 percent of the votes for U. S. House seats but took only 23 percent of the seats.[30]

Voter suppression. Another way you can keep political power is to reduce the number of supporters of the other party who vote. Finding ways to do this has become akin to a national sport.

One of the most important organizations in the conservative arsenal is the American Legislative Exchange Council (ALEC), which is funded by the Koch Brothers, the Coors family, and others in the conservative coalition. ALEC develops model conservative legislation and then cultivates, trains, and supports conservative legislators in each state to take the model bills back to their state. Progressives would do well to use this same approach to advance their policy agenda.

ALEC produced a model voter ID act that has influenced efforts in many states. For example, by requiring people to have state-approved ID cards to vote, you make it less likely that people without a driver's license will be able to vote. And if you require people to show a birth certificate to get a state-issued ID, you raise the cost to the person, who may have to pay to get a copy of that certificate. The Brennan Center for Justice estimates that millions of Americans are being disenfranchised by these laws. The Center found that in several states where such laws have been implemented, disproportionately fewer places where IDs can be obtained are in areas with high numbers of poor and minority voters.[31]

The distribution of Democrats. This is a problem we can't blame on the Republicans. Democrats tend to be concentrated in large cities. This fact has the same effect as gerrymandered districts. Some states and some cities in states have overwhelming majorities of Democrats and regularly elect Democrats. If those Democrats were more spread out, they might have fewer seats with huge majorities of Democrats and more seats in which they are competitive.

Of course, this would not be such a big problem if the party had continued the fifty-state strategy Howard Dean began. Party affiliation is not genetic. Democrats need to be persuading people in every part of the country.

Low voter turnout. Democratic voters tend to be poorer and younger than Republican voters. However, older and wealthier people are more likely to vote than younger or poorer people. If all the people who voted for Barack Obama in 2008 had turned out to vote in the 2010 Congressional elections, the Democrats might have held control of the House of Representatives, and our history could have been quite different. The tendency for older, wealthier people to vote has been around for a long time.

Thanks again to behavioral scientists, we are making progress on how to increase voter participation. If you go to Yale University's Institute for Social and Policy Studies website, you will find a list of strategies shown through rigorous randomized trials to increase voter turnout.

The Supreme Court. The U.S. Supreme Court will continue to have a conservative majority for the foreseeable future.

In summary, there are substantial obstacles to amplifying the voice of the people most harmed by our current political system. Yet there are ways to chip away at these obstacles. We can take back power in states Democrats have failed to compete in. As we do, we can overturn voter suppression laws and practices and reduce or eliminate gerrymandering. It is unlikely that we will change the structural impediments involved in our bicameral system of House and Senate, but we would not need to if progressives pursued a fifty-state strategy. And, yes, we can get rid of the electoral college or make it moot through laws that call for states to award their electoral votes to whomever wins the majority of votes nationally.

A Thorough Reform of Capitalism

Capitalism is a system in which market competition influences market actors to innovate in ways that are profitable. As I state at the outset of this book, such competition has influenced innovations that have vastly improved human well-being. Yet, as I have demonstrated repeatedly, devoid of any regulation, market actors will adopt practices that improve their profits but harm society.

Thus, a central tenet of our political movement should be the need to regulate capitalism in ways that minimize harms while retaining the benefits of market competition. As I have argued, we need to get people and organizations that have been combatting specific harmful practices—such as the marketing of cigarettes, unhealthful foods, and fossil fuels—to see that in every case, the fundamental problem is that their harmful practices produce profits. The principle that is implied is simple to state: we must eliminate *any* profit from the practices that produce more harm than benefit. Call it the *no-profit principle*.

It will be difficult to implement this principle throughout our economic system. But we will be far more likely to succeed if all the organizations opposing harmful corporate practices unite around this principle and work to bring our economic practices in line with our vision of a society in which everyone's well-being is advanced.

Policy Objectives

What shall we organize to do? Virtually all the policies suggested thus far could contribute to the kinds of reforms I have been advocating. Here are some of the major policy objectives I think we must pursue. And by "we," I do not mean just Democrats. We need to organize support for these policies in every community, in all segments of the population.

Income. The Democratic Party has endorsed a push to make the national minimum wage $15 an hour. As a former hardheaded realist, I knew this was far beyond what could get passed. But in the process, we let the other side make its right-of-center position seem like the accepted norm. Polls show that the majority in both parties support raising the national minimum wage.[32] The minimum wage can also be raised at the local and state levels. Indeed, given the differences in cost of living in different states, it may be better to set a minimum wage tied to the cost of living. This makes it a policy that can help to organize locally. Another policy that has proven benefit is the earned income tax credit, which provides added income to poor and moderate-income families and subsidies for rent.

There is also evidence of benefit from a universal basic income.[33] However, as with any other policy, this needs to be carefully evaluated through multiple experiments before it is enacted more widely.

Consumer protection. This issue pervades everyone's daily life. How many large corporations are nickel and diming you without your even knowing it? What hidden charges are in your credit card accounts, your phone bill, your cable service, your health insurance, your mutual funds, your car loan? Do a Google search on "hidden charges" and see all the different ones.

And have you read the fine print in all your contracts? Silly question! I haven't read one in years. They are written to not be read. But inside most of them these days is a provision that says you give up your right to sue them, and any dispute will be settled by a mediator. Guess who controls that process?

The situation demands empirical study of the ways in which consumers are harmed and the development and evaluation of regulations that eliminate harmful practices. And let there be no doubt that this will be an ongoing evolutionary arms race between regulators and companies that are continually innovating to give themselves an advantage.

Health care. At this writing, a number of Democratic presidential candidates have proposed setting up a single-payer system of health insurance: Medicare for All. There are strong arguments for doing this. The United States has the highest administrative costs for health care among eleven nations studied by Ryan Gamlin, a medical student and former health-care consultant.[34] He also found that we have the highest level of duplication of tests. And based on comparisons of Medicare and Medicaid costs with the costs of traditional health-insurance coverage, a single-payer system would control costs more effectively.[35] Of course, it may be difficult to achieve a single-payer system because all those highly profitable insurance companies will fight like hell to prevent it.

In whatever way this works out, Democrats are making a big mistake if they think ensuring that everyone has health care will reduce the huge disparities in health between this country and other developed countries or between poorer and wealthier Americans. As I point out in chapter 6, the poor health of Americans is much more a result of poverty, inequality, discrimination, the marketing of unhealthful substances, and Americans' unhealthful behaviors than a result of lack of health care. In addition, as presently constituted, our health-care system mostly spends money on treating illnesses that could have been prevented, wastes money on needless assessments, and often provides treatments that are useless or even harmful.

We are a long way from a well-functioning health-care system. We need to shift from a health-care *treatment* system to a *public health* system that focuses on preventing problems before they occur. *The Nurture Effect* details the power of prevention to achieve unprecedented improvements in public health at the same time that it reduces health-care costs. The most important policy change needed is much greater investment in prevention.

We also need to place controls on the amount of money that drug companies can charge. Thanks to effective lobbying, Americans pay far more for many drugs than people in other countries.

Education. I have outlined in *The Nurture Effect* the many ways in which we need to and can improve education. Reducing the costs of college education, increasing subsidies for attendance, and increasing the number and diversity of young people receiving higher education are needed. So are reforms that reduce punishment, promote prosocial behavior, teach more effectively, and reduce disparities in preschool through high school.[36]

Criminal Justice. In chapter 8, I describe the harm the criminal justice system is doing to millions of Americans. We can do much more to prevent crime, do a better job of rehabilitating offenders, reduce sentence length and racial and economic disparities in sentencing, and reduce the trauma that children experience as a result of their parents' involvement in the criminal justice system.

Regulation. In *This Fight Is Our Fight,* Elizabeth Warren reminds us of how much more corporations were regulated before the success of the conservative ascendancy. The harm that tobacco, alcohol, and unhealthful food cause, as well as the marketing of guns, fossil fuels, and opioids, are examples of harmful corporate practices we fail to regulate.

Union organizing. The conventional wisdom, which I must confess I generally accepted, was that unions were simply an anachronism. But unions have been systematically diminished by very successful efforts to undermine laws that allow organizing. Political scientists Jacob Hacker and Paul Pierson have documented the many ways in which union organizing has been undermined.[37] We need to change the law so union organizing is facilitated. It is in the public interest to have a labor force that has a strong voice in public affairs and the conduct of business.

Climate policy. As the climate crisis worsens, policies that had little chance ten years ago, thanks to the efforts of the fossil fuel industry, will become increasingly accepted. We need to pursue ambitious goals for reducing carbon use. I have carefully read the Green New Deal.[38] I think it is an excellent start on the huge changes needed if we are going to prevent further climate change. Thoughtful climate policy does not kill jobs, and, in fact, could reinvigorate local economies, including those that are declining because they are based on dying industries such as coal.

Let's Use Science!

How often have you heard a politician propose a policy and acknowledge that it might not work? In my experience, that is exceedingly rare. Because the "other side" will surely point out reasons to not support it, most policy makers would rather die than admit we can't really be sure a proposed policy will work.

Policies and programs are typically adopted by governments in a process that never examines the evidence that supports them or acknowledges that the program needs to be evaluated for effectiveness. For example, in a piece I wrote for *The New York Times,* I documented how we have poured billions of dollars into trying to defeat terrorism but have done very little research on how to prevent young men from being recruited to radical groups.[39]

This is changing. Empirical methods are increasingly being used to assess the impact of programs and policies. For example, the Arnold Foundation is funding experimental evaluations of numerous government programs, and we are beginning to identify those that work and those that don't.

But why should we tolerate *any* policy or program being implemented if we don't know if it will work—or even that it will do no harm? The traditional approach has been to not even raise the question. Evaluations are expensive and take time. Often, the argument is that the need for the program is so great that we can't wait around until it is evaluated.

This is nonsense. If we don't know what the effect of a program is, we may be wasting a lot of money for no benefit, or even doing harm. Recall the Scared Straight program, which was widely promoted for twenty years but eventually shown to *increase* crime.

No policy or program should be proposed without a plan for (1) evaluating its impact, using valid experimental methods, and (b) continuing to monitor its impact even after experiments have shown it can work. There is simply no reason to believe a program will continue to work, or will work in new settings, because it worked in a controlled experiment.

Appealing to the Whole Electorate

Fairly late in my writing of this book, I was discussing it with a Swedish friend and colleague, Magnus Johansson. We were on FaceTime, and he got a serious look on his face and said, "You really need to read *The Righteous Mind* by Jonathan Haidt."[40] He said this so firmly that I promised to read it. He was right. It is an important book.

Haidt is a social psychologist who studies morality. Morality has traditionally not gotten much attention from psychologists, perhaps because so many psychologists are secularists, and morality smacks of religious judgment. However, scientific methods can be applied to any phenomenon, and in my view, the empirical work that Haidt has done on moral judgment makes a critical contribution to how we might evolve a society that works well for far more people. However, I should warn you that if you think of yourself as a progressive, you may find some of what Haidt has learned difficult to accept.

Haidt identifies five orientations he sometimes refers to as *moral sentiments or intuitions*. Each reflects an almost automatic reaction to the world that has, on average, helped human groups survive. This is not to say that every person always reacts in this way. Instead, humans are prone to lean in the direction of these moral intuitions. Let me lay this out in terms of things humans have needed to do in order to survive.

- **Care vs. harm.** We had better care for our young. Humans take longer to raise their offspring than any other primate. If we had not evolved strong inclinations to care for our young, we could not have passed on the enormous amount of knowledge one generation teaches the next so it can master diverse and often hostile environments. Caring is not confined to taking care of our children. Human groups that care for all their members are more likely to survive.

- **Fairness vs. cheating.** Groups are more likely to survive if all members do their share of the work. We have evolved a sense of fairness so that we are quick to disapprove of people who shirk their responsibility to the welfare of the group. We got good at suppressing such behavior through gossip, criticism, shunning, and sometimes severe punishment. (Of course, ensuring the cooperation of group members can also be achieved through positive reinforcement of cooperation. But it is harder to learn the benefits of reinforcing others. Punishment is immediately reinforcing to the punisher, but you may not see the benefits of reinforcing behavior you want until much later.)

- **Loyalty vs. betrayal.** If our group is to succeed, we need all members to be loyal to it. Strong group loyalty is particularly important when other groups could be adversaries. Haidt points out that we tend to have stronger hatred for a traitor than an enemy.

- **Authority vs. subversion.** With the advent of agriculture, human evolution expanded beyond small groups of hunters and gatherers. Egalitarianism gave way to more-hierarchical social systems. The success of these groups depended on people having respect for authority. At the same time, this had to be balanced with the risk of allowing a leader to dominate in harmful ways.

- **Purity vs. degradation.** To survive, humans need to avoid pathogens. You are more likely to do that if you are easily disgusted by excrement, rot, noxious odors, and vermin. If you like cleanliness and purity, you are more likely to avoid disease. This moral intuition also has a spiritual quality; purity is also a matter of the degree to which we are pure in thoughts and behavior. Purity can be seen in devotion to the sacred, an orientation that transcends attraction to merely physical qualities.

Haidt argues that human beings' choices are driven much more by these almost automatic emotional reactions than any rational analysis of facts. We are far more likely to come up with reasons that support our emotional reactions than we are to make choices based on factual analysis.

Haidt is not arguing that these tendencies are entirely innate. Instead, he maintains that we are born with tendencies toward these orientations, which vary as any trait does in a population, and that we are further influenced by our social environments. For example, during the Vietnam War, many people of my generation soured on traditional loyalty to the nation because they felt that the war was immoral.

Haidt's analysis is particularly relevant to politics. His research has shown that progressives tend to both defend and promote their political positions on the basis of only two of these sentiments. Can you guess which? If you guessed caring and fairness, you are right. He shows, however, that conservatives tend to appeal to *all* of these sentiments, and, as a result, are more successful in appealing to segments of the electorate that are moved by values other than caring and fairness.

So how does Haidt's analysis line up with my promotion of the value of our seeing to the well-being of every person? With respect to caring and fairness, it lines up rather well. But if you are a progressive, you may be more reluctant to endorse the value of group loyalty because you see instances of "my country, right or wrong" that excuse things you abhor. Try thinking about it this way: If we are going to build a movement to reform capitalism, we will need tremendous solidarity. Be loyal to a movement that speaks to your most important values. Be loyal to your fellow Americans, including those who are less fortunate than you.

Then there is authority vs. subversion. You may be far less inclined than millions of other Americans to respect authority because you can think of so many authorities who are corrupt. In this case, I think the answer is to advocate respect for authorities who meet certain standards of leadership, such as listening to their followers rather than commanding them, and pursuing the kind of society you want to have. Think, for example of the leadership of the CSM Group of Companies I describe in chapter 5, which believes in the concept of *servant leadership*, whereby leaders are committed to helping employees reach their full potential.

As to the sentiment involving purity vs. degradation, those of us who are not religious tend to shy away from this dimension. However, think of it in terms of the environment. Aren't we massively degrading the environment? Isn't there a sense in which we need the purity of society that sees to the well-being of the planet?

Whether you agree that there are ways in which you could embrace these last three moral sentiments, consider how policies and candidates you support could gain more support from conservative-leaning voters by speaking about these moral sentiments. Here are some examples:

- Raising the minimum wage: Every American has the right to a decent income. To have it any other way is disloyal to the group we call Americans.

- Consumer protection: Unregulated corporate power is betraying the well-being of millions of Americans.

- Environmental policy: The purity of our environment is the birthright of every American. Those who pollute our environment are disloyal to the nation.

- Climate policy: To make God's earth unlivable is an affront to the sanctity of creation. Allowing greenhouse gas emissions to continue unabated is disloyal to future generations of Americans.

- Regulating social media: Social media companies that allow foreign nationals to systematically influence American voters are disloyal to the country.

- Regulating food and pharmaceutical companies: Corporations that market products with harmful ingredients are degrading Americans' bodies and their health.

- Tax law, environmental law: Corporations that intentionally evade or violate the law are showing no respect for authority.

In talking to people for whom the values of loyalty, respect for authority, and sanctity are important, we need to get generally better at showing them how the goals and policies we are pursuing speak to these values.

Making America Great

When Donald Trump promised to make America great again, it was a lie of historic proportions. Yet the Democrats' rejoinder that America was already great was not true, either. In the past half century, America has become a place of greater selfishness, poverty, economic inequality, and discrimination. It is true that many traditionally persecuted groups have gained greater freedom. But as I indicate earlier, the economic well-being of many minority groups has not improved. Nor do the recent increases in hateful treatment of minorities comport with the notion of greatness.[41]

In this book, I have described the many ways in which America is not as great as it could be, and how the conservative billionaire coalition has undermined millions of Americans' well-being by giving corporations free rein, advancing a selfish conception of what it means to be an American, and taking over the apparatus of government. Making America great will require that we reform every sector of society so that our capitalist system is guided by values, goals, policies, and practices that ensure the well-being of every person. I have provided a guide to specific steps we need to take to make us worthy of the appellation "great." I have suggested many things you can do to contribute to this change, including, especially, joining the Values to Action movement to reform every sector of society. I urge you to make a specific contribution to the change we need every day. If you take just twenty minutes a day to do something that helps, we can achieve great things.

Exactly two years before the day he died, Robert Kennedy spoke in Cape Town, South Africa, about the challenges each of us faces in trying to make a difference in the world.

> Few will have the greatness to bend history itself, but each of us can work to change a small portion of events, and in the total of all those acts will be written the history of this generation.... It is from numberless diverse acts of courage and belief that human history is shaped. Each time a man [sic] stands up for an ideal, or acts to improve the lot of others, or strikes out against injustice, he sends forth a tiny ripple of hope, and crossing each other from a million different centers of energy and daring those ripples build a current which can sweep down the mightiest walls of oppression and resistance.[42]

Speaking in South Africa at a time when apartheid oppression of black Africans seemed impregnable, his words were prophetic. We have huge challenges to creating a society in which each person is nurtured by those around him or her, in which our laws, norms, and values guide us toward an ever more caring society. But I submit that the very effort and sacrifice needed to create this society can make our lives more meaningful as we improve the lives of those around us.

Action Implications

Personal

Join Values to Action (valuestoaction.com).

You can join a team of people who are working to promote the reforms needed to our political system. You can do this at the local level or join statewide or nationwide efforts. There is much to be done.

Find, support, and work for progressive organizations.

If you go to valuestoaction.com/progressive, you will find a list. You can add to it.

Run for something.

One of the most exciting things about the transformation taking place in our politics is that all kinds of people are running for office who had never thought of doing so. Why not you? What better way to bring about the change we aspire to than to become a candidate for office? As I note, we need people to run for school boards, city councils, and all kinds of local governing boards. All the reforms I call for in previous chapters require that people who share our values get elected. If you have any interest in doing this, use your psychological flexibility skills—notice all the things your mind tells you about how you don't know enough, couldn't possibly, etc.—and take the plunge anyway. If you are turned off by the corrupt ways in which politics currently works—the negativity and viciousness—and think that that is what you must become to get elected, you can choose to live values of kindness and respect for others in the process of running and the process of serving. Be the kind of politician you choose to be.

Move to a place that needs more progressives.

This is a wild idea, but some people are actually doing it! You may be at a point in your life when you can start something new and important. Consider being a pioneer. Can you find a place you want to live that would benefit from having more people with your values? Vast shifts in demographics, such as the move of many young people to urban areas, have left many rural areas devoid of young people. However, the depopulation of many rural areas has left many places with room for people who want to build a new America.

Policy

Look at the policies I enumerate above.

Find one you think is particularly important and look for an organization that is working to advance it.

Connect with the State Innovation Exchange.

The State Innovation Exchange is doing for progressives what the American Legislative Exchange Council has been doing for conservatives: writing model legislation that state legislators can use to advance reforms. For example, among the polices they are addressing on criminal justice reform are use of force policies and de-escalation training, electronic recording of interrogations, and prohibitions on profiling.

Organizations

Help build the coalition of progressive organizations that our reform movement needs.

- The 2016 election results prompted the creation of a number of organizations that are working to bring about political change. Here are three that my wife and I have been supporting:

  - **Indivisible** was created by former Congressional staffers in the wake of the 2016 election. It has mobilized local groups throughout the nation who are mobilizing people to resist harmful Trump a dministration actions and elect progressives to office.

  - **Run for Something** was created to get more progressive people to run for office. It has helped hundreds of people run for office and win. Its founders understand that winning seats in the federal office requires that many more people get involved in local politics. I view this organization as vital to addressing the Democratic Party's failure to compete in every community.

  - **Flippable** is organized to flip political control in states to progressives. It has gotten a hundred thousand people involved in working to get ninety-five people elected in states. It has helped flip political control in seven states thus far.

- We need to find all the other organizations that are contributing to the change we want. Look at the organizations listed at valuestoaction. com/progressive. Add to this list. Find one or more that you would like to help and get involved. We need to forge a growing coalition that ultimately dwarfs the network of organizations created by the conservative billionaire coalition.

Conclusion

We mutually pledge to each other our Lives, our Fortunes,
and our sacred Honor.

— Declaration of Independence

I LOVE MY COUNTRY. It seems odd to say it. My social milieu consists almost entirely of progressives. Such sentiments are seldom spoken in these circles—largely, I think, because we see so many ways in which "flag waving" is used to justify huge military expenditures and exploits we do not support. Yet, in my circle of friends, there is tremendous devotion to the ideals of this nation.

Jonathon Haidt writes that after the 9/11 attacks, he was surprised to find that he wanted to put an American flag on his car.[1] I did the very same thing. I removed it when it became clear that the righteous indignation of Americans was going to be channeled into military misadventures, the curtailment of civil liberties, and a reduction in taxes for the wealthiest.

And yet if we are going to evolve the kind of society to which so many of us aspire, it is imperative that we find ways to bring people together to repair the damage that has been done in the past fifty years.

Robert Putnam cautions us not to assume that the conflicting segments of the electorate who are most vocal and get the most attention reflect the views of the majority of Americans. Therefore, our task is not a matter of changing the minds of people with strongly held political and moral beliefs that seem to differ from ours. Instead, our task is to organize a third party, so to speak—not really a political party, but a consensus of people who have been deeply concerned about the state of the nation, who are frustrated by the current stalemate, and who feel that we need to forge a new consensus. This will not involve settling the disputes that have so consumed us but require focusing on a new set of shared priorities in keeping with the highest ideals of the American project.

I have long felt that I had no connection with the spiritual. Yet, why do I choke up when I tell the story of how the D-Day landing mesmerized Americans? Why did I take my sons to the Lincoln Memorial and every other monument erected to the people who sacrificed to build the nation? I have often gone through the Second World War monument in Washington. As you walk into it, there are twenty-four bas-relief panels that tell the story of the men and women who worked so hard to win the war and defeat fascism. They commemorate not only the important battles of the war (Normandy, the Battle of the Bulge, Pearl Harbor) but also the people at home and in the military: the women who served, people who enlisted, bond drives, ship building. Americans united to win the war. I feel strong emotion just writing about it.

It was only when I studied Haidt's analysis of moral sentiments that I realized I do have what most would call a *spiritual side*. A sense of sacredness about something bigger than myself is what I feel about this country. Oh yes, I could go on and on about the terrible things that are happening in this country. The fact that so much of it is wrapped in the flag turns so many of us away from the whole idea of a nation with sacred principles.

Obama captured it in his 2008 run for the presidency. He acknowledged the shortcomings of the nation: racism, poverty, inequality. But he reminded us that the American ideal is aspirational. We can love and revere the highest ideals enshrined in the Declaration of Independence and the preamble to the Constitution and strive to strengthen and extend them. John Kennedy did so in his inaugural speech. Dr. Martin Luther King, Jr. did it in his leadership of the civil rights movement. Robert Kennedy did it when he reached out to and cared for starving children in Mississippi, oppressed farm workers in California, and black people striving to overturn apartheid in South Africa.

These images stir my strong sentiments to rebuild this country's moral fiber. They may not be what arouses such sentiments in you, but I urge you to find and embrace your own values and images of America's most noble aspirations. You need not rely on what has come before you.

You can, by your actions, add to the store of gallant examples of people bringing this nation to its highest ideals.

We need not turn our backs on American patriotism. Indeed, if Jonathan Haidt is correct, we need to shout out our vision of a true American as someone who sacrifices for the well-being of other Americans, as well as people around the world. We need to reclaim patriotism from those who have corrupted our ideals with calls for self-aggrandizement and hatred of those who are different from us.

We need to reach out to those who have been entranced by Trump's dishonesties and fabrications into believing that American greatness involves the vilification of people different from them. But it will not work to try to talk them out of what they believe. We must find ways to encourage them to move toward a different set of priorities—those that address their needs and the needs of others, and in the process, make them feel that they are proud members of a great nation. And to do this, we must work relentlessly for the political power that will enable the regulation of capitalism and the creation of laws and policies that steadily improve the well-being of all of us.

In helping others and acting to change public policy, we need to recognize that we are participating in the shared vision of a country that cares for every person. In this sense, the sacred ideals of the nation are bigger than any given act, yet consist of nothing more than those acts.

Acknowledgments

FIRST ON MY list and first in my heart is Georgia Layton, my partner of 50 years. What a journey. She has made me a better person, dampening down my worst instincts and guiding me through the many setbacks that life has brought us.

In the days after Donald Trump was elected, I kept having nightmares about the direction of the country. For a long time, I had been thinking about writing a book about capitalism and how we could evolve a more nurturing form of capitalism. I had hesitated because writing a book takes a long time and a lot of work.

But then I remembered how Jess Beebe, my editor when I wrote *The Nurture Effect*, had helped me. I called her. She shared my concerns about the direction of the country. We began a collaboration that resulted in this book. I thank her for her guidance and support. Just as she did for *The Nurture Effect*, she made this a far better book than it would have been.

In 2014, David Sloan Wilson, Steven Hayes, Dennis Embry, and I published a paper in *Behavioral and Brain Sciences* titled "Evolving the Future: Toward a Science of Intentional Change." It was the result of our coming together around the idea that evolutionary theory could organize the disparate fields of the human sciences in a way that would enable effective practical action to evolve societies that ensure everyone's well-being—including those who haven't been born. The present book is one branch of the tree we planted with that paper. I am deeply grateful for the opportunity to collaborate with David, Steven, and Dennis, each of whom is making enormous contributions to the evolution of more-nurturing societies.

I also thank two of my closest colleagues, Mark Van Ryzin and Magnus Johansson. Both are warm, amiable, and very competent behavioral scientists. Mark has continued to work with me on projects that we believe in but for which we have received no payment. I believe the papers we have collaborated on have advanced the science of cultural change. Magnus has collaborated on many of those papers as well, and he has provided steady, supportive, and sometimes critical feedback that has contributed greatly to this book.

Shaylor Murray has provided enthusiastic support for what I am trying to accomplish while also contributing his skills in marketing, which are critical to the success of bringing about the reforms needed in our current economic and political system.

Our son Mike has a knack for words. He came up with the title *Rebooting Capitalism*—which just might attract young people to a book that advocates not that we get rid of capitalism, but that we improve it. Mike also came up with "Values to Action," the name of the nonprofit we created to further the goals of the book.

I thank our other son, Sean, for consistently stimulating discussions about the issues I address in this book. His insight and span of knowledge have helped me understand the newest facet of cultural evolution, namely the Internet.

Katie Clawson is one of the most patient and upbeat people I have ever known. For the past three years she has managed my schedule and travel. More importantly, she has put in countless hours getting this book done and has always made me feel like this is a worthwhile project. I don't think we would have the book without her contributions.

Whitney Stratten has managed the financial aspects of my work in promoting nurturance in the world. What amazes me is that she does this in a very small amount of her time, but reliably gets things done that I fail to deal with.

For the past several years, Doug Carnine and I have been on parallel tracks, both trying to increase nurturance and kindness in the world. He has given me sometimes critical feedback on the book. On more than one occasion, I initially ignored his feedback, only to later conclude that he was right. Thanks for your patience and support, Doug!

Dee Dee Debartlo was the publicist who helped us get *The Nurture Effect* into the hands of thousands of people. When it came time to get this book out, she stepped in and helped us navigate the shoals of self-publishing. I thank her for taking this effort seriously and helping us get the attention I think it deserves.

I am also grateful for the network of people and organizations that are working to advance the use of science in solving the problems we have in the world—all of which are, at base, problems of human behavior. Diana Fishbein created the National Prevention Science Coalition, which is advocating very effectively for the use of prevention science. Maria Malott of the Association for Behavior Analysis International read *The Nurture Effect* and reached out to me, and together we assembled a coalition of behavioral science organizations that are advancing the use of behavioral science knowledge and methods.

Last but not least, I thank Kevin Moore for being my friend and colleague. He is one of the most insightful behavioral scientists I know. And whenever I need to just relax and feel appreciated, Kevin is there for me.

References

INTRODUCTION

1. U.S. Centers for Disease Control. Provisional Drug Overdose Death Counts, 2016. National Center for Health Statistics, National Vital Statistics System, 2017.

2. Child poverty. National Center for Child Poverty, 2019. http://www.nccp. org/topics/childpoverty.html. Accessed February 24, 2020.

3. Biglan A. *The Nurture Effect: How the Science of Human Behavior Can Improve Our Lives and Our World.* Oakland, CA: New Harbinger, 2015.

4. United Nations Framework Convention on Climate Change (UNFCCC). *IPCC Special Report on Global Warming of 1.5° C,* 2018.

5. World Health Organization. Tobacco. http://www.who.int/mediacentre/ factsheets/fs339/en/. Accessed January 7, 2020.

6. Kochanek KD, Murphy SL, Xu J, Tejada-Vera B. Deaths: Final Data for 2014. *National Vital Statistics Reports.* The Centers for Disease Control and Prevention, National Center for Health Statistics, National Vital Statistics System, 2016, 65(4):1-122.

7. U.S. Centers for Disease Control, Provisional Drug Overdose Death Counts.

8. Burrough B. *Days of Rage: America's Radical Underground, the FBI, and the Forgotten Age of Revolutionary Violence.* New York, NY: Penguin, 2015.

9. Hacker J, Pierson P. No cost for extremism: Why the GOP hasn't (yet) paid for its march to the right. The American Prospect, 2015. http://prospect. org/article/no-cost-extremism.

10. Powell LFJ. Attack of American Free Enterprise System,1971. https://lawdigitalcommons.bc.edu/cgi/viewcontent. cgi?article=1078&context=darter_materials.

11. Powell, Attack of American Free Enterprise System.

12. Powell, Attack of American Free Enterprise System.

13. Mayer J. *Dark Money: The Hidden History of the Billionaires Behind the Rise of the Radical Right.* New York, NY: Penguin Random House, 2016.

14. Smith A. *An Inquiry into the Nature and Causes of the Wealth of Nations.* New York, NY: The Modern Library (Original work published in 1776), 1937.

15. Friedman M, Friedman R. *Free to Choose: A Personal Statement. 1st ed.* New York, NY: Harcourt Brace Jovanovich, 1980.

16. Friedman, Friedman, *Free to Choose.*

17. Saez E, Zucman G. Wealth inequality in the United States since 1913: Evidence from capitalized income tax data. *The Quarterly Journal of Economics,* 2016, 131(2):519-578. doi:10.1093/qje/qjw004; Zucman G. *The Hidden Wealth of Nations: The Scourge of Tax Havens.* Chicago, IL: The University of Chicago Press, 2015; Putnam RD. *Our Kids: The American Dream in Crisis.* New York, NY: Simon & Schuster, 2016; Mayer, *Dark Money;* Hacker JS, Pierson P. *American Amnesia: How the War on Government Led Us to Forget What Made America Prosper.* New York, NY: Simon & Schuster, 2016; Stiglitz JE. *The Price of Inequality: How Today's Divided Society Endangers Our Future.* New York, NY: W. W. Norton, 2013; Stiglitz JE. *People, Power, and Profits: Progressive Capitalism for an Age of Discontent.* New York, NY: W. W. Norton, 2019; Stiglitz JE. *Globalization and Its Discontents.* New York, NY: W. W. Norton, 2002.

18. Hacker, Pierson. *American Amnesia;* Warren E. What Elizabeth Will Do, n.d. https://elizabethwarren.com/plans. Accessed January 7, 2020; Sanders B. Bernie Sanders on the Issues. n.d. https://berniesanders.com/issues/. Accessed January 7, 2020.

19. Biglan A. How cigarette marketing killed 20 million people. The Evolution Institute, 2020. https://evolution-institute.org/how-cigarette-marketing-killed-20-million-people. Accessed March 6, 2020; Biglan A. The right to sell arms. The Evolution Institute, 2020. https://evolution-institute.org/

the-right-to-sell-arms. Accessed March 13, 2020; Biglan A. How and why the food industry makes Americans sick. The Evolution Institute, 2020. https://evolution-institute.org/how-and-why-the-food-industry-makes-americans-sick. Accessed March 20, 2020; Biglan A. Big Pharma and the death of Americans. The Evolution Institute, 2020. https://evolution-institute.org/big-pharma-and-the-death-of-americans. Accessed March 27, 2020; Biglan A. How free market ideology resulted in the Great Recession. The Evolution Institute, 2020. https://evolution-institute.org/how-free-market-ideology-resulted-in-the-great-recession. Accessed April 3, 2020; Biglan A. The Fossil Fuel Industry: The greatest threat to human well-being. The Evolution Institute, 2020. https://evolution-institute.org/the-fossil-fuel-industry-the-greatest-threat-to-human-wellbeing. Accessed April 10, 2020; Biglan A. The crisis of capitalism. The Evolution Institute, 2020. https://evolution-institute.org/the-crisis-of-capitalism. Accessed April 17, 2020.

20. Obama B. *The Audacity of Hope: Thoughts on Reclaiming the American Dream.* New York, NY: Crown Publishing, 2006.

CHAPTER 1

1. Wilson DS. *Evolution for Everyone: How Darwin's Theory Can Change the Way We Think about Our Lives.* New York: Delacorte Press, 2007.

2. Stratmann T. Campaign contributions and congressional voting: Does the timing of contributions matter? *The Review of Economics and Statistics,* 1995, 77(1):127-136. doi:o.2307/2109998.

3. Wilson DS. Excerpt from "This View of Life" by David Sloan Wilson, 2019. https://evolution-institute.org/excerpt-from-this-view-of-life-by-david-sloan-wilson/. Accessed August 21, 2019.

4. Wilson DS, Hessen DO. How Norway Proves Laissez-Faire Economics Is Not Just Wrong, It's Toxic, 2015. http://evonomics.com/norway-toxic-trickle-down-david-sloan-wilson/. Accessed June 13, 2018.

5. Wilson, Excerpt from "This View of Life."

6. Guyenet S. By 2606, the US Diet Will Be 100 Percent Sugar, 2012. http://wholehealthsource.blogspot.com/2012/02/by-2606-us-diet-will-be-100-percent.html. Accessed November 1, 2018.

7. Marantz A. *Antisocial: Online Extremists, Techno-Utopians, and the Hijacking of the American Conversation.* New York, NY: Viking, 2019; Wylie C. *Mind F*ck: Inside Cambridge Analytica's Plot to Break the World.* New York, NY: Random House, 2019.

8. Dowd B. Tulip mania: When tulips cost as much as houses. Focus Economics, 2017. https://www.focus-economics.com/blog/tulip-mania-dutch-market-bubble; McBride W. America's shrinking corporate sector. The Tax Foundation, 2015. https://taxfoundation.org/america-s-shrinking-corporate-sector/. Accessed April 15, 2019.

9. Micklethwait J, Wooldridge A. From Sarajevo to September 11. *Policy Review*, 2003, 117(49-63).

10. *McCutcheon v. FEC,* 572 U.S., 2014.

11. *Citizens United v. Federal Election Commission.* 558 U.S., 2010; Center for Responsive Politics. SuperPACS, 2018. http://www.opensecrets.org/pacs/superpacs.php?cycle=2018. Accessed October 25, 2018.

12. Pew Research Center. More Americans favor raising than lowering tax rates on corporations, high household incomes. *Fact Tank: News in the Numbers,* 2017. https://www.pewresearch.org/fact-tank/2017/09/27/more-americans-favor-raising-than-lowering-tax-rates-on-corporations-high-household-incomes/. Accessed January 7, 2020.

13. Levitz E. The Trump tax cuts just got even more skewed to the rich. *New York Magazine, 2017. http://nymag.com/daily/intelligencer/2017/12/the-trump-tax-cuts-just-got-even-more-skewed-to-the-rich.html.*

14. Edwards-Levy A. Raising the minimum wage is a really, really popular idea: Most Americans say a higher minimum wage would help workers and nearly half want to see a $15-an-hour federal minimum. *HuffPost,* 2017. https://www.huffpost.com/entry/minimum-wage-poll_n_570ead92e4b08 a2d32b8e671.

15. 1968 United States Minimum Wage in Today's Dollars. DollarTimes, 2018. https://www.dollartimes.com/inflation/items/1968-united-states-minimum-wage. Accessed November 14, 2018.

16. Farias C. Americans agree on one thing: Citizens United is terrible. *HuffPost*, 2015. https://www.huffpost.com/entry/citizens-united-john-roberts_n_56oacdoce4boaf3706de129d.

17. Delk J. Poll: Few Americans support US withdrawal from Paris climate agreement. *The Hill*, 2017. http://thehill.com/blogs/blog-briefing-room/news/338550-poll-few-americans-support-us-withdrawal-from-paris-climate.

18. Rivlin G. How Wall Street defanged Dodd-Frank. *The Nation*, 2013. https://www.thenation.com/article/how-wall-street-defanged-dodd-frank/.

19. Biglan, How cigarette marketing killed 20 million people.

20. *United States v. Phillip Morris et al. Direct Written Examination of Anthony Biglan, PhD, submitted by the United States pursuant to order #471.* Civil No. 99-CV-02496 (GK).

21. Harris JL, Heard A, Schwartz MB. Older but still vulnerable: All children need protection from unhealthy food marking. *Rudd Brief*, 2014:1-14. http://www.uconnruddcenter.org/files/Pdfs/Protecting_Older_Children_3_14.pdf. Accessed March 5, 2019.

22. Strasburger VC, Donnerstein E. Children, adolescents, and the media: Issues and solutions. *Pediatrics*, 1999,103(1):129-139; Sutherland LA, Mackenzie T, Purvis LA, Dalton M. Prevalence of food and beverage brands in movies: 1996-2005. Pediatrics, 2010,125(3):468-474. doi:10.1542/peds.2009-0857.

23. U.S. Department of Health and Human Services. Childhood Obesity Facts, 2018. https://www.cdc.gov/healthyschools/obesity/facts.htm. Accessed November 1, 2018.

24. Olshansky SJ, Passaro DJ, Hershow RC, et al. A potential decline in life expectancy in the United States in the 21st century. *New England Journal of Medicine*, 2005, 352(11):1138-1145. doi:10.1056/NEJMsr043743. Commonwealth Fund. U.S. spends more on health care than other high-income nations but has lower life expectancy, worse health, 2015. https://www.commonwealthfund.org/press-release/2015/us-spends-more-health-care-other-high-income-nations-has-lower-life-expectancy?redirect_source=/publications/press-releases/2015/oct/us-spends-more-on-health-care-than-other-nations. Accessed October 24, 2018.

25. Biglan, Big Pharma and the death of Americans.

26. Katz J. Drug deaths in America are rising faster than ever. *The Upshot*, 2017. https://www.nytimes.com/interactive/2017/06/05/upshot/opioid-epidemic-drug-overdose-deaths-are-rising-faster-than-ever.html?_r=0. Accessed October 24, 2018.

27. Pollack A. Drug goes from $13.50 a tablet to $750, overnight. *The New York Times*, 2015. https://www.nytimes.com/2015/09/21/business/a-huge-overnight-increase-in-a-drugs-price-raises-protests.html?_r=0. Accessed March 5, 2019; Krantz M. Drug prices are high: So are the CEOs' pay. USA Today, 2016. https://www.usatoday.com/story/money/markets/2016/08/26/drug-money-pharma-ceos-paid-71-more/89369152/. Accessed March 5, 2019; Herper M. Why did that drug price increase 6,000%? It's the law. *Pharma & Healthcare, 2017. https://www.forbes.com/sites/matthewherper/2017/02/10/a-6000-price-hike-should-give-drug-companies-a-disgusting-sense-of-deja-vu/#37173338e71f5. Accessed March 5, 2019.*

28. Gun violence by the numbers. Everytown, 2018. https://everytownresearch.org/gun-violence-by-the-numbers/#foot_note_11.

29. Follman M, Lurie J, Lee J, West J. The true cost of gun violence in America. *Mother Jones*, 2015. http://www.motherjones.com/politics/2015/04/true-cost-of-gun-violence-in-america.

30. Reeves A, Stuckler D, McKee M, Gunnell D, Chang SS, Basu S. Increase in state suicide rates in the USA during economic recession. *Lancet*, 2012, 380(9856):1813-1814. doi:10.1016/s0140-6736(12)61910-2.

31. Maruthappu M, Watkins J, Noor AM, et al. Economic downturns, universal health coverage, and cancer mortality in high-income and middle-income countries, 1990–2010: A longitudinal analysis. *Lancet*, 2016, 388(10045):684-695. doi:10.1016/S0140-6736(16)00577-8.

32. Biglan, How cigarette marketing killed 20 million people; Biglan, The right to sell arms; Biglan, how and why the food industry makes Americans sick; Biglan, Big Pharma and the death of Americans; Biglan, How free market ideology resulted in the Great Recession; Biglan, The fossil fuel industry; Biglan, The crisis of capitalism.

33. Saez E, Zucman G. Wealth inequality in the United States; Zucman G. *The hidden wealth of nations.*

34. Biglan, Big Pharma and the death of Americans.

35. Biglan A, Cody C. Integrating the human sciences to evolve effective policies. *Journal of Economic Behavior & Organization*, 2013, 90S(Supplement):S152-S162.

36. Biglan, *The Nurture Effect*.

37. Dishion TJ, Snyder J. *Oxford Handbook of Coercive Relationship Dynamics*. New York, NY: Oxford University Press, 2016.

38. Loudenback T, Knueven. Mark Zuckerberg's net worth increased by over $1 billion after Facebook's FTC fine. *Business Insider*, August 16, 2019. https://www.businessinsider.com/facebook-mark-zuckerberg-net-worth-priscilla-chan-2017-10. Accessed January 29, 2020.

39. Kahneman D, Deaton A. High income improves evaluation of life but not emotional well-being. *Proceedings of the National Academy of Sciences*, 2010, 107(38):16489.

40. Isaacson W. *Steve Jobs*. New York, NY: Simon & Schuster, 2011.

41. Fabrega M. 35 powerful beliefs about money: From Trump to the Dalai Lama. Daring to Live Fully, n.d. https://daringtolivefully.com/powerful-beliefs-about-money. Accessed January 7, 2020.

42. Duff T. *The Buy Side: A Wall Street Trader's Tale of Spectacular Excess*. New York, NY: Crown Publishing, 2014; Lattman P. A tale of Wall St. excess. *The New York Times*, June 3, 2013.

43. Pizzigati S, Anderson S. *Executive Excess 2016: The Wall Street CEO Bonus Loophole*. Washington, DC: Institute for Policy Studies, 2016.

44. Astin AW. *The American freshman: Thirty-Five Year Trends, 1966–2001*. Los Angeles, CA: Higher Education Research Institute, 2002.

45. Twenge J. Status and gender: The paradox of progress in an age of narcissism. *Sex Roles*, 2009, 61(5-6):338-340; Twenge JM, Campbell WK. Increases in positive self-views among high school students: birth-cohort changes in anticipated performance, self-satisfaction, self-liking, and self-competence. *Psychological Science*, 2008, 19(11):1082-1086.

46. Biglan, How cigarette marketing killed 20 million people; Biglan, The right to sell arms; Biglan, how and why the food industry makes Americans sick; Biglan, Big Pharma and the death of Americans; Biglan, How free market ideology resulted in the Great Recession; Biglan, The fossil fuel industry; Biglan, The crisis of capitalism.

CHAPTER 2

1. Hayes SC. *A Liberated Mind: How to Pivot Toward What Matters.* New York: NY: Penguin Publishing Group, 2019.

2. Biglan, How cigarette marketing killed 20 million people; Biglan, The right to sell arms; Biglan, how and why the food industry makes Americans sick; Biglan, Big Pharma and the death of Americans; Biglan, How free market ideology resulted in the Great Recession; Biglan, The fossil fuel industry; Biglan, The crisis of capitalism.

3. Kabat-Zinn J. *Wherever You Go, There You Are: Mindfulness Meditation in Everyday Life.* New York, NY: Hachette Books, 1994.

4. Yadavaia JE, Hayes SC, Vilardaga R. Using Acceptance and Commitment Therapy to increase self-compassion: A randomized controlled trial. *Journal of Contextual Behavioral Science,* 2014, 3(4):248-257. doi:10.1016/j.jcbs.2014.09.002.

5. Jazaieri H, Jinpa GT, McGonigal K, et al. Enhancing compassion: A randomized controlled trial of a compassion cultivation training program. *Journal of Happiness Studies,* 2013,14(4):1113-1126.

6. Yadavaia et al., Using Acceptance and Commitment Therapy.

7. Hayes SC. *Get Out of Your Mind and Into Your Life.* Oakland, CA: New Harbinger Publications, 2005.

8. Hayes, *A Liberated Mind.*

9. Harris R. *The Happiness Trap: How to Stop Struggling and Start Living: A Guide to ACT.* Boston, MA: Trumpeter Books, 2008.

10. Grewal D. How wealth reduces compassion. *Scientific American,* 2012. https://www.scientificamerican.com/article/how-wealth-reduces-compassion/. Accessed January 8, 2020.

11. National Academies of Sciences, Engineering, Medicine. *Fostering Healthy Mental, Emotional, and Behavioral Development in Children and Youth: A National Agenda.* Washington, DC: National Academy of Sciences, 2019.

12. Worline MC, Dutton JE, Sisodia R. *Awakening Compassion at Work: The Quiet Power That Elevates People and Organizations.* Oakland, CA: Berrett-Koehler Publishers, 2017.

13. Tirch, D. Personal communication.

14. Paluck EL, Green DP. Prejudice reduction: What works? A review and assessment of research and practice. *Annual Review of Psychology,* 2009, 60:339-367.

15. Van Ryzin MJ, Roseth CJ. Cooperative learning in middle school: A means to improve peer relations and reduce victimization, bullying, and related outcomes. *Journal of Educational Psychology,* 2018, 110(8):1192-1201.

16. Bezrukova K, Spell CS, Perry JL, Jehn KA. A meta-analytical integration of over 40 years of research on diversity training evaluation. *Psychological Bulletin,* 2016, (11):1227-1274.

17. Butz DA, Plant EA. Prejudice control and interracial relations: The role of motivation to respond without prejudice. *Journal of Personality,* 2009, 77(5):1311-1342.

18. Hayes SC, Bissett RT, Roget N, et al. The impact of acceptance and commitment training and multicultural training on the stigmatizing attitudes and professional burnout of substance abuse counselors. *Behavior Therapy,* 2004, 35(4):821-835.

19. Lillis J, Hayes SC. Applying acceptance, mindfulness, and values to the reduction of prejudice: A pilot study. *Behavior Modification,* 2007, 31(4):389-411.

20. Plant EA, Devine PG. The antecedents and implications of interracial anxiety. *Personality and Social Psychology Bulletin,* 2003, 29(6):790-801.

21. Vezzali L, Stathi S, Giovannini D, Capozza D, Trifiletti E. The greatest magic of Harry Potter: Reducing prejudice. *Journal of Applied Social Psychology,* 2015, 45(2):105-121. doi:10.1111/jasp.12279.

22. Hornsey MJ, Oppes T, Svensson A. "It's OK if we say it, but you can't": Responses to intergroup and intragroup criticism. *European Journal of Social Psychology*, 2002, 32(3):293-307. doi:10.1002/ejsp.90.

23. Transcript: Barack Obama's Speech on Race. NPR, 2008. https://www.npr.org/templates/story/story.php?storyId=88478467. Accessed February 12, 2020.

24. Hornsey MJ, Trembath M, Gunthorpe S. 'You can criticize because you care': Identity attachment, constructiveness, and the intergroup sensitivity effect. *European Journal of Social Psychology*, 2004, 34(8):499-518. doi:10.1002/ejsp.212.

25. Miller WR. Motivational interviewing: Research, practice, and puzzles. *Addictive Behaviors*, 1996, 21(6):835-842.

26. Glaser PA, Glaser SR. *Be Quiet, Be Heard: The Paradox of Persuasion.* Eugene, OR: Communication Solutions Publishing, 2006.

27. Cohen GL, Sherman DK. The psychology of change: Self-affirmation and social psychological intervention. *Annual Review of Psychology*, 2014, 65(1):333-371. doi:10.1146/annurev-psych-010213-115137.

28. Stone J, Whitehead J, Schmader T, Focella E. Thanks for asking: Self-affirming questions reduce backlash when stigmatized targets confront prejudice. *Journal of Experimental Social Psychology*, 2011, 47(3):589-598. doi:10.1016/j.jesp.2010.12.016.

29. Camerota A. Man calls voting for Trump 'biggest mistake' [video online], 2018, 1:13. https://www.cnn.com/videos/politics/2018/08/07/voter-panel-regret-vote-biggest-mistake-trump-idiot-camerota-newday-sot-vpx.cnn. Accessed January 30, 2020.

30. New data says Youngstown has worst unemployment rate in the state. WFMJ, 2018. https://www.wfmj.com/story/39516247/new-data-says-youngstown-has-worst-unemployment-rate-in-the-state. Accessed February 24, 2020.

31. Youngstown, Ohio. Wikipedia, 2020. https://en.wikipedia.org/wiki/Youngstown,_Ohio#2010_Census. Accessed February 24, 2020.

32. Fishkin J, Diamond L. This experiment has some great news for our democracy. *The New York Times,* October 2, 2019. https://www.nytimes.com/2019/10/02/opinion/america-one-room-experiment.html. Accessed October 4, 2019.

33. Ambrose SE. *D Day: June 6, 1944: The Climactic Battle of World War II.* New York, NY: Simon & Schuster, 1995.

34. Biglan, *The Nurture Effect.*

35. Harris, *The Happiness Trap.* Harris R. *ACT with Love: Stop Struggling, Reconcile Differences, and Strengthen Your Relationship with Acceptance and Commitment Therapy.* Oakland, CA: New Harbinger, 2009.

36. Hayes, *Get Out of Your Mind and Into Your Life.* Hayes, *A Liberated Mind.*

37. Tirch D. *The Compassionate-Mind Guide to Overcoming Anxiety: Using Compassion-Focused Therapy to Calm Worry, Panic, and Fear.* Oakland, CA: New Harbinger, 2012.

38. Edsall TB. Don't feed the troll in the oval office. *The New York Times,* June 28, 2018. https://www.nytimes.com/2018/06/28/opinion/trump-immigration-democrats-response.html. Accessed November 1, 2019.

39. Embry DD. The Good Behavior Game: A best practice candidate as a universal behavioral vaccine. *Clinical Child and Family Psychology Review, 2002, 5(4):273-297.*

CHAPTER 3

1. Dishion, Snyder, *Oxford Handbook;* Wilson DS, Hayes SC, Biglan A, Embry DD. Evolving the future: Toward a science of intentional change. *The Behavioral and Brain Sciences,* 2014, 37(4):395-416. doi:10.1017/s0140525x13001593; Biglan A, Prinz R. Progress in nurturing human well-being. *Clinical Child and Family Psychology Review,* 2017, 20(1):1-2. doi:10.1007/s10567-017-0231-8; Zettle RD, Barnes-Holmes D, Hayes SC, Biglan A. *The Wiley Handbook of Contextual Behavioral Science.* New York, NY: John Wiley & Sons, 2016. University of Washington Center for Communities That Care. Research and Results. n.d. https://www.communitiesthatcare.net/research-results/. Accessed January 8, 2020.

2.   Biglan, Cody, Integrating the human sciences; Evonomics: The next evolution of economics. n.d. http://evonomics.com/. Accessed November 16, 2018; Gowdy JM, Dollimore DE, Wilson DS, Witt U. Economic cosmology and the evolutionary challenge. *Journal of Economic Behavior & Organization*, 2013, 90, Supplement(0):S11-S20.

3.   Institute of Medicine et al., *Preventing Mental, Emotional, and Behavioral Disorders Among Young People: Progress and Possibilities.* Washington, DC: The National Academies Press, 2009.

4.   Kasser T. Materialistic values and goals. *Annual Review of Psychology*, 2016, 67:489-514. doi:10.1146/annurev-psych-122414-033344.

5.   Kasser, Materialistic values and goals.

6.   Kasser, Materialistic values and goals.

7.   Carroll JS, Dean LR, Call LL, Busby DM. Materialism and marriage: Couple profiles of congruent and incongruent spouses. *Journal of Couple & Relationship Therapy*, 2011, 10(4):287-308. doi:10.1080/15332691.2011.613306.

8.   Kasser, Materialistic values and goals.

9.   Kasser, Materialistic values and goals.

10. Mayer, *Dark Money.*

11. Liebal K, Behne T, Carpenter M, Tomasello M. Infants use shared experience to interpret pointing gestures. *Developmental Science*, 2009, 12(2):264-271.

12. Güth W, Kocher MG. More than thirty years of ultimatum bargaining experiments: Motives, variations, and a survey of the recent literature. *Journal of Economic Behavior & Organization*, 2014, 108(396-409).

13. Frank RH, Gilovich T, Regan DT. Does studying economics inhibit cooperation? *The Journal of Economic Perspectives*, 1993, 7(2):159-171.

14. Frank T. *One Market Under God: Extreme Capitalism, Market Populism, and the End of Economic Democracy.* Toronto, Ontario: Anchor Canada, 2001.

15. Lieberman MD. *Social: Why Our Brains Are Wired to Connect.* New York, NY: Crown Publishing, 2013.

16. Boehm C. *Moral Origins: The Evolution of Virtue, Altruism, and Shame.* New York, NY: Basic Books, 2013.

17. Biglan, *The Nurture Effect.*

18. Dishion, Snyder, *Oxford Handbook.*

19. Dishion TJ, Spracklen KM, Andrews DW, Patterson GR. Deviancy training in male adolescent friendships. *Behavior Therapy*, 1996, 27(3):373-390; Capaldi DM, Dishion TJ, Stoolmiller M, Yoerger K. The contribution of male adolescent friendships to aggression toward female partners in young adulthood in an at-risk sample. *Developmental Psychology*, 2001, 37(1):61-73.

20. Case A, Deaton A. *Deaths of Despair and the Future of Capitalism.* Princeton, NJ: Princeton University Press, 2020.

21. Gloster AT, Meyer AH, Lieb R. Psychological flexibility as a malleable public health target: Evidence from a representative sample. *Journal of Contextual Behavioral Science*, 2017, 6(2):166-171. doi:10.1016/j.jcbs.2017.02.003.

22. Bach PB. Smoking as a factor in causing lung cancer. *Journal of the American Medical Association*, 2009, 301(5):539–541. doi:10.1001/jama.2009.57.

23. Schroeder SA. We can do better: Improving the health of the American people. *The New England Journal of Medicine*, 2007, 357(12):1221-1228. doi:10.1056/NEJMsa073350.

24. Stolberg HO, Norman G, Trop I. Randomized controlled trials. *American Journal of Roentgenology*, 2004, 183(6):1539-1544. doi:10.2214/ajr.183.6.01831539.

25. Barr AC, Castleman BL. *Advising Students To and Through College: Experimental Evidence from the Bottom Line Advising Program*, 2016. https://www.bottomline.org/sites/default/files/Bottom%20Line%20 Evaluation%20Report%2002_11_2016.pdf. Accessed January 30, 2020.

26. Petrosino A, Turpin-Petrosino C, Buehler J. Scared Straight and other juvenile awareness programs for preventing juvenile delinquency: A systematic review of the randomized experimental evidence. *The ANNALS of the American Academy of Political and Social Science*, 2003, 589(1):41-62. doi:10.1177/0002716203254693.

27. Biglan A. Healthcare for all is essential: And it's not enough. Medium, 2019. https://medium.com/@tony_71103/healthcare-for-all-is-essential-and-its-not-enough-86ad4feda3d8. Accessed January 8, 2020; Biglan A. If corporations want to help they will have to forgo some profits. Medium, 2019. https://medium.com/@tony_71103/if-corporations-want-to-help-they-will-have-to-forgo-some-profits-ad7d5d8bfe68. Accessed January 8, 2020.

CHAPTER 4

1. Saez, Zucman, Wealth inequality.

2. Matthews DR. The Republican tax bill got worse: Now the top 1% gets 83% of the gains. Vox, 2017. https://www.vox.com/policy-and-politics/2017/12/18/16791174/republican-tax-bill-congress-conference-tax-policy-center Accessed March 8, 2019.

3. Biglan A. Creating a grand coalition to foster human wellbeing. The Evolution Institute, 2015. https://evolution-institute.org/creating-a-grand-coalition-to-foster-human-wellbeing/. Accessed November 22, 2019.

4. Biglan A, Brennan PA, Foster SL, Holder HD. *Helping Adolescents at Risk: Prevention of Multiple Problem Behaviors*. New York, NY: Guilford, 2004.

5. Biglan, *The Nurture Effect;* Institute of Medicine et al., *Preventing Mental, Emotional, and Behavioral Disorders*.

6. Bradshaw CP, Mitchell MM, Leaf PJ. Examining the effects of schoolwide positive behavioral interventions and supports on student outcomes: Results from a randomized controlled effectiveness trial in elementary schools. *Journal of Positive Behavior Interventions*, 2010, 12(3):133-148; Embry, The Good Behavior Game; Flay BR, Allred CG. The Positive Action Program: Improving academics, behavior, and character by teaching comprehensive skills for successful learning and living. In: Lovat T, Toomey R, Clement N, eds. *International Research Handbook on Values Education and Student Wellbeing*. New York, NY: Springer Science and Business Media, 2010, 471-501.

7. Rankin K. Study reveals the financial impact of mass incarceration on families. Color Lines, 2015. https://www.colorlines.com/articles/study-reveals-financial-impact-mass-incarceration-families. Accessed March 8, 2019.

8. Eddy JM, Martinez CR, Schiffmann T, et al. Development of a multisystemic parent management training intervention for incarcerated parents, their children and families. *Clinical Psychology: A Publication of the Division of Clinical Psychology of the American Psychological Association,* 2008, 12(3):86-98. doi:10.1080/13284200802495461.

9. McGinnis JM, Williams-Russo P, Knickman JR. The case for more active policy attention to health promotion. *Health Affairs,* 2002, 21(2):78-93. doi:10.1377/hlthaff.21.2.78.

10. Biglan, *The Nurture Effect;* Leslie LK, Mehus CJ, Hawkins JD, et al. Primary health care: Potential home for family-focused preventive interventions. *American Journal of Preventive Medicine,* 2016, 51(4):S106-S118. doi:10.1016/j.amepre.2016.05.014; Kaplan RM. *More than Medicine: The Broken Promise of American Health.* Cambridge, MA: Harvard University Press, 2019.

11. Khazan O. Why 80 percent of addicts can't get treatment. *The Atlantic,* 2015. https://www.theatlantic.com/health/archive/2015/10/why-80-percent-of-addicts-cant-get-treatment/410269/. Accessed April 24, 2019.

12. Hawkins J, Oesterle S, Brown EC, Abbott RD, Catalano RF. Youth problem behaviors 8 years after implementing the communities that care prevention system: A community-randomized trial. *JAMA Pediatrics, 2014, 168(2):122-129.*

13. Leachman M, Masterson K, Figueroa E. A punishing decade for school funding. Center on Budget and Policy Priorities, 2017. https://www.cbpp.org/research/state-budget-and-tax/a-punishing-decade-for-school-funding. Accessed March 8, 2019.

14. Preschool teacher salaries. Glassdoor, 2019. https://www.glassdoor.com/Salaries/preschool-teacher-salary-SRCH_KOo,17.htm. Accessed May 10, 2019.

15. Average behavioral health specialist salary. Payscale, n.d. http://www.payscale.com/research/US/Job=Behavioral_Health_Specialist/Hourly_Rate. Accessed May 10, 2019.

16. How much does a lawyer make? *U.S. News,* n.d. http://money.usnews.com/careers/best-jobs/lawyer/salary. Accessed May 10, 2019. Average salary for people with jobs as physicians/doctors. Payscale, n.d. http://www.payscale.

com/research/US/People_with_Jobs_as_Physicians_%2F_Doctors/Salar.
Accessed May 10, 2019. Chamberlain A. CEO to worker pay ratios: Average
CEO earns 204 times median worker pay. Glassdoor, 2015. https://www.
glassdoor.com/research/ceo-pay-ratio/. Accessed May 10, 2019. Adams A.
How much do hedge fund managers make? *Management Jobs*, 2018. http://
work.chron.com/much-hedge-fund-managers-make-23556.html. Accessed
May 10, 2019.

17. Martin J. Barrington: Executive compensation. Salary, 2017. https://
www1.salary.com/Martin-J-Barrington-Salary-Bonus-Stock-Options-for-
ALTRIA-GROUP-INC.html. Accessed May 10, 2019.

18. Pierce J, Gilpin E, Choi W. Sharing the blame: Smoking experimentation
and future smoking-attributable mortality due to Joe Camel and Marlboro
advertising and promotions. *Tobacco Control*, 1999, 8(1):37-44.

19. Biglan, *The Nurture Effect*.

20. Leachman et al., A punishing decade.

21. Van Ryzin M, Fishbein D, Biglan A. The promise of prevention science
for addressing intergenerational poverty. *Psychology, Public Policy, and Law*,
2018, 24(1):128-143. doi:10.1037/law0000138; Kaplan, *More than Medicine*.

22. What we do. Bill and Melinda Gates Foundation, n.d. https://local.
gatesfoundation.org/our-work/what-we-do. Accessed February 24, 2020.

23. Van Ryzin et al., The promise of prevention science.

24. Bill Gates: Biography and political campaign contributions.
CampaignMoney, n.d. https://www.campaignmoney.com/biography/
bill_gates.asp. Accessed March 8, 2019.

25. Goodwin DK. *The Bully Pulpit: Theodore Roosevelt, William Howard Taft, and
the Golden Age of Journalism*. New York, NY: Simon & Schuster, 2014.

26. Seldon R. Green group pushes for sustainable rebuilding of Joplin, MO.
Security and Sustainability Forum, 2012. https://ssfonline.org/green-
group-pushes-for-sustainable-rebuilding-of-joplin-mo-2576. Accessed
March 8, 2019.

27. Kania J, Karmer M. Collective impact. *Stanford Social Innovation Review*, 2011.
https://ssir.org/articles/entry/collective_impact. Accessed April 24, 2019.

CHAPTER 5

1. U.S. Department of Labor. Occupational Safety and Health Administration: Commonly Used Statistics, n.d. https://www.osha.gov/oshstats/commonstats.html. Accessed April 15, 2019.

2. A global community of leaders. B Lab, n. d. https://bcorporation.net. Accessed February 24, 2020.

3. Wilson DS, Hessen DO. Blueprint for the global village. The Evolution Institute, 2014. https://evolution-institute.org/article/blueprint-for-the-global-village.

4. Mackey J, Sisodia R. *Conscious Capitalism.* Boston, MA: Harvard Business School, 2014.

5. Mackey, Sisodia, *Conscious Capitalism.*

6. McBride W. America's shrinking corporate sector. The Tax Foundation, 2015. https://taxfoundation.org/america-s-shrinking-corporate-sector/. Accessed April 15, 2019.

7. Leonhardt D. When the rich said no to getting richer. *The New York Times,* September 5, 2017. https://www.nytimes.com/2017/09/05/opinion/rich-getting-richer-taxes.html. Accessed January 8, 2020.

8. National Center for Employee Ownership. Employee Stock Ownership Plan, n.d. https://www.esop.org/. Accessed November 1, 2019.

CHAPTER 6

1. Kaplan, *More Than Medicine.*

2. National Center for Health Statistics. *Health, United States, 2015: With Special Feature on Racial and Ethnic Health Disparities.* Hyattsville, MD: Library of Congress, 2016.

3. Center for Medicare and Medicaid Services. National Health Expenditures 2015 Highlights, 2015. https://www.cms.gov/Research-Statistics-Data-and-Systems/Statistics-Trends-and-Reports/NationalHealthExpendData/downloads/highlights.pdf; Squires D, Anderson C. *U.S. Health Care from a Global Perspective: Spending, Use of Services, Prices, and Health in 13 Countries.* The Commonwealth Fund, 2015.

4. OECD. *Society at a Glance 2011: OECD Social Indicators*, 2011.

5. Gonzales S, Sawyer B. How does U.S. life expectancy compare to other countries? 2017. https://www.healthsystemtracker.org/chart-collection/u-s-life-expectancy-compare-countries/#item-u-s-lowest-life-expectancy-birth-among-comparable-countries. Accessed June 13, 2018.

6. Olshansky SJ, Antonucci T, Berkman L, et al. Differences in life expectancy due to race and educational differences are widening, and many may not catch up. *Health Affairs*, 2012, 31(8):1803-1813. doi:10.1377/hlthaff.2011.0746.

7. Chen A., Oster E., Williams H. Why is infant mortality higher in the United States than in Europe? *American Economic Journal: Economic Policy*, May 2016, 8(2), 89-124. doi:10.1257/pol.20140224

8. Biglan, Big Pharma and the death of Americans.

9. Gawande A. The cost conundrum: What a Texas town can teach us about health care. *Annals of Medicine*, 2009. https://www.newyorker.com/magazine/2009/06/01/the-cost-conundrum. Accessed May 10, 2019.

10. Gawande, The cost conundrum.

11. Gawande, The cost conundrum.

12. Herman B. Profits are booming at health insurance companies. *Axios*, 2017. https://www.axios.com/profits-are-booming-at-health-insurance-companies-1513302495-18f3710a-cob4-4ce3-8b7f-894a755e6679.html. Accessed May 9, 2019.

13. Small L. Highest-paid health insurance CEO earned $22M in 2016. FierceHealthCare, 2017. https://www.fiercehealthcare.com/payer/health-insurance-ceo-pay-tops-out-at-22m-2016. Accessed May 10, 2019.

14. Bakalar N. Nearly 20 million have gained health insurance since 2010. *The New York Times*, May 22, 2017.

15. M.J. Why Republicans hate Obamacare. *The Economist*, 2016. https://www.economist.com/the-economist-explains/2016/12/11/why-republicans-hate-obamacare. Accessed May 10, 2019.

16. Cox A. Why are the Koch brothers so keen to repeal Obamacare? 2017. https://www.quora.com/Why-are-the-Koch-brothers-so-keen-to-repeal-Obamacare. Accessed May 10, 2019.

17. Ernst D. Koch Brothers' group vows millions to Republicans who vote against health care bill. *Washington Times*, 2017. https://www.washingtontimes.com/news/2017/mar/23/koch-brothers-group-vows-millions-to-republicans-w/. Accessed May 10, 2019.

18. Salam R. The anti-Obamacare FAQ: Everything you need to know about why conservatives want to repeal the president's health care law. Slate, 2014. https://slate.com/news-and-politics/2014/11/obamacare-faq-everything-you-need-to-know-about-why-conservatives-want-to-repeal-the-presidents-health-care-law.html. Accessed January 8, 2020.

19. Salam, The anti-Obamacare FAQ.

20. Schroeder, We can do better.

21. Mokdad AH, Marks JS, Stroup JS, Gerberding JL. Actual causes of death in the United States, 2000. *Journal of the American Medical Association*, 2004, 291(10):1238-1245.

22. McGinnis et al., The case for more active policy attention.

23. Schroeder, We can do better.

24. Stringhini S, Carmeli C, Jokela M, et al. Socioeconomic status and the 25 × 25 risk factors as determinants of premature mortality: A multicohort study and meta-analysis of 1·7 million men and women. *Lancet*, 2017, 389(10075):1229-1237. doi:10.1016/S0140-6736(16)32380-7.

25. Biglan, *The Nurture Effect*.

26. Kaplan, *More than Medicine*.

27. Jarjoura R, Triplett R, P. Brinker G. Growing up poor: Examining the link between persistent childhood poverty and delinquency. *Journal of Quantitative Criminology*, 2002, 18(2):159-187; Pampel FC, Krueger PM, Denney JT. Socioeconomic disparities in health behaviors. *Annual Review of Sociology*, 2010, 36:349-370. doi:10.1146/annurev.soc.012809.102529.

28. Dishion, Snyder, *Oxford Handbook*.

29. Biglan et al., *Helping Adolescents at Risk.*

30. Wickrama KK, O'Neal CW, Lee TK, Wickrama T. Early socioeconomic adversity, youth positive development, and young adults' cardio-metabolic disease risk. *Health Psychology,* 2015, 34(9):905-914. doi:10.1037/hea0000208.

31. Miller GE, Lachman ME, Chen E, Gruenewald TL, Karlamangla AS, Seeman TE. Pathways to resilience: Maternal nurturance as a buffer against the effects of childhood poverty on metabolic syndrome at midlife. *Psychological Science,* 2011, 22(12):1591-1599.

32. Miller GE, Chen E, Parker KJ. Psychological stress in childhood and susceptibility to the chronic diseases of aging: moving toward a model of behavioral and biological mechanisms. *Psychological Bulletin,* 2011, 137(6):959-997. doi:10.1037/a0024768.

33. Miller GE, Chen E, Fok AK, et al. Low early-life social class leaves a biological residue manifested by decreased glucocorticoid and increased proinflammatory signaling. *Proceedings of the National Academy of Sciences,* 2009, 106(34):14716-14721.

34. Miller et al., Psychological stress in childhood.

35. Olshansky et al., Differences in life expectancy.

36. Krogstad JM, Lopez G. Roughly half of Hispanics have experienced discrimination. Pew Research Center, June 29, 2016. http://www.pewresearch.org/fact-tank/2016/06/29/roughly-half-of-hispanics-have-experienced-discrimination/. Accessed May 10, 2019.

37. Harrell JP, Hall S, Taliaferro J. Physiological responses to racism and discrimination: An assessment of the evidence. *American Journal of Public Health,* 2003, 93(2):243-248. doi:10.2105/AJPH.93.2.243.

38. Miller et al., Pathways to resilience.

39. Mays VM, Cochran SD. Mental health correlates of perceived discrimination among lesbian, gay, and bisexual adults in the United States. *American Journal of Public Health,* 2001, 91(11):1869-1876.

40. Kishi K. Assaults against Muslims in U.S. surpass 2001 level. Pew Research Center, November 15, 2017. http://www.pewresearch.org/fact-tank/2017/11/15/assaults-against-muslims-in-u-s-surpass-2001-level/. Accessed May 10, 2019.

41. Johnstone M, Jetten J, Dingle GA, Parsell C, Walter ZC. Discrimination and well-being amongst the homeless: The role of multiple group member membership. *Frontiers in Psychology*, 2015, 6:739-739. doi:10.3389/fpsyg.2015.00739; Shaw KM, Theis KA, Self-Brown S, Roblin DW, Barker L. Chronic disease disparities by county economic status and metropolitan classification, behavioral risk factor surveillance system, 2013. *Preventing Chronic Disease*, 2016, 13:E119. doi:10.5888/pcd13.160088.ship.

42. National Center for Child Poverty, Child poverty.

43. Wilkinson R, Pickett K. *The Spirit Level: Why Equality Is Better for Everyone*. New York, NY: Bloomsbury Press, 2010.

44. Johnson J. 'What a rigged economy looks like': Top 10% now own 77% of American wealth. Bill Moyers website, 2017. https://billmoyers.com/story/top-10-percent-wealth/. Accessed June 14, 2018.

45. Wilkinson, Pickett, *The Spirit Level*.

46. American Civil Liberties Union. A Pound of Flesh: The Criminalization of Private Debt. ACLU website, 2018. https://www.aclu.org/sites/default/files/field_document/022318-debtreport_0.pdf. Accessed January 31, 2020.

47. Calvey M. Failure pays big at Wells Fargo, judging by these executive bonuses. *San Francisco Business Times*, 2017. https://www.bizjournals.com/sanfrancisco/news/2017/03/17/wells-fargo-bank-wfc-executive-pay-scandal-bonuses.html. Accessed March 5, 2019.

48. Burrows S. 85% of people hate their jobs, Gallup poll says. Return to Now website, 2017. https://returntonow.net/2017/09/22/85-people-hate-jobs-gallup-poll-says/. Accessed June 7, 2019.

49. Wilkinson, Pickett, *The Spirit Level*.

50. Fitz N. Economic inequality: It's far worse than you think. *Scientific American*, 2015. https://www.scientificamerican.com/article/economic-inequality-it-s-far-worse-than-you-think/ Accessed March 5, 2019.

51. Norton MI, Ariely D. Building a better America: One wealth quintile at a time. *Perspectives on Psychological Science, 2011, 6(1):9-12.*

52. Wealth inequality in America [video online], 2012. https://www.youtube.com/watch?v=QPKKQnijnsM. The Editorial Board. The tax bill that inequality created. *The New York Times,* December 16, 2017. https://www.nytimes.com/2017/12/16/opinion/sunday/tax-bill-inequality-created.html. Accessed March 5, 2019.

53. Gawande, The cost conundrum.

54. Daggett L. Physician salary 2017: Doctors' earnings on the rise. 2017. https://weatherbyhealthcare.com/blog/physician-salary-2017. Accessed May 16, 2019.

55. Daggett, Physician salary; Rampell C. How much do doctors in other countries make? *The New York Times,* July 15, 2009. https://economix.blogs.nytimes.com/2009/07/15/how-much-do-doctors-in-other-countries-make/. Accessed May 16, 2019.

56. Krantz, Drug prices are high.

57. Herman B. The sky-high pay of health care CEOs. *Axios,* 2017. https://www.axios.com/the-sky-high-pay-of-health-care-ceos-1513303956-d5b874a8-b4a0-4e74-9087-353a2ef1ba83.html. Accessed March 5, 2019.

58. Chaloupka FJ, Cummings KM, Morley CP, Horan JK. Tax, price and cigarette smoking: Evidence from the tobacco documents and implications for tobacco company marketing strategies. *Tobacco Control,* 2002, 11(Suppl I):i62-i72.

59. Brody GH, Murry VM, Gerrard M, et al. The Strong African American Families Program: Translating Research Into Prevention Programming. *Child Development,* 2004, 75(3):900-917.

60. Brody GH, Yu T, Chen E, Miller GEJHP. Prevention moderates associations between family risks and youth catecholamine levels. *Health Psychology,* 2014, 33(11):1435.

61. Biglan, *The Nurture Effect.*

62. Kellam SG, Brown CH, Poduska JM, et al. Effects of a universal classroom behavior management program in first and second grades on young adult behavioral, psychiatric, and social outcomes. *Drug and Alcohol Dependence,* 2008, 95(Supplement 1):S5-S28.

63. Forgatch MS, Patterson GR, Gewirtz AH. Looking forward: the promise of widespread implementation of parent training programs. *Perspectives on Psychological Science,* 2013, 8(6):682-694; Webster-Stratton C, Reid MJ, Stoolmiller M. Preventing conduct problems and improving school readiness: Evaluation of the Incredible Years Teacher and Child Training Programs in high-risk schools. *Journal of Child Psychology & Psychiatry,* 2008, 49(5):471-488; Connell AM, Dishion TJ, Yasui M, Kavanagh K. An adaptive approach to family intervention: Linking engagement in family-centered intervention to reductions in adolescent problem behavior. *Journal of Consulting and Clinical Psychology,* 2007, 75(4):568-579.

64. Beets MW, Flay BR, Vuchinich S, et al. Use of a social and character development program to prevent substance use, violent behaviors, and sexual activity among elementary-school students in Hawaii. *American Journal of Public Health,* 2009, 99(8):1438-1445. doi:10.2105/ajph.2008.142919.

65. See the Pax Good Behavior Game website, https://www.goodbehaviorgame.org/.

66. See the PBIS website, https://www.pbis.org/.

67. Estabrooks P, Pagoto S, Otten J, et al. The Society of Behavioral Medicine (SBM) and public policy advocacy: A call to action. *Translational Behavioral Medicine,* 2011, 1(3):492-496. doi:10.1007/s13142-011-0073-8.

68. Hawkins, J., Oesterle, S., Brown, E. C., Abbott, R. D., Catalano, R. F. Youth problem behaviors 8 years after implementing the communities that care prevention system: a community-randomized trial. *JAMA Pediatrics,* 2014, 168(2), 122-129. Retrieved from http://dx.doi.org/10.1001/jamapediatrics.2013.4009.

69. Komro KA, Tobler AL, Delisle AL, O'Mara RJ, Wagenaar AC. Beyond the clinic: improving child health through evidence-based community development. *BMC Pedriatrics,* 2013, 13(1):172. doi:10.1186/1471-2431-13-172.

70. Biglan, *The Nurture Effect*.

71. Biglan A. Where terrorism research goes wrong. *The New York Times*, March 8, 2015. https://www.nytimes.com/2015/03/08/opinion/sunday/where-terrorism-research-went-wrong.html?_r=o. Accessed April 24, 2019.

72. Schroeder, We can do better.

73. Vargas AJ, Schully SD, Villani J, Ganoza Caballero L, Murray DM. Assessment of prevention research measuring leading risk factors and causes of mortality and disability supported by the US National Institutes of Health. *Journal of the American Medical Association Network Open*, 2019, 2(11):e1914718-e1914718.

74. Kaplan, *More than Medicine*.

75. Curtin SC, Warner M, Hedegaard H. Increase in suicide in the United States, 1999-2014. NCHS Data Brief, no 241. Hyattsville, MD: National Center for Health Statistics, 2016.

76. Rudd RA, Aleshire N, Zibbell JE, Matthew Gladden R. Increases in drug and opioid overdose deaths: United States, 2000–2014. *American Journal of Transplantation*, 2016, 16(4):1323-1327. doi:10.1111/ajt.13776.

77. U.S. Substance Abuse and Mental Health Services Administration. *Results From the 2010 National Survey on Drug Use and Health: Summary of National Findings*. Rockville, MD: Author, 2014.

78. Merikangas KR, He JP, Burstein M, et al. Lifetime prevalence of mental disorders in U.S. adolescents: Results from the National Comorbidity Survey Replication, Adolescent Supplement (NCS-A). *Journal of the American Academy of Child and Adolescent Psychiatry*, 2010, 49(10):980-989. doi:10.1016/j.jaac.2010.05.017.

79. Mojtabai R, Olfson M, Han B. National trends in the prevalence and treatment of depression in adolescents and young adults. *Pediatrics*, 2016, 138(6):e20161878. doi:10.1542/peds.2016-1878.

80. Fredrickson BL, Joiner T. Reflections on positive emotions and upward spirals. *Perspectives on Psychological Science: A Journal of the Association for Psychological Science*, 2018, 13(2):194-199.

doi:10.1177/1745691617692106. Fredrickson BL. Research. University of North Carolina at Chapel Hill PEP Lab website, n.d. http://peplab.web. unc.edu/research/. Accessed May 10, 2019.

81. Carnine D. *How Love Wins: The Power of Mindful Kindness.* Mindful Kindness Project, 2017.

CHAPTER 7

1. Gross N. Professors are overwhelmingly liberal. Do universities need to change hiring practices? *The Los Angeles Times,* May 20, 2016. https://www. latimes.com/opinion/op-ed/la-oe-gross-academia-conservatives-hiring-20160520-snap-story.html. Accessed April 24, 2019.

2. Consortium of Social Science Associations. COSSA Releases 2017 Rankings of Social and Behavioral Science Funding at Colleges and Universities, 2016. https://www.cossa.org/2016/12/13/cossa-releases-2017-rankings-of-social-and-behavioral-science-funding-at-colleges-and-universities/. Accessed April 24, 2019.

3. Weigley S, Hess AEM. Universities getting the most government money. *24/7 Wall St.,* 2013. https://247wallst.com/special-report/2013/04/25/universities-getting-the-most-government-money/#ixzz2RbGnuBBc. Accessed May 10, 2019.

4. Kaplan, *More than Medicine.*

5. Zettle et al., *The Wiley Handbook.*

6. Biglan A, Hayes SC. Should the behavioral sciences become more pragmatic? The case for functional contextualism in research on human behavior. *Applied and Preventive Psychology,* 1996, 5(1):47-57.

7. Schneider SM. *The Science of Consequences: How They Affect Genes, Change the Brain, and Impact Our World.* Amherst, NY: Prometheus Books, 2012.

8. Frank RH. *The Darwin Economy: Liberty, Competition, and the Common Good.* Princeton, NJ: Princeton University Press, 2011.

9. Perry MJ. New US homes today are 1,000 square feet larger than in 1973 and living space per person has nearly doubled, 2016. http://www.aei.org/ publication/new-us-homes-today-are-1000-square-feet-larger-than-in-1973-and-living-space-per-person-has-nearly-doubled/. Accessed April 24, 2019.

10. Bowerman M. It's not just you, weddings are more expensive, extravagant. *USA Today*, 2017. https://www.usatoday.com/story/life/nation-now/2017/05/17/wedding-planning-costs-almost-double-what-did-10-years-ago/322763001/. Accessed April 24, 2019.

11. Biglan, How free market ideology resulted in the Great Recession.

12. Martin E. 65% of Americans save little or nothing, and half could end up struggling in retirement. *CNN*, 2018. https://www.cnbc.com/2018/03/15/bankrate-65-percent-of-americans-save-little-or-nothing.html. Accessed May 2, 2019.

13. Sekera J. *Economics and the Near-Death Experience of Democratic Governance* [working paper]. Global Development and Environment Institute at Tufts University, *2015*.

14. Lewis M. *The Fifth Risk*. New York, NY: W.W. Norton, 2018.

15. Anteby M. Why business schools need business ethics. *The Guardian*, 2013. https://www.theguardian.com/commentisfree/2013/oct/22/business-schools-need-ethics. Accessed April 24, 2019.

16. McDonald D. *The Golden Passport: Harvard Business School, the Limits of Capitalism, and the Moral Failure of the MBA Elite*. New York, NY: HarperCollins, 2017.

17. Biglan, How free market ideology resulted in the Great Recession.

18. Jiang D, Santos R, Mayer T, Boyd L. Latent transition analysis for program evaluation with multivariate longitudinal outcomes. Quantitative Psychology Research: The 80th Annual Meeting of the Psychometric Society, Beijing, 2015, 377-388. Sugai GM, Horner RH, Lewis TJ. Schoolwide Positive Behavior Support: Implementers' blueprint and self-assessment. Eugene, OR: Center on Positive Behavioral Interventions and Supports, U.S. Department of Education, Office of Special Education Programs, 2009; Flay, Allred, The Positive Action Program; Domitrovich CE, Cortes RC, Greenberg MT. Improving young children's social and emotional competence: A randomized trial of the preschool 'PATHS' curriculum. *Journal of Primary Prevention*, 2007, 28(2):67-91.

CHAPTER 8

1. List of Countries, by Incarceration Rate. Wikipedia, n.d. https://en.wikipedia.org/wiki/List_of_countries_by_incarceration_rate#Incarceration_rates. Accessed April 25, 2019.

2. Cullen J. The History of Mass Incarceration, 2018. https://www.brennancenter.org/blog/history-mass-incarceration. Accessed April 25, 2019.

3. Statistics of Incarcerated African-American Males. Wikipedia, n.d. https://en.wikipedia.org/wiki/Statistics_of_incarcerated_African-American_males. Accessed April 25, 2019.

4. Alexander M. *The New Jim Crow: Mass Incarceration in the Age of Colorblindness.* New York, NY: The New Press, 2010.

5. Woodward CV, McFeely WS. *The Strange Career of Jim Crow.* New York, NY: Oxford University Press, 1955.

6. Lai KKR, Lee JC. Why 10% of Florida adults can't vote: How felony convictions affect access to the ballot. *The New York Times,* October 6, 2016. https://www.nytimes.com/interactive/2016/10/06/us/unequal-effect-of-laws-that-block-felons-from-voting.html?_r=o. Accessed April 25, 2019.

7. SpearIt. Shackles beyond the sentence: How legal financial obligations create a permanent underclass. *1 Impact,* 2015, 46. Accessed April 25, 2019.

8. Kennedy M. ACLU sues over Florida law that requires felons to pay fees, fines before voting. NPR, 2019. https://www.npr.org/2019/07/01/737668646/aclu-sues-over-florida-law-that-requires-felons-to-pay-fees-fines-before-voting. Accessed November 1, 2019.

9. Sterbenz C. Why Norway's prison system is so successful. *Business Insider,* 2014. https://www.businessinsider.com/why-norways-prison-system-is-so-successful-2014-12. Accessed April 25, 2019.

10. Newman J. Trauma of witnessing police violence is not lost on children. *The Chicago Reporter,* 2016. http://chicagoreporter.com/trauma-of-witnessing-police-violence-is-not-lost-on-children/. Accessed April 25, 2019.

11. Davis LM, V. MM, Derose KP, et al. The impact of incarceration on families: Key findings. *Understanding the Public Health Implications of Prisoner Reentry in California: State-of-the-State Report*. Santa Monica, CA: RAND Corporation, 2011.

12. Morsy L, Rothstein R. Mass Incarceration and Children's Outcomes. Economic Policy Institute, 2016. https://www.epi.org/publication/mass-incarceration-and-childrens-outcomes/. Accessed April 25, 2019.

13. Eisen LB. Inside private prisons: An American dilemma in the age of mass incarceration. Brennan Center for Justice, 2017. https://www.brennancenter.org/our-work/analysis-opinion/inside-private-prisons-american-dilemma-age-mass-incarceration. Accessed November 1, 2019.

14. Simon C. DOJ: Private prisons are more dangerous than government prisons—for inmates and guards. *Business Insider*, 2016. http://www.businessinsider.com/report-finds-that-private-prisons-are-more-dangerous-than-public-ones-2016-8. Accessed April 25, 2019.

15. Lipsey MW. The primary factors that characterize effective interventions with juvenile offenders: A meta-analytic overview. *Victims and Offenders*, 2009, 4(2):124-147. doi:10.1080/15564880802612573; Landenberger NA, Lipsey MW. The positive effects of cognitive-behavioral programs for offenders: A meta-analysis of factors associated with effective treatment. *Journal of Experimental Criminology*, 2005, 1(4):451-476. doi:10.1007/s11292-005-3541-7.

16. Lipsey, The primary factors that characterize effective interventions; Landenberg, Lipsey, The positive effects of cognitive-behavioral programs.

17. Larson CR. Prisoner rehabilitation around the world. CounterPunch, 2016. https://www.counterpunch.org/2016/02/26/prisoner-rehabilitation-around-the-world/. Accessed November 15, 2019.

18. Larson, Prisoner rehabilitation.

19. Leslie et al., Primary health care.

20. Biglan A. Unleashing the power of prevention. *HuffPost*, 2016. https://www.huffingtonpost.com/entry/unleashing-the-power-of-p_b_11099386.html. Accessed April 25, 2019.

21. La Vigne NG, Davies E, Palmer T, Halberstadt R. Release planning for successful reentry: A guide for corrections, service providers, and community groups. The Urban Institute, 2008. https://www.urban.org/ research/publication/release-planning-successful-reentry. Accessed November 12, 2019.

22. The Way Home: Lane County Reentry Collaborative, project overview, 2018.

23. Biglan, *The Nurture Effect.*

24. Truman JL, Morgan RE. Criminal victimization, 2015. U.S. Department of Justice, Office of Justice Programs, 2016.

25. Biglan, *The Nurture Effect.*

26. Jails to Jobs. From jails to jobs: A how-to guide to becoming employed, n.d. https://jailstojobs.org/. Accessed November 15, 2019; UNICOR. Employing former offenders, n.d. https://www.unicor.gov/Inmate_ Employment.aspx. Accessed November 15, 2019; Hope for Prisoners. Reimagining re-entry, n.d. https://hopeforprisoners.org/. Accessed November 15, 2019.

27. Monahan M. Exceptional nonprofits in criminal justice reform. Namaste website, 2016. https://www.namaste.org/blog/exceptional-nonprofits-in-criminal-justice-reform. Accessed January 11, 2020.

CHAPTER 9

1. Frank T. *What's the Matter with Kansas?: How Conservatives Won the Heart of America.* New York, NY: Henry Holt, 2005.

2. Marantz A. *Antisocial: Online Extremists, Techno-Utopians, and the Hijacking of the American Conversation.* New York, NY: Viking, 2019.

3. Kaleem J, Jarvie J. Neo-Nazi website unleashed Internet trolls against a Jewish woman, lawsuit says. *Los Angeles Times*, April 18, 2017. http://www.latimes.com/nation/la-na-neonazi-website-lawsuit-20170418-story.html. Accessed May 10, 2019.

4. Phillips K. Founder of neo-Nazi site Daily Stormer argues 'troll storm' against Jewish woman is free speech. *Internet Culture*, 2017. https://www.washingtonpost.com/news/the-intersect/wp/2017/12/03/neo-nazi-argues-that-troll-storm-against-jewish-woman-is-free-speech/. Accessed May 10, 2019.

5. Katz AJ. Fox News and MSNBC are No. 1 and No. 2 most-watched cable networks in August. *TV Newser*, 2017. http://www.adweek.com/tvnewser/basic-cable-network-ranker-august-2017/339773. Accessed May 10, 2019.

6. Katz, Fox News and MSNBC.

7. Cadwalladr C. Facebook's Role in Brexit—and the Threat to Democracy. TED Talk, 2019. https://www.ted.com/talks/carole_cadwalladr_facebook_s_role_in_brexit_and_the_threat_to_democracy?language=en#t-553128. Accessed November 1, 2019.

8. Jamieson KH. *Cyberwar: How Russian Hackers and Trolls Helped Elect a President: What We Don't, Can't, and Do Know*. New York, NY: Oxford University Press, 2018; Yglesias M. Russia's hacking campaign revealed a sophisticated understanding of US politics. Vox, 2017. https://www.vox.com/policy-and-politics/2017/7/11/15952666/russia-dnc-hacks-timing. Accessed May 10, 2019; Entous A, Timberg C, Dwoskin E. Russian operatives used Facebook ads to exploit America's racial and religious divisions. *The Washington Post*, September 25, 2017. https://www.washingtonpost.com/business/technology/russian-operatives-used-facebook-ads-to-exploit-divisions-over-black-political-activism-and-muslims/2017/09/25/4a011242-a21b-11e7-ade1-76d061d56efa_story.html. Accessed May 10, 2019.

9. Wylie, *Mind F*ck*.

10. Jamieson KH. *Cyberwar: How Russian Hackers and Trolls Helped Elect a President: What We Don't, Can't, and Do Know*. New York, NY: Oxford University Press, 2018; Mueller RS. *Report on the Investigation into Russian Interference in the 2016 Presidential Election*. Washington, DC: U.S. Department of Justice, 2019; Isaac M, Wakabayashi D. Russian influence reached 126 million through Facebook alone. *The New York Times*, October 30, 2017. https://www.nytimes.com/2017/10/30/technology/facebook-google-russia.html Accessed November 1, 2019; Pierce CP. Some useful idiots were even more useful to the Russians than we thought. *Esquire*,

2018. https://www.esquire.com/news-politics/politics/a25605936/
russia-2016-influence-bernie-sanders-jill-stein/. Accessed November
1, 2019; Hohmann J. The daily 202: Russian efforts to manipulate
African Americans show sophistication of disinformation campaign.
The Washington Post, December 17, 2018. https://www.washingtonpost.
com/news/powerpost/paloma/daily-202/2018/12/17/daily-202-
russian-efforts-to-manipulate-african-americans-show-sophistication-of-
disinformation-campaign/5c1739291b326b2d6629d4c6/. Accessed
November 1, 2019.

11. Stein J, Crowe K. Russian trolls stoked racial tension after Milwaukee
rioting. *Milwaukee Journal Sentinel*, March 15, 2018. https://www.
jsonline.com/story/news/politics/2018/03/15/russian-twitter-trolls-
stoked-racial-tension-wake-sherman-park-riots-milwaukee-before-2016-
election/421439002/#. Accessed November 1, 2019.

12. Constine J. Facebook should ban campaign ads: End the lies. *TechCrunch*,
2019. https://techcrunch.com/2019/10/13/ban-facebook-campaign-
ads/. Accessed November 1, 2019.

13. Taplin J. *Move Fast and Break Things: How Facebook, Google, and Amazon
Cornered Culture and Undermined Democracy*. New York, NY: Little, Brown,
2017; McNamee, R. *Zucked: Waking Up to the Facebook Catastrophe*. New York,
NY: Penguin, 2019.

14. Largest companies by market cap today. Dogs of the Dow, n.d. http://
dogsofthedow.com/largest-companies-by-market-cap.htm. Accessed August
21, 2019.

15. Taplin, *Move Fast*.

16. About Facebook. Facebook, n.d. https://about.fb.com/company-info/.
Accessed November 22, 2019; Number of active Amazon customer
accounts worldwide from 1st quarter 2013 to 1st quarter 2016. Statista,
n.d. https://www.statista.com/statistics/476196/number-of-active-amazon-
customer-accounts-quarter/. Accessed November 22, 2019; 63 fascinating
Google search statistics. BlueList.co, 2018. https://seotribunal.com/blog/
google-stats-and-facts/. Accessed November 22, 2019.

17. How many Roman Catholics are there in the world? *BBC News*, 2013.
https://www.bbc.com/news/world-21443313. Accessed November 22, 2019.

18. Curran D. Are you ready? Here is all the data Facebook and Google have on you. *The Guardian*, March 30, 2018. https://www.theguardian.com/ commentisfree/2018/mar/28/all-the-data-facebook-google-has-on-you-privacy. Accessed February 24, 2020.

19. McNamee, *Zucked*.

20. Granville K. Facebook and Cambridge Analytica: What you need to know as fallout widens. *The New York Times*, March 19, 2018. https://www. nytimes.com/2018/03/19/technology/facebook-cambridge-analytica-explained.html. Accessed November 1, 2019.

21. Entous A, Dwoskin E, Timberg C. Obama tried to give Zuckerberg a wake-up call over fake news on Facebook. *The Washington Post*, September 24, 2017. https://www.washingtonpost.com/business/economy/ obama-tried-to-give-zuckerberg-a-wake-up-call-over-fake-news-on-facebook/2017/09/24/15d19b12-ddac-4ad5-ac6e-ef909e1c1284_story. html. Accessed June 10, 2019.

22. Stewart E. Facebook is refusing to take down a Trump ad making false claims about Joe Biden. *Vox*, 2019. https://www.vox.com/policy-and-politics/2019/10/9/20906612/trump-campaign-ad-joe-biden-ukraine-facebook. Accessed November 1, 2019; Ivanova I. Facebook expects to sell over $400 million of political ads next year. *CBS Moneywatch*, 2019. https://www.cbsnews.com/news/facebook-earnings-call-political-ads-to-bring-in-350-million-this-year/. Accessed November 22, 2019.

23. Rand A. *Atlas Shrugged*. New York, NY: Dutton, 1957.

24. Rand, *Atlas Shrugged*.

25. Taplin, *Move fast*.

26. Liberto D. Facebook, Google digital ad market share drops as Amazon climbs. *Company News*, 2019. https://www.investopedia.com/news/ facebook-google-digital-ad-market-share-drops-amazon-climbs/. Accessed November 22, 2019.

27. Cadwalladr, Facebook's role in Brexit.

28. U.S. Department of Health and Human Services. Reduce screen time. n.d. https://www.nhlbi.nih.gov/health/educational/wecan/reduce-screen-time/index.htm. Accessed November 22, 2019; U.S. Department

of Health and Human Services. Bullying. n.d. https://www.nichd.nih. gov/health/topics/bullying. Accessed November 22, 2019; Riley WT, Oh A, Aklin WM, et al. Commentary: Pediatric digital health supported by the National Institutes of Health. *Journal of Pediatric Psychology*, 2018, 44(3):263-268. doi:10.1093/jpepsy/jsy108.

29. Ma HK. Internet addiction and antisocial internet behavior of adolescents. *Scientific World Journal, 2011, 11:2187-2196. doi:10.1100/2011/308631.*

30. Burkitt L. Behavioral ads offer a windfall for marketers. *Forbes*, 2010. https://www.forbes.com/2010/03/24/behavioral-targeted-ads-advertising-ftc-privacy-cmo-network-ads.html#19be50976042 Accessed November 22, 2019.

31. Rosenberg Y. Confessions of a digital Nazi hunter. *The New York Times*, December 27, 2018. https://www.nytimes.com/2017/12/27/opinion/ digital-nazi-hunter-trump.html. Accessed February 24, 2020.

32. Silverstein H. Twitter posts (suspended account), December 23–25, 2016.

33. Sherr I. Germany is putting an end to hate speech on the Internet. Cnet. com, 2015. https://www.cnet.com/news/germany-is-putting-an-end-to-hate-speech-on-the-internet/. Accessed May 10, 2019.

34. Atkins PWB, Wilson DS, Ryan RM, Hayes SC. *Prosocial: Using Evolutionary Science to Build Productive, Equitable, and Collaborative Groups*. Oakland, CA: New Harbinger, 2019.

35. Wilson DS, Ostrom E, Cox ME. Generalizing the core design principles for the efficacy of groups. *Journal of Economic Behavior & Organization*, 2013, 90:S21-S32. doi:https://doi.org/10.1016/j.jebo.2012.12.010.

36. Atkins et al., *Prosocial.*

37. Prosocial World. *Prosocial Magazine*, n.d. https://www.prosocial.world/ magazine. Accessed November 22, 2019.

38. Atkins et al., *Prosocial.*

39. City of Kindness. About us, n.d. http://cityofkindness.org/about-us/ Accessed August 15, 2019.

40. Bomey N. Newspapers, digital news operations hit with layoffs as disruption. *USA Today*, 2019. https://www.usatoday.com/story/money/2019/08/01/newspaper-layoffs-digital-journalism-job-cuts-pew-research-center/1877757001/. Accessed November 22, 2019.

41. King G, Schneer B, White A. How the news media activate public expression and influence national agendas. *Science*, 2017, 358(6364):776-780. doi:10.1126/science.aao1100.

42. King et al., How the news media activate.

43. Number of monthly active Twitter users in the United States from 1st quarter 2010 to 1st quarter 2019 (in millions). Statista, n.d. https://www.statista.com/statistics/274564/monthly-active-twitter-users-in-the-united-states/. Accessed May 10, 2019.

44. Weise E. Your mom and 58% of Americans are on Facebook. *USA Today*, 2015. https://www.usatoday.com/story/tech/2015/01/09/pew-survey-social-media-facebook-linkedin-twitter-instagram-pinterest/21461381/. Accessed May 10, 2019; Mazie S. Do you have too many Facebook friends? Big Think, 2014. https://bigthink.com/praxis/do-you-have-too-many-facebook-friends. Accessed May 10, 2019.

45. Biglan, Creating a grand coalition.

CHAPTER 10

1. Funk M. *Windfall: The Booming Business of Global Warming.* New York, NY: Penguin Press, 2014.

2. Cho R. Why thawing permafrost matters. The Earth Institute, Columbia University, 2018. https://blogs.ei.columbia.edu/2018/01/11/thawing-permafrost-matters/. Accessed August 15, 2019.

3. Nyman P. Methane vs. carbon dioxide: A greenhouse gas showdown. One Green Plant, 2014. https://www.onegreenplanet.org/animalsandnature/methane-vs-carbon-dioxide-a-greenhouse-gas-showdown/. Accessed May 10, 2019.

4. Samenow J. It was 84 degrees near the Arctic Ocean this weekend as carbon dioxide hit its highest level in human history. *The Washington Post,* 2019. https://www.washingtonpost.com/weather/2019/05/14/it-was-degrees-near-arctic-ocean-this-weekend-carbon-dioxide-hit-its-highest-level-human-history/?utm_term=.f4aa34500e2f. Accessed June 11, 2019.

5. Steffen, W., Rockström, J., Richardson, K., Lenton, T., Folke, C., Liverman, D... Schellnhuber, H. Trajectories of the earth system in the anthropocene. *Proceedings of the National Academy of Sciences,* 2018. 115, 201810141. doi:10.1073/pnas.1810141115.

6. Kulp SA, Strauss BH. New elevation data triple estimates of global vulnerability to sea-level rise and coastal flooding. *Nature Communications,* 2019, 10(1):4844. Doi:10.1038/s41467-019-12808-z.

7. Nyman, Methane vs. carbon dioxide.

8. What is an engineering standard? What are the advantages and disadvantages of using standards in engineering? *TryEngineering,* n. d. http://trynanotechnology.org/ask-expert/what-engineering-standard-what-are-advantages-and-disadvantages-using-standards. Accessed February 24, 2020.

9. Lynch D, Marschall K. *Titanic: An illustrated history.* 2nd ed. London, UK: Hodder & Stoughton, 1997.

10. Cruz AM. Engineering contribution to the field of emergency management. *FEMA,* n.d. https://training.fema.gov/hiedu/docs/emt/engineering%20contribution.pdf. Accessed October 24, 2018.

11. Biglan A, Barnes-Holmes Y. Acting in light of the future: How do future-oriented cultural practices evolve and how can we accelerate their evolution? *Journal of Contextual Behavioral Science,* 2015, 4(3):184-195. Doi:http://dx.doi.org/10.1016/j.jcbs.2015.06.002.

12. Thunberg G. The disarming case to act right now on climate change. [video online], 2019. https://www.youtube.com/watch?v=H2QxFM9yotY. Accessed November 15, 2019.

13. U.S. Government Accountability Office. Climate Change: Analysis of Reported federal Funding, 2018. https://www.gao.gov/products/GAO-18-223 Accessed May 10, 2019.

14. Economists' statement on carbon dividends. *The Wall Street Journal,* January 17, 2019. https://clcouncil.org/economists-statement. Accessed February 24, 2020.

15. Abrahamse W, Steg L, Vlek C, Rothengatter T. A review of intervention studies aimed at household energy conservation. *Journal of Environmental Psychology,* 2005, 25(3):273-291. Doi:https://doi.org/10.1016/j.jenvp.2005.08.002.

16. Biglan A, Ary D, Yudelson H, Duncan TE, Hood D. Experimental evaluation of a modular approach to mobilizing antitobacco influences of peers and parents. *American Journal of Community Psychology,* 1996, 24(3):311-339.

17. Fisher J, Irvine K. Reducing household energy use and carbon emissions: The potential for promoting significant and durable changes through group participation. *Proceedings of the IESD PhD Conference: Energy and Sustainable Development,* 2010; Reshaping the future: How local communities are catalyzing social, economic and ecological transformation in Europe [press release]. Mountain View, CA: ECOLISE, the European network for community-led initiatives on climate change and sustainability, 2019.

18. Biglan A, Ary DV, Smolkowski K, Duncan TE, Black C. A randomized control trial of a community intervention to prevent adolescent tobacco use. *Tobacco Control,* 2000, 9:24-32.

19. Marris E. How to stop freaking out and tackle climate change: Here's a five-step plan to deal with the stress and become part of the solution. *The New York Times,* January 10, 2020. https://www.nytimes.com/2020/01/10/opinion/how-to-help-climate-change.html?smid=nytcore-ios-share. Accessed January 10, 2020.

20. Climate Store. Top 50 non-prof organizations working to stop climate change, n.d. https://climatestore.com/take-action/get-involved/non-profit-organizations-working-on-climate-change. Accessed November 15, 2019.

CHAPTER 11

1. PK. Income percentile calculator for the United States in 2018. DQYDJ, 2019. https://dqydj.com/income-percentile-calculator/ Accessed March 7, 2019.

2. PK. Income percentile calculator.

3. Violent Crime Control and Law Enforcement Act. Wikipedia, n.d. https://en.wikipedia.org/wiki/Violent_Crime_Control_and_Law_Enforcement_Act#Federal_Death_Penalty_Act. Accessed April 25, 2019.

4. Waldron T. Capital gains tax cuts 'by far' the biggest contributor to growth in income inequality, study finds. Think Progress, 2013. https://thinkprogress.org/capital-gains-tax-cuts-by-far-the-biggest-contributor-to-growth-in-income-inequality-study-finds-9f7e6b4a8058/. Accessed January 9, 2020.

5. Kolhatkar S. The growth of Sinclair's conservative media empire. *The New Yorker*, 2018. https://www.newyorker.com/magazine/2018/10/22/the-growth-of-sinclairs-conservative-media-empire. Accessed November 1, 2019.

6. Enron was done in by its own greed: California, nation should put a halt to energy deregulation. Consumer Watchdog, 2002. https://consumerwatchdog.org/newsrelease/lesson-enron-electricity-deregulation-disaster. Accessed November 1, 2019.

7. Scott, RE. Trade deficit with Mexico has resulted in 682,900 U.S. jobs lost or displaced. Economic Policy Institute, October 12, 2011. https://www.epi.org/publication/trade-deficit-mexico-resulted-682900-jobs. Accessed February 24, 2020.

8. Job losses due to trade since NAFTA deepen Pennsylvania's manufacturing crisis. The Keystone Research Center, 2003. https://www.keystoneresearch.org/sites/default/files/krc_pa_jobs_NAFTA.pdf. Accessed February 24, 2020.

9. Congressional Budget Office. Wikipedia, n.d. https://en.wikipedia.org/wiki/Congressional_Budget_Office. Accessed April 25, 2019.

10. Mason J, Rasco A. Obama: 20 million Americans insured thanks to 'Obamacare'. Reuters, 2016. http://www.reuters.com/article/us-usa-healthcare-obama-idUSKCN0W52KF. Accessed April 25, 2019.

11. Gimein M. Who really dug us out of the Great Recession? *Time,* 2016. http://time.com/money/4176949/who-really-dug-us-out-of-the-great-recession/. Accessed April 25, 2019.

12. Obama's Speech on Reducing the Budget (Text). *The New York Times,* April 13, 2011. https://www.nytimes.com/2011/04/14/us/politics/14obama-text.html. Accessed February 24, 2020.

13. Krugman P. The case for cuts was a lie. Why does Britain still believe it? The austerity delusion. *The Guardian,* 2015. https://www.theguardian.com/business/ng-interactive/2015/apr/29/the-austerity-delusion. Accessed April 25, 2019.

14. AIG Bonus Payments Controversy. Wikipedia, n.d. https://en.wikipedia.org/wiki/AIG_bonus_payments_controversy. Accessed April 25, 2019.

15. Federal White Collar Crime Prosecutions At 20-Year Low. Transactional Records Access Clearinghouse, 2015. http://trac.syr.edu/tracreports/crim/398/. Accessed April 25, 2019.

16. Javed A. Six years on, 30% of Dodd-Frank rules yet to be finalized. Bloomberg, 2016. https://www.bloomberg.com/professional/blog/six-years-30-dodd-frank-rules-yet-finalized/. Accessed April 25, 2019.

17. Great Recession in the United States. Wikipedia, n.d. https://en.wikipedia.org/wiki/Great_Recession_in_the_United_States. Accessed May 10, 2019; Schoen JW. Study: 1.2 million households lost to recession. *NBC News,* 2010. http://www.nbcnews.com/id/36231884/ns/business-eye_on_the_economy/t/study-million-households-lost-recession/. Accessed May 10, 2019; Brenner MH. *The Impact of Unemployment on Heart Disease and Stroke Mortality in European Union Countries.* Publications Office of the EU, 2016; Reeves A, McKee M, Stuckler D. Economic suicides in the Great Recession in Europe and North America. *The British Journal of Psychiatry,* 2014, 205(3):246-247. doi:10.1192/bjp.bp.114.144766.

18. Chart book: The legacy of the Great Recession. Center on Budget and Policy Priorities, *2019. https://www.cbpp.org/research/economy/chart-book-the-legacy-of-the-great-recession. Accessed May 10, 2019.*

19. Percentage of black families in the U.S. who live below the poverty level from 1990 to 2017. Statista, n.d. https://www.statista.com/statistics/205059/percentage-of-poor-black-families-in-the-us/. Accessed May 10, 2019.

20. Asante-Muhammed D, Collins C, Hoxie J, Nieves E. *The Ever-Growing GAP: Without Change, African-American and Latino Families Won't Match White Wealth for Centuries.* CFED: The Institute for Policy Studies, 2016.

21. Alexander D. How Bill And Hillary Clinton made $240 Million in the last 15 years. Forbes, 2016. https://www.forbes.com/sites/danalexander/2016/11/08/how-bill-house-hillary-clinton-made-240-million-how-much-earnings-rich-white/#688491437a16. Accessed April 25, 2019.

22. McCalmont L. Orszag's income detailed. Politico, 2014. https://www.politico.com/story/2014/03/peter-orszag-citigroup-omb-money-104525. Accessed November 1, 2019.

23. Powell, Attack of American free enterprise.

24. Drutman L. The real civil war in the Democratic Party. *The New York Times,* July 26, 2017. https://www.nytimes.com/2017/07/26/opinion/democrats-divided-new-plan.html?_r=0. Accessed April 25, 2019.

25. McLeod, S. Solomon Asch–Conformity Experiment. SimplyPsychology, December 28, 2018. https://www.simplypsychology.org/asch-conformity.html. Accessed February 24, 2020.

26. Run For Something, 2017. https://www.runforsomething.net/. Accessed April 25, 2019.

27. Alesina A, Glaeser EL. *Fighting Poverty in the US and Europe: A World of Difference.* Oxford, UK: Oxford University Press, 2004.

28. 2012-2020 federal representation by people per House seat, Senate seat, and electors. The Green Papers, n.d. https://www.thegreenpapers.com/Census10/FedRep.phtml. Accessed May 10, 2019.

29. Selby WG. Republicans won more House seats than more popular Democrats, though not entirely because of how districts were drawn. Politifact, 2013. http://www.politifact.com/texas/statements/2013/nov/26/lloyd-doggett/democrats-outpolled-republicans-who-landed-33-seat/. Accessed May 10, 2019.

30. Wolf TJ, Miller P. How gerrymandering kept Democrats from winning even more seats Tuesday. *The Washington Post*, 2018. https://www.washingtonpost.com/outlook/2018/11/08/how-gerrymandering-kept-democrats-winning-even-more-seats-tuesday/?utm_term=.732b62511ad3 Accessed June 7, 2019.

31. Gaskins K, LIyer S. The challenge of obtaining voter identification. The Brennan Center for Justice, 2012. http://www.brennancenter.org/publication/challenge-obtaining-voter-identification. Accessed June 11, 2019.

32. Elis N. Poll: Bipartisan majority supports raising minimum wage. The Hill, 2017. http://thehill.com/homenews/335837-poll-bipartisan-majority-supports-raising-minimum-wage. Accessed May 10, 2019.

33. Heller N. Who really stands to win from universal basic income? *The New Yorker*, 2018. https://www.newyorker.com/magazine/2018/07/09/who-really-stands-to-win-from-universal-basic-income. Accessed November 1, 2019.

34. Gamlin R. Administrative costs are killing U.S. healthcare. Medical Economics, 2016. https://www.medicaleconomics.com/medical-economics-blog/administrative-costs-are-killing-us-healthcare. Accessed May 10, 2019.

35. Archer D. Medicare is more efficient than private insurance. Health Affairs, 2011. http://healthaffairs.org/blog/2011/09/20/medicare-is-more-efficient-than-private-insurance/. Accessed May 10, 2019.

36. Biglan, *The Nurture Effect*.

37. Hacker, Pierson, *American Amnesia*.

38. Green Party of the United States. Green New Deal, n.d. https://www.gp.org/green_new_deal. Accessed August 15, 2019.

39. Biglan, Where terrorism research goes wrong.

40. Haidt J. *The Righteous Mind: Why Good People Are Divided by Politics and Religion.* New York, NY: Pantheon Books, 2012.

41. Smith G, Trotta D. U.S. hate crimes up 20 percent in 2016, fueled by election campaign: report. Reuters, 2017. https://www.reuters.com/article/us-usa-crime-hate/u-s-hate-crimes-up-20-percent-in-2016-fueled-by-election-campaign-report-idUSKBN16LoBO. Accessed May 10, 2019.

42. Kennedy, RF. Day of affirmation address, University of Capetown, Capetown, South Africa, June 6, 1966. https://www.jfklibrary.org/learn/about-jfk/the-kennedy-family/robert-f-kennedy/robert-f-kennedy-speeches/day-of-affirmation-address-university-of-capetown-capetown-south-africa-june-6-1966. Accessed February 24, 2020.

CONCLUSION

1. Haidt, *The Righteous Mind.*

CPSIA information can be obtained
at www.ICGtesting.com
Printed in the USA
LVHW050717020721
691686LV00015B/2175